Boys and Schooling in the Early Years

Boys' underachievement in education has now become a global concern, taxing the minds of governments across the Western world. *Boys and Schooling in the Early Years* represents the first major study of its kind to focus specifically on young boys and achievement. It makes a powerful argument for the need to begin tackling the problem of boys' lower educational performance in the early years.

The book includes one of the most detailed and up-to-date analyses of national evidence regarding gender differences in educational achievement – from the early years through to the end of compulsory schooling. Together with original and in-depth case studies that vividly capture the differing experiences and perspectives of 5–6-year-old boys, the book sets out the nature of the problems facing young boys in education and highlights a number of practical ways in which these can begin to be addressed.

This is essential reading for all those working in the early years, who are concerned about boys' lower levels of achievement, and want to know what they can do about it.

Dr Paul Connolly is Reader in Education at Queen's University, Belfast.

Boys and Schooling in the Early Years

Paul Connolly

RoutledgeFalmer
Taylor & Francis Group

LONDON AND NEW YORK

First published 2004
by RoutledgeFalmer
11 New Fetter Lane, London EC4P 4EE

Simultaneously published in the USA and Canada
by RoutledgeFalmer
29 West 35th Street, New York, NY 10001

RoutledgeFalmer is an imprint of the Taylor & Francis Group

© 2004 Paul Connolly

Typeset in Sabon by
HWA Text and Data Management, Tunbridge Wells
Printed and bound in Great Britain by
Biddles Ltd, King's Lynn, Norfolk

British Library Cataloguing in Publication Data
A catalogue record for this book is available from the British
Library

Library of Congress Cataloging in Publication Data
A catalog record for this book has been requested

ISBN 0–415–29840–7 (hbk)
ISBN 0–415–29841–5 (pbk)

Dedicated to my children – Mary (aged 4), Orla (aged 3) and Rory (aged 2) – who are teaching me just how important the early years are!

Contents

Figures

Tables

Acknowledgements

There are a number of people I would like to thank who have helped me write this book. First and foremost I would like to thank the young children, parents and staff at 'South Park' and 'North Parade' Primary Schools for their invaluable time and willingness to participate in the research. I am also extremely grateful to Julie Healy and Karen Winter for conducting the interviews with the parents on my behalf. A particular thank you is also due to the statistics division within the Department for Education and Skills who have been extremely helpful and supportive in supplying a wealth of data upon which much of Chapter 1 is based.

I am also indebted to Jannette Elwood, Becky Francis and Tony Gallagher who kindly agreed to read various parts of the book in draft and whose comments I have found extremely useful. A particular thank you is due to Christine Skelton who agreed to read through a whole draft of the book and who has played an invaluable role in keeping me focused!

Finally, and as always, I am most indebted to my partner, Karen Winter, who has made all of this possible. She has also read through and commented on the whole of the book and has really helped me to develop and refine my ideas. Karen has also made huge sacrifices to create space for me to work on the book. Most importantly she is my best friend and soul mate who I love very much and couldn't be without.

Abbreviations

DE	Department of Education (Northern Ireland)
DfES	Department for Education and Skills (England)
EOC	Equal Opportunities Commission (Britain)
GCSE	General Certificate of Secondary Education
GNVQ	General National Vocational Qualification
HESA	Higher Education Statistics Agency (UK)
INLA	Irish National Liberation Army (republican)
IRA	Irish Republican Army (republican)
LVF	Loyalist Volunteer Force (loyalist)
NISRA	Northern Ireland Statistics and Research Agency
Ofsted	Office for Standards in Education
UDA	Ulster Defence Association (loyalist)
UFF	Ulster Freedom Fighters (loyalist)
UVF	Ulster Volunteer Force (loyalist)
ZPD	Zone of Proximal Development

Introduction

Interviewer:	Do you think it's important to go to school?
Cameron (Aged 5):	Nooo!
Davey (Aged 5):	Nah!
Interviewer:	Why? Does it not matter if you go to school?
Davey:	No.
Cameron:	I hate it.
Interviewer:	In school what about sums, do you like doing sums?
Adrian (Aged 5):	No.
Tommy (Aged 6):	No.
Interviewer:	Why?
Adrian:	Because too boring.
Interviewer:	What makes it boring?
Adrian:	Because you have to, like/
Tommy:	/You have to, you have to think about it and write the number – a hundred plus a thousand an' all.
Adrian:	[*in agreement*] I know.
Interviewer:	What about reading, do you like reading?
Jamie (Aged 6):	No.
Cameron:	No.
Interviewer:	No? Why not?
Cameron:	I don't.
Jamie:	It's wick! It takes my memory away!

The tendency for boys to lag behind girls in education is a problem that can be traced right back to the early years. As indicated above, some young boys at this age are already becoming disillusioned with schooling (see also Myhill, 2002) and, within just a few years, there is evidence to suggest that some of these boys will have started attaching a stigma to working hard in school (Adler *et al.*, 1992). Indeed, all of the trends and patterns in relation to gender differences at GCSE – that have been the focus for so much public concern – are all clearly evident in Key Stage 1 test results. And yet, while the issue of 'boys' underachievement' has now become a global phenomenon, taxing the minds of governments across the Western world (Ofsted, 1993; Johnson, 1996; Epstein *et al.*, 1998a; Arnot *et al.*, 1999; Martino and Berrill, 2003), hardly any attention at all has been paid to the early years. Remarkably, although there is now a plethora of books, pamphlets and training materials in the UK alone aimed at providing guidance and advice to teachers to help improve the performance of boys and thus close this apparent gender gap (see, for example, Pickering, 1997; Bleach, 1998a; Hannan, 1999; Noble and Bradford, 2000; Wilson, 2003; Ofsted, 2003a, 2003b), there is a real absence of detailed work available aimed explicitly at this issue in the early years.

This is the purpose of the present book. It represents one of the first major studies of its kind to look explicitly at the issue of boys' achievement in the early years. It draws upon a comprehensive analysis of national statistical data as well as in-depth case studies of the experiences and perspectives of 5–6-year-old boys to help identify the nature of the issues involved as well as the reasons for the gender differences that already exist at this age in terms of educational achievement. The book also includes a detailed discussion of the implications of the findings for those working with young boys in the early years and makes a number of suggestions regarding how to develop an effective strategy to begin raising young boys' educational achievement.

The structure of the book

The book is separated into four, inter-related parts that combine together to provide a detailed and comprehensive assessment of the problems faced in relation to the schooling of young boys.

Part I: the rhetoric and reality of 'boys' underachievement'

The first part of the book examines the issue of 'boys' under-achievement' generally and how it relates to the early years more specifically. Chapter 1 focuses on the available national evidence on gender and achievement and shows how all of the key patterns and trends in terms of the differences between boys and girls at the end of compulsory schooling (i.e. in terms of GCSE results) are already evident in the early years. The chapter begins, therefore, with a careful analysis of data relating to GCSE results before then tracing the key differential patterns right back to Key Stage 1. In doing this, the chapter also shows that things are not as bleak as the popular rhetoric surrounding 'boys' underachievement' tends to suggest and that they are also considerably more complex. Most notably, and as will be seen, not all young boys are 'underachieving' and, equally, not all young girls are achieving well. It will be shown that social class and ethnicity tend to have a far greater impact on the educational performance of young children than gender. Moreover, while it will be shown that boys do tend to lag behind girls in the early years whatever social class or ethnic group one looks at, the size of the gender gap is greatest among those groups that tend to already be doing badly in education (i.e. working class young children in the context of this book) and is smallest among those who tend to already be doing well (i.e. middle class young children).

Chapter 2 then goes onto re-evaluate the key arguments put forward for 'boys' underachievement' to date in light of the actual evidence discussed in Chapter 1. Not surprisingly, many of these explanations have been offered with older boys in mind. However, the aim of the chapter in re-assessing these debates is to attempt to identify some of the key factors that can help to account for the gender differences that exist at GCSE level. This in turn provides the starting point from which the book can then 'work backwards' to assess to what extent these factors are relevant to the early years.

The chapter shows that a number of explanations have been put forward ranging from a focus on innate biological differences between boys and girls to those that blame schools in one way or another. It will be argued, however, that most of these explanations are based upon crude generalisations about all boys and all girls and simply fail to account for the more complex patterns of gender differences in attainment as outlined in Chapter 1. Having carefully looked at all of the main arguments put forward, the chapter concludes that the only explanation that has been proposed to date that can begin to account for the differences involved is masculinity itself and the differing ways it is appropriated and reproduced in young boys' lives. This, then, provides the rationale for the choice of case studies to be reported in Part III of the book that provide an in-depth study of the differing forms of masculinity that tend to be found between two groups of 5–6-year-old boys – one from a school located in a deprived, working class area and the other from a school in an affluent middle class area in Northern Ireland – and examines how these forms of masculinity tend to impact upon their dispositions towards education and schooling.

Part II: theorising boys and masculinities in the early years

Before launching into the case studies, however, it is important to first consider the ways in which young children have been theorised and understood. This is particularly so in relation to the focus of the present book given the way in which traditional accounts of child development – based largely around the influential work of Piaget (1962, 1965, 1977) – have provided little space for a consideration of gender (Yelland, 1998; MacNaughton, 2000). For example, the emphasis on universal stages of development has tended to remove gender from the analysis – treating boys and girls as if they all naturally and uniformly follow the same developmental pathway. Moreover, Piaget's notion of child-centred development and his concept of 'readiness' have also relegated the role of adults in children's learning to the sidelines. While adults have a responsibility to ensure that young children have exposure to a rich variety of experiences, there remains a tendency to frown upon any direct forms of intervention in children's activities and play. As MacNaughton (2000) has argued, this has tended to powerfully discourage and restrict any attempts by those working in the early years to work directly with young children about gender issues.

The purpose of the second part of the book (Chapter 3), therefore, is to discuss some of these problems in more detail as well as to suggest an alternative way of theorising young children's learning and development that can accommodate the issue of gender. This is done through the work of Vygotsky (1978) that not only allows for an understanding of gender but also provides the rationale and methods for undertaking more direct work with young children about this issue. The chapter identifies some elements of Vygotsky's overall approach that have largely remained under-developed and suggests how these can be addressed through incorporating some of the insights found in the work of Bourdieu (1977, 1990) and Elias (1978).

Part III: case studies of boys and schooling in the early years

This theoretical framework is applied in Part III of the book (Chapters 4–8) that reports the findings of two in-depth case studies of 5–6-year-old working class and middle class boys respectively. The aim of the case studies is to get beneath the surface of the statistical evidence discussed in Chapter 1 and to begin to identify some of the reasons for the tendency for young boys to lag behind girls and why this differs in relation to social class. The case studies include: observations of the boys throughout all aspects of the school day, in-depth interviews with them as well as interviews with parents and teachers and an analysis of the broader communities in which the two groups of boys live. In contrasting young boys from a deprived working class area ('North Parade') and an affluent middle class area ('South Park'), the two case studies clearly demonstrate the overriding importance of social class in determining the very different forms of masculinity adopted by the boys and thus their attitudes towards education and learning. In locating the boys within their wider social contexts, the case studies also stress the deeply engrained nature of their masculine identities and how they have come to reflect those differing contexts.

More specifically, Chapter 4 introduces the two case studies, describes the methodology employed and outlines the nature of the two respective areas in which the boys live. Chapters 5 and 6 then focus on the young middle class boys in South Park, while Chapters 7 and 8 focus on their working class counterparts in North Parade. For both groups of boys, the analysis begins with an exploration of the perspectives of parents and teachers, and thus the broader contexts of home and school within which the young boys are located, before then examining, in some detail, the actual experiences of and perspectives towards schooling of the boys themselves.

Part IV: Implications for practice

Chapter 9 represents the final part of the book and provides a summary of the key findings that have emerged through the earlier chapters before then considering their implications for practice. While it is not appropriate nor possible to provide detailed lesson plans for those wishing to work with young boys, it is possible to set out the key issues that need to be considered and addressed when devising an effective strategy for working with young boys. As will be argued, such strategies need to bear in mind issues of social class (in this case) as well as gender and the chapter concludes by discussing a number of broader suggestions for teachers and early years practitioners wanting to begin to raise young boys' levels of educational achievement.

Companion website

As mentioned at the beginning of this chapter, there is now a substantial body of research as well as a plethora of resources available on the issue of boys and achievement. Moreover, new research and additional resources are appearing all the time. In an attempt to help you navigate your way through all of this material and to keep on top of latest developments, a companion website has been created for this book. It contains regularly up-dated information on research and links to a wide range of resources relating to boys and achievement as well as equity issues in the early years more generally. The website can be found at: http://www.routledgefalmer.com/companion/0415298415/.

Part I

The rhetoric and the reality of 'boys' underachievement'

Chapter 1

'Boys' underachievement'

The evidence

Introduction

Before we can begin to set about trying to explain gender differences in educational performance in the early years we first need to ascertain whether such differences actually exist and, if they do, what their precise nature and form is. This is the purpose of the present chapter. The main aim of the chapter is to demonstrate that a high level of continuity exists between the differences in achievements between boys and girls in the early years (i.e. at Key Stage 1) and those found through successive key stages and onto GCSEs (and beyond). As will be seen, all of the key trends and patterns found in relation to gender differences in GCSE results have their origins right back in Key Stage 1. This is an important point to demonstrate in terms of stressing the need for any strategies aimed at addressing the poorer performance of boys in education to begin in the early years.

To do this, the chapter will therefore spend some time looking at gender differences in GCSE examination results in order to identify the major trends and patterns that exist at the end of compulsory schooling. With these trends and patterns in mind, the chapter will then 'work backwards' through each key stage to show how they all have their origins in the early years.

'Keeping a sense of proportion': the gender gap in GCSE performance

One additional benefit of starting the analysis with GCSE results is that it can show, quite effectively, the difference between the rhetoric and the reality of 'boys' underachievement'. Much of the data to be analysed below relate to the examination results of 2002.

Interestingly, the media response at the time of their publication in August of that year certainly demonstrates the rhetoric that has now become firmly established and continues to be expressed, year-by-year, since the mid-1990s (Arnot *et al.*, 1999). Headlines in the 'quality' papers, for example, reported that: 'Boys Fall Further Behind in GCSE Exams' (*Times Educational Supplement*, 22 August 2002) and 'GCSE Gender Gap Continues to Grow' (*The Guardian*, 22 August 2002). The taken-for-granted sense in which this is a *growing* problem is illustrated in the introductory lines of the report accompanying the headline in *The Guardian*:

> Ministers' efforts to close the gender gap at GCSE foundered this year as girls once again extended their lead over boys, figures published last night on the eve of results day showed.
>
> Margaret Hodge, education minister, acknowledged the government's concern admitting that the 'achievement gap between boys and girls remains unacceptable'. Head teachers blamed a 'laddish culture' which was putting government performance targets at risk.
>
> (*The Guardian*, 22 August 2002)

The rhetoric then is one of boys being disadvantaged compared to girls within education and, moreover, that this disadvantage continues to worsen year on year (Yates, 1997; Esptein *et al.*, 1998a; Raphael Reed, 1999; Martino and Berrill, 2003). As we will now see, the reality is rather different to this.

In examining the actual nature of the evidence, it is useful to use the measure of GCSE performance that encouraged the headlines and reactions above – that is the proportions of boys and girls gaining five or more GCSEs grades A*–C or their equivalent,[1] sometimes referred to as the 'GCSE benchmark'. There are, of course, a number of alternative ways of analysing differences in GCSE achievements.[2] However, given the fact that the GCSE benchmark is now widely understood and used (not least in the construction of school league tables in England) and that similar overall patterns of difference tend to emerge whatever alternative measure of GCSE performance is used (Demack *et al.*, 2000),[3] this will be the measure that will provide the focus for the analysis to follow.

Figure 1.1 illustrates the differential trends in performance of boys and girls from 1974/5 to 2001/2 in England in relation to this GCSE benchmark or its earlier equivalent.[4] As can be seen, while

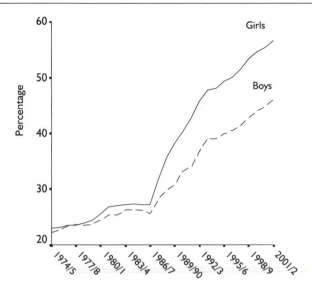

Figure 1.1 Proportions of school leavers in England gaining five or more GCSEs grades A*–C or their equivalent, by gender, 1974/5–2001/2

Source: Analysis of data supplied by DfES.

boys have always slightly under-performed compared to girls, there does seem to be evidence of a *growing* gap between boys' and girls' levels of achievement since the mid-1980s and, moreover, one that is continuing to increase. It is certainly easy to see why such a conclusion is reached given that the actual size of the gap represented by the vertical distance between the two lines has clearly increased over this period. Indeed it is this percentage point gap that is most commonly quoted by politicians and the media. For 2001/2, for example, there was a 10.6 point gap with 46.0 per cent of boys gaining five or more GCSEs grades A*–C compared to 56.6 per cent of girls. In comparison, in 1991/2 the gap was only 8.6 percentage points with 34.1 per cent of boys and 42.7 per cent of girls gaining the required five passes at this time.

While such a way of measuring changes in gender differences over time may be simple and easy to understand, it does actually produce a fundamentally misleading picture. Given the central role that this particular measure plays in fuelling the moral panic over boys' underachievement it is worth outlining briefly what the nature of the problem is with it. In essence, and as Gorard (1999, 2001) has pointed out, at the heart of the problem lies the confusion between percentage point differences and differences in percentage increases in performance between boys and girls. Perhaps the simplest way of illustrating this is to continue with this comparison between the figures for 1991/2 and 2001/2. As can be seen in Table 1.1 the overall proportions of boys and girls achieving the GCSE benchmark are shown for these two years together with the percentage point gaps. By focusing solely on the change in the *percentage point gap* it would certainly appear that boys have lagged further behind girls over the last ten years. However, a different picture emerges when we look at the *percentage increase* in performance for boys and girls respectively over this same period. As can be seen, boys have actually increased their performance at a slightly greater rate than girls over this time. Thus there was a 34.9 per cent increase in the number of boys gaining five or more GCSEs grades A*–C over the last ten years compared to a 32.6 per cent increase for girls. Contrary to the generally-accepted picture of boys lagging further behind, therefore, these trends actually provide a little room for optimism.

The main reason for this discrepancy is that it is misleading to simply compare the actual percentage point gaps from year to year without taking into account the overall proportions of boys and girls achieving the GCSE benchmark. As Gorard (2001) argues, there is, quite simply, a need to keep these differences in proportion. For example, if only 5 per cent of boys and 10 per cent of girls passed a particular GCSE examination the percentage point difference (i.e. 10 – 5 = 5 percentage points) would be the same as if 90 per cent of boys and 95 per cent of girls had passed that exam (i.e. 95 – 90 = 5 percentage points). However, we would generally be more concerned about the differences evident in the former case than the latter. To understand why we need to look at it proportionately. Thus, in the first instance girls are twice as likely to pass the examination than

Table 1.1 Comparison of the proportions of boys and girls in England gaining five or more GCSEs grades A*–C between 1991/2 and 2001/2

Year	% Boys	% Girls	% Point gap	Increase for the boys (%)	Increase for the girls (%)	No. of boys per 100 girls
1991/2	34.1	42.7	8.6	–	–	79.9
2001/2	46.0	56.6	10.6	34.9	32.6	81.3

Source: Secondary analysis of data supplied by DfES.

boys (i.e. $10 \div 5 = 2$) whereas, in the second instance, girls are only marginally (1.06 times) more likely to pass the examination than boys (i.e. $95 \div 90 = 1.06$). In this way, 'keeping a sense of proportion' requires us to calculate the relative chances of boys and girls achieving the required examination passes.

Going back to Table 1.1 and the comparison of the proportions of boys and girls gaining five or more GCSE grades A*–C in 1991/2 and 2001/2, then we need to similarly divide the proportion of boys who have been successful by the equivalent proportion of girls to provide an indication of the relative chances of boys achieving this GCSE benchmark compared to girls. For 1991/2, dividing the proportion of boys by the proportion of girls gives 0.799 (i.e. $34.1 \div 42.7 = 0.799$). In other words, boys are only 0.799 times as likely as girls to achieve five or more GCSE grade A*–C passes. To help in the interpretation of this figure we can simply multiply it by 100. This then gives the number of boys per 100 girls achieving the GCSE benchmark (Arnot *et al.*, 1998). As can be seen, for 1991/2 this gives 79.9 boys to every 100 girls. Interestingly, when we do the same calculation for 2001/2 we find that the number has increased slightly so that 81.3 boys are now gaining five or more GCSEs grades A*–C per 100 girls. This small improvement therefore more accurately reflects the slightly greater rate of increase in boys' achievement over the ten year period compared to girls.

It is this measure of the difference in performance between boys and girls that will be used, where necessary, throughout the remainder of this chapter. Stated as the number of boys per 100 girls achieving the required standard, it is not only easy to comprehend but more crucially it provides a much more valid way of examining changes over time (Gorard, 1999, 2001). With this in mind, we can therefore re-present the data shown in Figure 1.1 using this measure. This has been done in Figure 1.2 that shows the number of boys per 100 girls achieving five or more GCSEs grades A*–C (or their equivalent) between 1974/5 and 2001/2.[5] As can be seen, from a period of relative stability from the mid-1970s through to the mid-1980s where about 95 boys to every 100 girls achieved the required benchmark, the relative performance of boys compared to girls did reduce quite significantly from the mid- to the late 1980s. However, from the beginning of the 1990s onwards the relative performance of boys compared to girls has stabilised once again with about 80 boys to every 100 girls achieving the stated GCSE benchmark (Arnot *et al.*, 1998). Indeed, and in line with the data in Table 1.1, there do appear

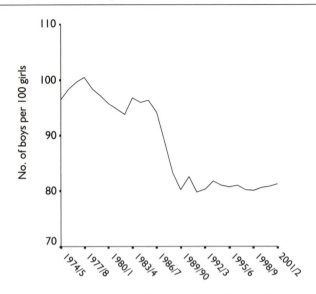

Figure 1.2   Number of boys per 100 girls in England gaining five or more GCSEs grades A*–C or their equivalent, 1974/5–2001/2

Source: Adaptation of figure in Arnot *et al*. (1998: 11) with more recent data supplied by DfES.

to be some signs of a slight improvement for boys over recent years with their relative performance compared to girls beginning to increase marginally. Rather than boys continuing to lag further behind girls in relation to GCSE performance as the rhetoric so strongly suggests, therefore, the actual reality is that while there is a difference between the achievements of boys and girls it has actually been stable over the last decade and, if anything, boys are now showing some limited signs of beginning to catch up with girls.

Gender differences in GCSE subject passes achieved

Alongside the misleading picture created in relation to overall trends, there are two other areas in which the rhetoric concerning boys' underachievement has tended to distort the reality. The first relates to the way in which these overall aggregate results tend to overlook differences in achievements between boys and girls in relation to specific subjects. Table 1.2 provides details of the overall proportions of young people leaving school in 2002 with GCSE grades A*–C

Table 1.2 Proportions of school leavers in England gaining a GCSE grade A*–C by subject in 2001/2, by gender (%)[a]

Subject	Boys	Girls	No. of boys per 100 girls
Home Economics	0.2	4.6	4.3
Social Studies	0.6	2.0	30.0
Drama	6.5	14.6	44.5
Art and Design	13.4	25.4	52.8
Religious Studies	7.0	12.9	54.3
Any modern language	30.0	45.4	66.1
Music	3.9	5.8	67.2
Humanities	1.2	1.7	70.6
English Literature	42.8	59.8	71.6
Design and Technology	29.0	39.3	73.8
English	45.1	61.0	73.9
History	17.8	20.3	87.7
Science (double award)	35.8	40.6	88.2
Mathematics	45.9	48.2	95.2
Geography	20.4	18.9	107.9
Business Studies	8.2	7.1	115.5
Information Technology	10.0	8.5	117.6
Biological Sciences	6.5	5.0	130.0
Chemistry	6.4	4.7	136.2
Physics	6.5	4.4	147.7
Physical Education	11.8	7.5	157.3

Source: Secondary analysis of data from DfES (2002b).

Note: a Stated as a percentage of the total population of school leaving age.

passes in particular subjects in England. Undoubtedly, some of the differences evident in the table will be due to the different proportions of boys and girls who have chosen particular subjects and have consequently been entered for a specific examination. However, the key point to draw out from the data in the table is that these are *outcome figures* – they simply provide an indication of the relative odds of boys and girls leaving school with a higher grade pass in a particular GCSE subject regardless of the reasons why.

If we look at the final column of Table 1.2 showing the number of boys per 100 girls achieving a grade A*–C pass in each subject then it is clear that significant variations exist. In relation to the core subjects, it can be seen that boys are significantly less likely to gain a higher grade GCSE pass in English or modern languages than girls. They also lag behind to a lesser extent in double award science and, while they are also behind in relation to mathematics, the difference is marginal. However, it is also important to note that the rhetoric of 'failing boys' tends to ignore the fact that there are subjects where boys are still more likely to leave school with higher grade GCSE passes than girls. This is certainly noticeable in relation to named science subjects as well as subjects such as business studies and information technology. These early differential patterns of specialisation are particularly significant given the fact that these latter subjects can give boys greater access to a number of highly-rewarded occupations (Arnot *et al.*, 1999; Francis, 2000).

Overall, the key point to emerge from these differences in attainment between subjects is that they represent the start of a process of increasing differentiation that continues through further and higher education whereby young men and women still tend to follow well-defined career pathways. This is illustrated by Figure 1.3 that shows the gender breakdown of those achieving first degrees in particular subjects within the UK in 2002. As can be seen, clear differences still remain in relation to particular subjects that continue to be male- or female-dominated. Moreover, in relation to languages, computer science and engineering and technology degrees, they reflect differences that, as we have seen, are already emerging at GCSE level. This is certainly a point that is overlooked by the rhetoric

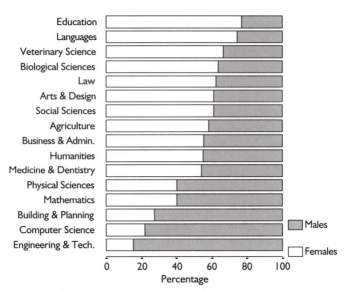

Figure 1.3   First degrees awarded in the UK in 2002 by gender
Source: Secondary analysis of data from HESA (2003).

of boys' underachievement that simply casts boys universally as the victims. The reality, however, is a little more complex than this with boys continuing to outperform girls in a small number of subjects and, moreover, with both boys and girls finding themselves in a situation where their educational and career opportunities are still significantly constrained in terms of their gender.

The effects of social class and ethnicity on gender differences in GCSE performance

The final area in which the rhetoric of boys' underachievement tends to significantly distort the reality that will be highlighted here derives from the tendency simply to compare the performance of *all* boys with that of *all* girls as if they represent two distinct and homogeneous categories (Mac an Ghaill, 1996b; Epstein *et al.*, 1998b; Jackson, 1998). The problem with this, as Lucey and Walkerdine (2000) make clear, is that:

> all too often simplistic, statistical interpretations which concentrate entirely on gender differences serve to shore up a universal notion of boys' underachievement and present a picture which powerfully obscures and confuses enduring inequalities in attainment.
>
> (Lucey and Walkerdine, 2000: 38)

Thus it is not that all boys are uniformly underachieving and that all girls are performing well in education. Rather, such levels of achievement are strongly determined by the social class and ethnic backgrounds of boys and girls (Epstein *et al.*, 1998b). This is a point clearly illustrated by the data in Table 1.3 that shows the effects of social class and ethnicity on the proportions of boys and girls in England and Wales gaining five or more GCSEs grades A*–C in 2000/1. As can be seen, not all boys are 'underachieving' with 72.1 per cent of boys from higher professional backgrounds, for example, achieving the GCSE benchmark and 67.4 per cent of Chinese boys. Both these proportions are well above the national average for all school leavers of just 51.1 per cent. Similarly, not all girls are 'succeeding'. Only 37.4 per cent of girls from routine occupational backgrounds achieved the GCSE benchmark and, similarly, girls from lower supervisory occupational backgrounds as well as Black and

Table 1.3 Proportions of boys and girls in England and Wales gaining five or more GCSEs grades A*–C in 2000/1 by social class and ethnicity (%)

Category	Total	Boys	Girls	No. of boys per 100 girls
Social class				
Higher professional	77.1	72.1	82.6	87.3
Lower professional	64.5	58.9	70.1	84.0
Intermediate	51.8	46.7	56.6	82.5
Lower supervisory	34.9	29.5	40.8	72.3
Routine	31.8	26.1	37.4	69.8
Ethnicity				
Chinese	68.9	67.4	70.5	95.6
Indian	59.6	51.3	67.8	75.7
White	51.6	46.6	56.7	82.2
Bangladeshi	41.5	33.9	50.0	67.8
Pakistani	40.2	35.7	45.1	79.2
Black	36.3	32.0	40.2	79.6
Total	51.1	46.1	56.2	82.0

Source: Based upon secondary analysis of the Youth Cohort Study 2002.

Pakistani girls were all significantly underachieving compared with the national average.

Thus the rhetoric of boys' underachievement has tended to focus contemporary discussions of educational inequalities onto gender at the expense of a consideration of inequalities related to social class and ethnicity. And yet, as the evidence consistently shows, it is social class and ethnicity that tend to have a much greater impact on the chances of young people achieving in education compared to gender (Demack et al., 2000; Gillborn and Mirza, 2000). This last point can also be illustrated through a further analysis of the data presented in Table 1.3. As can be seen the findings in the table have been derived from the most recent cohort of the Youth Cohort Study of England and Wales. It comprises a sample of 16,707 young people selected randomly from across England and Wales who left school in 2001 and who were first surveyed early in 2002. A logistic regression analysis has been conducted on this dataset and the results are summarised in Figure 1.4. The mathematics behind such an analysis are fairly complex and need not concern us here. For those interested, the full results of the analysis are provided in the Appendix.

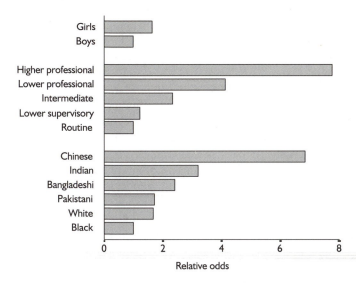

Figure 1.4 Relative odds of school leavers in England and Wales gaining five or more GCSEs grades A*–C in 2000/1 by gender, social class and ethnicity[a]

Source: Based upon a secondary analysis of the Youth Cohort Study 2002.

Note: a Relative odds calculated by means of a binary logistic regression analysis. See Appendix for full details.

The main point to note about the analysis is that it calculates the relative odds of particular categories of young people in the sample gaining five or more GCSEs grades A*–C. In this instance, and as can be seen from Figure 1.4, this has been done in relation to the three main variables – gender, social class and ethnicity respectively. While all three variables have been included in the same diagram, only the categories within each variable should be directly compared. Basically, for each variable, the bars indicate the relative odds of that category of young people achieving the GCSE benchmark compared to the reference category (i.e. the lowest one whose relative odds are 1.0). For example, if we look at ethnicity then it can be seen that Chinese young people in the sample are nearly seven times (6.8) more likely to gain five or more GCSEs grades A*–C than Black young people (who in this case represent the reference category with odds of 1.0). Similarly, those in the Indian category are over three times (3.2) more likely than Black young people and so on. If we look at social class then we can see that those from the highest social class category (Higher professional) are nearly eight times (7.7) more likely to achieve the GCSE benchmark than those from the lowest category (Routine), who are the reference category in this case. Finally, and as can be seen in relation to gender, girls are a little over one and a half times (1.6) more likely than boys to gain five higher grade GCSE passes.

One key point to make concerning the findings presented in Figure 1.4 is that these relative odds for the categories in each variable have been calculated once the other two variables have been 'controlled for'. Thus we can say that Chinese young people are nearly seven times more likely to gain five or more higher grade GCSE passes than Black young people once gender and social class have been controlled for. Similarly, girls are 1.6 times more likely to achieve the GCSE benchmark once social class and ethnicity have been controlled for. With this in mind, two key points are worth drawing out from the analysis. The first is that there is a tendency for boys to underachieve compared to girls across all social class and ethnic groups. As we have already seen in Table 1.3, boys' underachievement is therefore not simply confined to particular social class or ethnic groups. Once the effects of social class and ethnicity have been controlled for, it can be seen that girls are still, on average, 1.6 times more likely to achieve the GCSE benchmark than boys. However, and this is the second point, the overall difference that exists between boys and girls is relatively small and is certainly overshadowed by the differences that exist in relation to social class and ethnicity. As Figure 1.4 illustrates quite clearly, while the gender of a young person affects their chances of gaining five or more GCSEs grades A*–C by a factor of 1.6, their social class background can affect their chances by a factor of 7.7 and their ethnic background by a factor up to 6.8.

What this analysis of the effects of social class and ethnicity clearly shows is that it is not possible to simply make generalisations about all boys or all girls as the rhetoric concerning 'boys' underachievement' would suggest. Rather, there are different groups of boys and girls from a diverse range of backgrounds with very different experiences and attitudes towards education and learning. As will be discussed later in the next chapter, it is in recognition of this point that we cannot simply talk of a universal form of masculinity in relation to boys but only of a diverse range of masculinities, reflecting the very different backgrounds and experiences that exist among boys and men. It is also for this reason that the two detailed qualitative case studies to be discussed in Part III of the book have been chosen specifically with social class in mind, offering a contrast between boys in a working class and middle class school respectively. One final issue to examine with the data is whether the gender differences that exist remain relatively constant across social class and ethnic groups or, alternatively, whether it is the case that gender differences are more pronounced among some groups than others. If the differences in achievement among boys and girls do vary between social class categories, for example, then this would indicate that an 'interaction effect' is evident between gender and social class. In other words, it is not simply that gender and social class exert independent effects on a young person's levels of educational achievement but that they tend to combine in specific ways to either increase or decrease their achievement further. In relation to boys and schooling, for example, there is now a considerable amount of in-depth qualitative research that would certainly suggest that an interaction effect may exist between social class and gender. Ever since the classic studies conducted by Hargreaves (1967), Lacey (1970) and Willis (1977), successive studies of working class boys have shown how their general alienation and lack of success in school has provided the tendency for some to seek alternative status through the development of exaggerated forms of masculinity that, in turn, leads to the creation of strong anti-school sub-cultures. In this sense, social class is not likely to have the same effects on all working class children but is likely to impact more heavily on boys than girls because of the mediating influence of these exaggerated forms of masculinity. In contrast, while dominant forms of masculinity among middle class boys are also likely to provide an obstacle to them learning in comparison with middle class girls, their social class background this time is likely to reduce the adverse effects of masculinity. As a number of studies have shown, particular forms of middle class masculinity tend to incorporate a sense of competitiveness based partly around displays of academic success, particularly when that success can be shown to have been gained naturally, with little effort (Bourdieu and Passeron, 1977; Aggleton, 1987; Mac an Ghaill, 1994; Frosh et al., 2002).

If we return to Table 1.3 then there is certainly evidence of an interaction effect consistent with the findings of these qualitative studies. As can be seen, the number of boys per 100 girls achieving the GCSE benchmark does seem to decrease as one progresses down the social class categories. While 87.3 boys per 100 girls achieved five or more higher grade GCSE passes from higher professional backgrounds, only 69.8 boys per 100 girls did so from routine occupational backgrounds. A trend does, therefore, appear to exist such that the lower the levels of achievement that are apparent within any particular group the greater the differences that exist between boys and girls. Interestingly, this trend can be shown graphically in Figure 1.5 where the overall performance of each of the social class categories has been plotted against the number of boys per 100 girls achieving the GCSE benchmark in each group.

It can be seen that an extremely strong, linear relationship does actually exist. In fact the correlation between overall GCSE performance and gender differences is extremely high ($r = 0.964$, $p = 0.008$). This suggests that once we know the total proportion of young people in a specific social class category who have gained five or more higher grade GCSE passes we can actually predict the size of the gender differences in achievement that exist within that group with 93 per cent accuracy.[6] Clearly, therefore, while there is

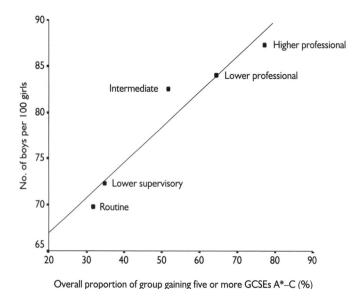

Figure 1.5 Relationship between overall GCSE performance of different social class groups and the number of boys per 100 girls in those groups gaining five or more GCSEs grades A*–C in England and Wales, 2000/1

Source: Based upon a secondary analysis of the Youth Cohort Study 2002.

evidence of boys slightly underachieving compared to girls across all social class categories, the extent of the problem is certainly greater among children from lower social class backgrounds. A similar finding is also evident, to a slightly lesser extent, in relation to ethnicity such that gender differences tend to be greatest among those ethnic groups where levels of performance are the lowest (see Connolly, 2003b).

Gender differences in Key Stage tests

So far we have seen that the reality of boys' educational underachievement is a little more complex than the rhetoric tends to suggest. From the foregoing discussion we can draw out four key trends when examining the differences in GCSE performance between boys and girls:

- In general, and across all social groups, boys do tend to achieve less well than girls – relatively marginally in terms of mathematics and science but more significantly in relation to English and languages;
- Rather than the 'gap' in performance continuing to increase between boys and girls it has actually been fairly stable for over a decade and, if anything, there is evidence over the last few years that it is slowly beginning to reduce;
- Such overall comparisons between boys and girls are misleading, however, and tend to mask the significant effects of social class and ethnicity on the achievement levels of particular groups of boys and girls;
- The differences in educational achievement between boys and girls tend to be greatest among those social class and ethnic groups with the lowest levels of achievement generally.

With these key trends in mind, we can now examine the national data from key stage assessments to ascertain at what age they first begin to emerge. The data have been collected for England since 1995 in relation to the performance of boys and girls in tests and teacher assessments at the end of Key Stages 1, 2 and 3 (corresponding to 7-, 11- and 14-year-olds) in English, mathematics and science. Following the approach taken in relation to the analysis of GCSE results, the analysis will look first at overall differences in educational performance between boys and girls before then assessing the impact of social class and ethnicity on these differences.

Figure 1.6 shows the number of boys per 100 girls at the end of Key Stage 1 achieving or exceeding the expected standards in English, Science and Mathematics between 1995 and 2002. As can be seen, while boys are only marginally behind girls in terms of science and mathematics, there is a more significant gap in relation to English – suggesting that the problems faced by boys in this subject are already evident in the early years. Over this period, around 90 boys to every 100 girls have tended to reach or exceed the expected standards in English. However, and as is also evident, there are some signs for optimism in relation to the slight improvement in performance of boys in English relative to girls over the last few years. This again tends to mirror the later trends found at GCSE.

Table 1.4 provides data on the performance of boys and girls at all three key stages in 2002 and shows how gender differences in performance in science, mathematics and English tend to change with age. It can be seen that the very slight gender differences in mathematics and science found at Key Stage 1 remain relatively stable through Key Stages 2 and 3. However, in contrast, it appears that

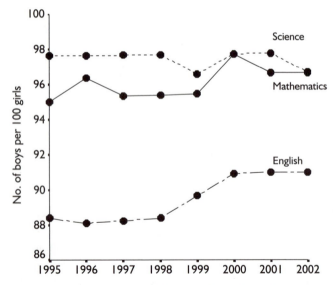

Figure 1.6 Number of boys per 100 girls in England reaching or exceeding expected standards* in National Curriculum Assessments of 7-year-olds in English, Mathematics and Science

Source: Secondary analysis of data supplied by DfES.

Note: * Level 2 or above at Key Stage 1 (Teacher Assessment Results).

the tendency for boys to achieve less well than girls in English at Key Stage 1 worsens through each successive stage. Thus while 91.0 boys to every 100 girls reached or exceeded the expected standards in English at the age of seven, this reduced to 85.9 boys at the age of 11 and 78.7 boys by the age of 14.

This trend for the worsening performance of boys in English compared to girls with age is also a stable feature across time as shown in Figure 1.7. As can be seen, for every year from 1995 to 2002, boys' achievements in English do get progressively worse compared to girls at each key stage. However, again, it should also be noted that Figure 1.7 also provides some room for optimism given the modest increases in the performance of boys relative to girls for all three key stages over this period.

Alongside these overall differences between boys and girls, we can also examine the effects of social class and ethnicity. Table 1.5 presents data on the proportions of 7-year-olds achieving expected standards at Key Stage 1 by ethnicity and free school meal band. The latter is a rather crude measure of a child's social class background. It relates to the percentage of children in the child's school in receipt of free school meals. It therefore provides some indication

Table 1.4 Proportions of children in England reaching or exceeding expected standards* in National Curriculum Assessments of 7-, 11- and 14-year-olds in 2002, by gender

	Boys (%)	Girls (%)	No. of boys per 100 girls
Key Stage 1 (7-year-olds)			
English	81	89	91.0
Mathematics	87	90	96.7
Science	88	91	96.7
Key Stage 2 (11-year-olds)			
English	67	78	85.9
Mathematics	74	75	98.7
Science	82	83	98.8
Key Stage 3 (14-year-olds)			
English	59	75	78.7
Mathematics	69	72	95.8
Science	66	69	95.7

Source: Secondary analysis of data supplied by DfES (Teacher Assessment Results).

Note: *Level 2 or above at Key Stage 1; Level 4 or above at Key Stage 2; and Level 5 or above at Key Stage 3.

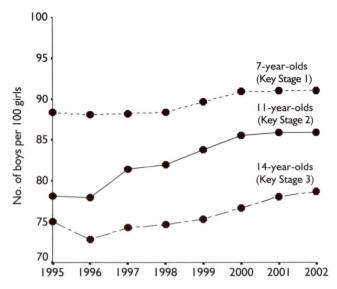

Figure 1.7 Number of boys per 100 girls in England reaching or exceeding
expected standards* in National Curriculum Assessments of 7-, 11-
and 14-year-olds in English

Source: Secondary analysis of data supplied by DfES – Teacher Assessments.

Note: * Level 2 or above at Key Stage 1; Level 4 or above at Key Stage 2;
Level 5 or above at Key Stage 3.

of the overall social class background of the school and therefore,
by implication, of the child. While it is far from perfect as a measure
it is the only one available for social class and thus will have to
suffice for the purposes of the present chapter.

There are a number of points to note from this table. First, social
class and ethnicity tend to exert a far greater effect on educational
performance at this early age than gender. This can be seen when
comparing the overall performance levels for each of the social class
and ethnic categories with the data presented earlier in Table 1.4. In
relation to English at Key Stage 1, we have seen that 81 per cent of
boys achieved the expected standards compared to 89 per cent of
girls. However, in relation to social class the variation is much wider
between the highest and lowest bands (i.e. 93 per cent and 72 per
cent respectively) and similarly in relation to ethnicity (89 per cent
and 73 per cent respectively). Similar patterns are also evident in
relation to mathematics and science. Just as with the GCSE results,

Table 1.5 Gender differences in the proportions of 7-year-old children in England reaching or exceeding expected standards* in National Curriculum Assessments in 2002, by free school meal band and ethnicity

Category	English		Mathematics		Science	
	Total	Boys per 100 girls	Total	Boys per 100 girls	Total	Boys per 100 girls
Free School Meal Band**						
0–5%	93	94.7	94	98.9	96	99.0
>5% and <=9%	90	93.5	92	98.9	94	98.9
>9% and <=13%	88	92.4	91	97.8	92	97.8
>13% and <=21%	85	91.0	89	97.8	90	97.8
>21% and <=35%	80	88.2	85	96.5	85	96.6
>35%	72	85.9	79	95.1	78	95.1
Ethnicity						
Chinese	89	92.4	95	97.9	91	95.7
Indian	88	94.5	91	97.8	90	96.7
White	86	91.1	89	96.7	90	96.7
Black	80	88.2	83	95.3	83	94.2
Pakistani	75	90.0	80	97.5	77	97.4
Bangladeshi	73	92.1	80	98.8	77	100.0
Total	85	91.0	89	96.7	89	96.7

Source: Secondary analysis of data supplied by DfES (Teacher Assessment Results).

Notes:
* Level 2 or above at Key Stage 1.
** Children categorised by the proportion of children in their school receiving free school meals.

therefore, it is clear that even at the age of 7, children's social class and ethnic backgrounds have a much greater impact upon their likelihood of achieving the expected standards in key curriculum subjects than gender.

Second, while we should not overemphasise the importance of gender differences at this age, it is evident from Table 1.5 that, with just one exception (i.e. Bangladeshi children's performance in science), girls are on average already outperforming boys in English, mathematics and science across all social class and ethnic groups. Many of these differences are relatively small at this age, particularly in relation to mathematics and science. However, the key point to draw out from this is that the more substantial gender differences we have already seen at GCSE are clearly already beginning to emerge across all three subject areas and in relation to all social class and ethnic groups at this early age.

Third, and finally, there is evidence in relation to social class (but not ethnicity at this age) of a relationship between the overall performance of a particular social class group and the size of the gender differences within that group. Just as with GCSE performance, therefore, it can be seen from Table 1.5 that as the overall proportion of children achieving the expected standard in a particular subject falls, so too do the number of boys per 100 girls achieving that standard. In simple terms, even at the age of 7 it is clear that the lower the social class background (as roughly indicated by their FSM band) the greater the gap between boys and girls in terms of their educational performance. Just as we illustrated this relationship at GCSE level earlier in Figure 1.5, we can do exactly the same here with the data for free school meal bands. As can be seen in Figure 1.8, an almost perfect line can be plotted for these 7-year-olds in terms of English ($r = 0.993$, $p < 0.0005$) indicating, again, that as soon as we know what the overall proportion of children is that is achieving the required standards in English, we can predict the gender differences for that group with 98.6 per cent accuracy. While not shown here, very similar relationships are also evident in relation to mathematics ($r = 0.982$, $p < 0.0005$) and science ($r = 0.990$, $p < 0.0005$).

Conclusions

This chapter has focused on the latest national evidence available to illustrate the nature and extent of the differences that exist between

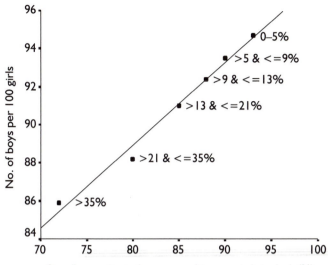

Figure 1.8 Relationship between overall proportions of 7-year-olds within different FSM bands* reaching expected standards** in English and the numbers of boys per 100 girls in those bands reaching these standards in England, 2002

Source: Based upon an analysis of data supplied by DfES.

Notes:
* Percentage of children receiving free school meals in the school that the child attends.
** Level 2 or above at Key Stage 1 (Teacher Assessment Results).

young boys and girls in terms of their educational achievement. As we have seen, the reality is somewhat different from the rhetoric concerning 'boys' underachievement' that has tended to paint a very dire picture of boys continuing to lag further and further behind girls. In fact the evidence presented above certainly supports the view that the rhetoric surrounding the issue of 'boys' underachievement' can legitimately be characterised as a 'moral panic' as defined by Cohen (1972). In this sense the media, with the help of some key educationalists and politicians, has exaggerated and amplified public concern about the issue out of all proportion to the actual size of the problem.

However, and as shown, the reality is rather more complex than is commonly suggested. In particular, four key trends can be identified in relation to gender differences in educational performance between boys and girls – all four of which are already evident in the early years. First, boys tend to perform less well than girls across all social class and ethnic categories. However, the overall difference between boys and girls is relatively small and overshadowed by the differences created by ethnicity and social class. Second, these differences have been stable for a while now and, if anything, there are some signs over recent years that the gap is beginning to close. Third, the gap between boys and girls is not the same for all groups but tends to be largest among those groups that, as a whole, are already the most likely to perform least well (i.e. lower social class groups in the case of this present book). Fourth, and finally, because of the above two points it is wrong to generalise about all boys and all girls. There are particular groups of boys who are achieving well above the national average in GCSE results and, similarly, specific groups of girls who are significantly underachieving.

Chapter 2

'Boys' underachievement'

The explanations

Introduction

The previous chapter has examined the statistical evidence regarding boys' educational performance compared to girls and has helped to distinguish between the rhetoric and the reality of 'boys' underachievement'. With this in mind, it is now possible to re-evaluate some of the key explanations that have been put forward over the years for the lower educational performance of boys. Given the preoccupation with gender differences in GCSE results, most of these explanations have been offered with older boys in mind. However, many of these explanations can be applied to younger boys. Either way, it is important to examine these in a fair amount of detail in order to identify what some of the key reasons are for boys' poor educational performance at this later stage. This can then guide the approach taken in the case studies of the young boys to follow in Part III and, in particular, can be used to assess the extent to which these reasons have their origins in the early years.

Such explanations can be organised into six main camps: those that focus on biological explanations; those that claim that schools are now biased in favour of girls ('feminine schools'); those that blame boys' lower levels of educational attainment on poor or mediocre teaching more generally ('failing schools'); those that focus on the adverse effects of wider changes within society on boys and men (the 'crisis of masculinity'); those that cite the impact of feminism and the increase in girls' aspirations; and finally those that identify boys' laddish behaviour as the principal cause of boys' poor performance. Each of these explanations will be examined in turn and their adequacy assessed against the evidence presented in the previous chapter. It will be argued that what is missing from all of these explanations (with the exception of the last one) is a focus on masculinity itself as appropriated and expressed by boys in school. With this in mind, the chapter concludes with a consideration of how masculinity has been theorised and understood. This, in turn, provides the basic starting point for the more detailed qualitative case studies to follow in later chapters.

Biological differences

> Belonging to the culture of manhood is important to almost every boy. To impugn his desire to become 'one of the boys' is to deny that a boy's biology determines much of what he prefers and is attracted to. Unfortunately, by denying the nature of boys, education theorists can cause them much misery.
>
> (Hoff Sommers, 2000,
> quoted in Martino and Berrill, 2003: 99)

There remains a strong underlying belief among many people that the differences between boys and girls are natural and thus inevitable. The fact that boys tend to be more active and aggressive than girls, it is argued, is simply the result of their hormones (and particularly, the higher levels of testosterone that boys tend to produce). In a similar vein, it is maintained that the fact that girls excel in English and languages whereas boys tend to do better at mathematics and science can be explained by differences in their respective brain structures. The power of these arguments lies in their simplicity and the fact that they appear to give scientific legitimacy to differences that are deeply engrained and that most of us tend to experience as natural. However, the consequences of such arguments are dangerous. If boys and girls are naturally different then there is nothing that we can, or should, do to address these differences. Rather, the only option available is to respect and work with the different behaviours and preferences that exist between boys and girls. Thus, in relation to education, if boys are achieving less well than girls then we need to change the way they are taught and the content of what they are expected to learn to appeal to their innate masculine tendencies. Such proposals for making schools more 'boy-friendly' have certainly provided an undercurrent to some of the populist advice given to schools regarding 'boys' underachievement' (see, especially, Hannan, 1999) and will be outlined and discussed in a little more detail in the next section. As will be argued, not only does this approach to distorting the curriculum and the organisation of schools tend to alienate and disadvantage girls but it also simply encourages and reinforces the expression of dominant forms of masculinity among boys (which, ironically, remain the main cause for their poor performance in school compared to girls as we will see below and in the chapters to follow).

Given the popularity of such biological explanations and the dangerousness of their implications for school practice, it is important that we briefly examine the evidence available in relation to these. We will look, in turn, at perhaps the two most commonly used arguments based around hormones and brain differences respectively.[1] In relation to hormones, as Head (1999: 13) explains, there is sufficient evidence to suggest that they do tend to affect mood and behaviour. Moreover, it is evident that men and women do tend to produce differing types of hormones – androgens and oestrogens respectively. As regards androgens, one of the most commonly known is testosterone and there is certainly evidence of a relationship between higher levels of testosterone and behavioural traits such as aggression. Armed with these biological 'facts', some commentators proceed to explain much of boys' behaviour in terms of their higher levels of testosterone and use this as a basis for providing advice on how best to deal with boys in school. Biddulph (1997) provides one such example of this:

> Testosterone ... affects mood and energy ... There's no doubt it causes energetic and boisterous behaviour ... It can grow more muscles and less fat, and it can make you go bald and bad tempered! ... Testosterone influences the brain and makes boys more concerned with rank and competition ...
>
> Boys feel insecure and in danger if there isn't enough structure in a situation. If no-one is in charge, they begin to jostle with each other to establish a pecking-order. Their testosterone-driven make-up leads them to want to set up hierarchies, but they can't always do it because they are all the same age. If we provide structure, then they can relax. For girls, this is not so much a problem.
>
> (Biddulph, 1997: 39–41)

The key problem with arguments such as this is that they are based upon a false premise. As Head (1999) contends, while there is a link between levels of testosterone and certain forms of behaviour, particularly aggression, it is not the one most commonly claimed.

Rather than changes in levels of testosterone simply causing behavioural change, it has been found that changes in behaviour also tend to cause changes in the amount of testosterone excreted in the body. For example, studies involving rhesus monkeys have shown that males, following a fight, experience increased levels of testosterone whereas, in contrast, another study has shown that men suffering from depression find that their bodies release lower levels of testosterone (Head, 1999: 13). The main point from this is that our behaviour is not simply determined by the chemicals in our body. A much more complex process is clearly in operation (Stainton Rogers and Stainton Rogers, 2001). Thus while our immediate behaviour may be influenced by the levels of hormones in our body, the production of these hormones is also directly influenced by our behaviour. For boys and girls, given that they do tend to be raised in different ways, it is not surprising that over time their bodies will tend to produce different levels of particular hormones as a consequence. Ultimately, therefore, while boys as a whole may be found to be more aggressive than girls, it is inadequate simply to explain this in terms of higher levels of testosterone. This does not, in itself, explain why they have higher levels of testosterone in the first place. To answer this question we need to look at how boys are being raised and the different experiences they have and types of behaviour they are encouraged to adopt. More specifically, if higher levels of aggression result in the production of higher levels of testosterone then we need to ask ourselves what it is about society that leads boys and men to behave in a more aggressive way.

Similar arguments are also evident in relation to the second issue of differences in brain structure between boys and girls. There have been two main arguments put forward at various times regarding gender differences in the brain – one involving overall differences in size, the other focusing on differences in the way men's and women's brains are structured. As regards the former, it has been shown that men's brains are on average slightly larger than women's. Historically, this has certainly led some to argue that this proves that men are more intelligent than women (Head, 1999). Of course one of the problems with this argument is the fact that the evidence from examination performance, as we have seen, no longer bears this out! More generally, it is now widely accepted that it is not the size of the brain that determines intellectual capacity as such but the complexity of the connections between brain cells, called neurones.

In terms of current debates concerning intellectual differences between boys and girls, it is the second argument concerning differences in brain structure that still tends to predominate. In essence it is pointed out that the brain is separated into different sections with each being responsible for specific thoughts and actions. Moreover, the brain is separated into two halves and while there are a relatively high number of neurones connecting both halves of the brain in women, there are significantly fewer in men. With characteristic simplicity, Biddulph (1997) explains the implications of these differences for boys and education:

> The right half in a boy's brain is richer in internal connections but poorer in cross connections to the other half. This is one possible explanation of boys' greater success in mathematics, which is largely a 'right side of the brain' activity ... [However], if your brain is somewhat less connected from right to left, then you will have trouble doing things well which need both sides of the brain. This involves skills such as reading, talking about feelings and solving problems through quiet introspection rather than by beating people over the head! Do all these problems sound familiar to you? So now can you see the importance of all this brain research?
>
> (Biddulph, 1997: 60)

Such explanations are certainly seductive in their simplicity and in their ability, apparently, to account for many of the differential trends in achievement highlighted in the previous chapter. However, as with arguments surrounding hormones, the reality is rather more complex than this. First of all, the research evidence to date that has examined gender differences in the neural systems connecting the two halves of the brain (known as the corpus callosum) has been inconclusive with no clear proof that the corpus callosum is actually significantly larger for women than men (Gilbert and Gilbert, 1998). Second, it is too simplistic to claim that mental functions map so directly onto specific areas of the brain. As Head (1999) explains, while this may be true for certain simple motor functions, it is not the case for higher mental functions, especially those acquired through learning. Memories, for example, tend to be stored through connected sets of thousands of neurones spread across the whole area of the brain. Moreover, research has shown that particular functions tend to use different parts of the brain on different occasions (Gilbert and Gilbert, 1998).

Third, the development and growth of neurones does not happen automatically but reflects the activities of individuals and how, basically, they use their brains. Just as with hormones, it is not so much that the structure of the brain simply causes certain forms of behaviour but, rather, that certain forms of behaviour over time cause the structure of the brain to develop in specific ways (Head, 1999; Gilbert and Gilbert, 1998). Again, even if differences in brain structures are found between boys and girls we need to ask ourselves what it is about the differing ways that boys and girls have been raised and the differing experiences they have had that has led to these differences.

Overall, biological explanations provide little help in accounting for gender differences in educational achievement. Indeed, whatever the particular biological explanation posited, it is difficult to square such explanations with the realities of educational performance outlined in the previous chapter. If the differences between boys and girls are so clearly biologically-driven then how can the differential performance of specific groups of boys and girls be explained? How, for example, can we account for the fact that middle class boys tend to significantly outperform working class girls in English and modern languages? If boys' and girls' brains are biologically structured so differently then such anomalies should not arise. However, this is not to deny that our day-to-day behaviour and intellectual capacity may well be influenced, at least in part, by deeply-embedded biological factors. However, as has been seen, these factors are neither natural nor inevitable aspects of our being male or female. Rather, they represent the cumulative ways in which our bodies have been moulded and shaped by our past experiences and behaviour. As Edley and Wetherell (1995) argue, it is for this reason that it makes no sense to separate out biological and cultural explanations of gender. It is also because the cultural and biological are so deeply entwined that there is so much diversity between differing groups of boys and girls in terms of their educational achievements. Ultimately, what this shows is that our search for some of the reasons behind the differences between boys and girls in relation to educational performance needs to look further afield, to the ways in which society tends to influence and structure the lives of boys and girls differently.

Feminine schools

A second collection of explanations regarding boys' poor educational performance focuses more specifically on schools themselves. Schools, it is argued, are now rather alien environments for boys. For example, the content of the curriculum no longer reflects boys' interests. The change of assessment procedures to include more projects and coursework rather than examinations has also favoured girls' rather than boys' learning styles. Moreover, the general lack of male teachers or role models, especially in primary schools, tends to reinforce this 'feminisation' of the school and classroom. It has been argued that many of these changes have been brought about as a consequence of concerns expressed from the late 1970s through to the 1980s regarding inequalities in education faced by girls. While such improvements in the opportunities for girls are to be welcomed, so the argument goes, things have now probably gone too far. There is thus a need to 'redress the balance' to ensure that schools are made a little more 'boy-friendly'.

As will be seen, these arguments are based upon rigid and stereo-typical notions of differences between boys and girls. They also tend to follow logically from the type of biological perspectives outlined above. Thus if it is believed that there are significant, biological differences between the behaviour, interests and intellectual abilities of boys and girls then the only option for schools is to ensure that they work with these differences (see, for example, Biddulph, 1997; Hannan, 1999). However, it is certainly not the case that everyone in this camp will subscribe to these beliefs about biological differ-ences. For some, it is more a sense of pragmatism and a simple concern with raising boys' levels of achievement 'by any means necessary'. Whether the differences between boys and girls are caused by biology or society, the key thing is that they are perceived to exist. These differences are therefore simply taken-for-granted and existing school practices are assessed, and advice consequently given, on what is likely to work 'for boys' (see, for example, Bleach, 1998a; Noble and Bradford, 2000).

To gain a greater appreciation of the arguments associated with this perspective and the problems related to them, it is worth looking briefly at two key areas in turn – first, changes to the curriculum and, second, the apparent 'feminisation' of schools. There are a number of arguments relating to the way in which changes to curriculum have possibly influenced gender differences in attainment. It is intended to examine just one here – the way that changes in the curriculum have been felt to favour what are perceived to be the learning styles of girls over boys. In their extensive review of the evidence, Arnot *et al.* (1998) summarise the overall differences that have been found between the learning styles of girls and boys in the following way:

- There is evidence that girls are more attentive in class and more willing to learn. They do better than boys on sustained tasks that are open-ended, process-based, related to realistic situations, and that require pupils to think for themselves.
- Boys show greater adaptability to more traditional approaches to learning which require memorising abstract, unambiguous facts and rules that have to be acquired quickly. They also appear to be more willing to sacrifice deep understanding, which requires sustained effort, for correct answers achieved at speed.

(Arnot *et al.*, 1998: 28)

Even before we examine some of the ways these findings have been used to inform practice in schools, it is important to stress again the problems of making such blanket comparisons between all girls and all boys. Two points are worth making in this respect. First, the actual size of the cognitive differences between boys and girls as a whole is small (Hyde, 1981). Thus while the average scores of girls may be slightly higher than boys their overall distributions will overlap substantially. Second, we need to be reminded of the significant effects of social class and ethnicity on the differential achievements of boys and girls as highlighted earlier in the previous chapter. Both points taken together mean that it is impossible to predict with any degree of certainty what the learning style and preferences will be for a particular boy or girl simply based upon their gender.

However, these points have not prevented a number of commentators from treating these differences in learning styles as relatively fixed and clear and using this as the basis to explain boys' poor performance. In particular, boys' lower levels of attainment overall compared to girls in English is often explained not only in terms of the open-ended emphasis on reflection and reading and the writing of long prose but also in terms of the choice of literature that tends, through a focus on the 'classics', to place emphasis on 'feminine' concerns such as emotion and relationships (Arnot *et al.*, 1998; Head,

1999). However, such arguments are not just confined to English but tend to be applied across the curriculum, even to areas that have been traditionally associated with boys. As Hannan (1999) explains in his manual for teachers aimed at *Improving Boys' Performance*:

> The prime understanding for the provision and delivery of Equal Opportunities is that BOYS AND GIRLS HAVE DIFFERING LEARNING STYLES.
>
> Rightly or wrongly, the English National Curriculum is much more girl-friendly than boy-friendly. This 'feminisation' is easy to see in the changed outcome patterns in subjects such as technology, geography and history ... Technology is boy-friendly when it is about doing and making things. The pre- and post-realisation emphasis of the National Curriculum places it now firmly in the girl-friendly reflective and analytical arena. Boys hold on well to factual information and like working with it. A history curriculum that is centred in fact is boy-friendly, whereas one based on evidence seeking and analysis is girl-friendly.
>
> (Hannan, 1999: 15, original emphasis)

These arguments have, in turn, led to the provision of a range of tips and advice for teachers in relation to helping them raise boys' achievement by making their lessons more 'boy-friendly'. There have been calls, for example, for a return to traditional methods of teaching including far more structure in class with shorter lessons and children being set a number of short-term goals to appeal to boys' more immediate learning styles (Noble and Bradford, 2000). There have also been calls for the introduction of more class tests and a greater emphasis on competition and examinations as well as the use of more activity-based, hands-on tasks that all, again, appeal particularly to boys' learning preferences (Skelton, 2001; Martino and Berrill, 2003). Moreover, alongside these differing teaching styles, it has been suggested that the material covered in the curriculum should be 'masculinised'. Noble (1998: 33), for example, provides a number of suggestions regarding how lessons can be presented to boys including the 'use of phrases and techniques like "word-attack skills" which appeal to boys' sense of competition'. Bleach (1998b: 25) recommends 'choosing books with good covers, showing males as central characters', whereas Hannan (1999) offers a number of 'handy tips' to make lessons more 'boy-friendly', including:

Early foreign language learning could become a space journey to an alien planet where the brave astronauts are preparing themselves for mankind's [sic] first contact. The Key Stage 3 science class could become a laboratory team seeking a new industrial process for using magnets. Maths can become code-breaking.

Communicating challenge at the start of a more traditional lesson will help to motivate the pupils. Tell the class that they are going to find today's lesson difficult ... they'll be able to do it ... but they are going to find it hard! And you are helping immediately to make it more 'boy-friendly'.

(Hannan, 1999: 17)

These just represent the 'tip of the iceberg' in relation to the type of guidance and advice that can be gleaned from the books and manuals on dealing with 'boys' underachievement'. However, they do give a good taste of the kind of approach taken. Overall, there are at least three problems with these explanations for the lower educational performance of boys and the advice that springs from them. First, and most obviously, this emphasis on the increasing trend towards 'girl-friendly' schools as an explanation of boys' growing 'underachievement' does not square with the evidence. If schools are becoming more hostile places for boys then we would expect that boys would be becoming increasingly alienated from school and that their achievement levels would be falling as a result. However, as we saw from the long-term trends presented in Figure 1.1 in the previous chapter, boys' overall levels of achievement have been increasing year-on-year, and without fail, for the best part of three decades and indeed continue to do so. More specifically, and as we also saw from Table 1.1, the numbers of those gaining five or more GCSEs grades A*–C have increased by over a third (34.9 per cent) over the decade since 1991/2 (roughly the time when the National Curriculum was introduced in schools). These figures certainly do not suggest a growing tide of alienation and disaffection among boys. Moreover, the same evidence undermines the more specific argument about the adverse effects on boys' performance of the increasing emphasis on coursework through the introduction of GCSEs. As Figure 1.2 shows, girls were already improving their performance relative to boys prior to the introduction of GCSEs and more recent studies have shown that even when coursework has been reduced, girls still continue to outperform boys (Elwood, 1995, 1999; Ofsted/EOC, 1996; Arnot et al., 1998).

Second, the advice that emanates from such explanations will simply act to distort the curriculum and thus fundamentally limit and distort the learning and development of boys and girls. For girls, there is evidence that this blanket approach to making lessons much more structured and competitive will disadvantage them (Boaler, 1997) and, certainly, the emphasis on just a limited range of (boy-friendly) material will certainly act to alienate some girls. Moreover, such approaches will also simply reinforce and tie boys further into dominant modes of masculinity. This, in turn, will continue the process whereby their learning and development remains severely restricted to just a narrow range of topics and skills. If boys do currently find it difficult to work on open-ended tasks, to critically reflect upon their learning and to deal with issues such as relationships and emotions then surely these are aspects of their learning that need to be focused on rather than simply avoided.

Third, and finally, the key problem underpinning such explanations for boys' poor performance and the advice and guidance that stem from them is that they take boys' expressions of masculinity for granted. However, as already highlighted in terms of the debates surrounding biological influences, there is nothing natural nor inevitable about boys' masculinities. Indeed, and as we will see, it is precisely these dominant forms of masculinity that lie at the heart of boys' poor educational performance. Rather than pandering to them, it will be shown through the chapters to follow that effective strategies in school need to work with boys and girls to challenge boys' expressions of masculinity (Salisbury and Jackson, 1996; Gilbert and Gilbert, 1998). Only through such a process will boys (and girls) be enabled to significantly broaden their learning opportunities and development. The irony of the type of advice and guidance associated with this perspective is that it simply tends to reinforce boys' current forms of masculinity and thus, ultimately, tends to contribute further to the precise factors that limit their overall educational development.

The other main aspect within this 'feminine schools' approach is the notion that schools as organisations have become 'feminised' mainly through the dominance of female teachers and thus the lack of male role models. As Bleach (1998c) has argued, for example:

In infant and junior schools – and increasingly in secondary schools – teachers are usually female. Some boys are not taught by a male until the secondary phase ... The result is that boys

are not exposed to the 'masculine' dimension of some values ...
Also, many boys find themselves in a world of learning that is
not associated with a masculine figure in their formative years;
hence the activities it involves – principally reading and writing
– are devalued in their eyes.

(Bleach, 1998c: 9–10)

Alongside encouraging more male teachers into primary schools,
such an explanation has generated a number of 'tips' for increasing
the profile of boys and men in schools. Popular suggestions include
encouraging men to act as role models by coming into school and
reading to children and then discussing 'their enjoyment of reading
and what part education has played in their success' (Bleach, 1998b:
30). Moreover, as Raphael Reed (1999: 101) points out, at least
one school has gone a stage further and established a mentoring
system for boys where they shadow businessmen to see 'what
being busy and organised at work really means'. Such a scheme
includes, as she goes on to describe, 'being picked up by a male
manager at 6.45 am in the morning to attend a business meeting
over breakfast'. In addition, some commentators have focused on
increasing boys' profile and positive experiences of the school. Advice
in this instance has included the need to 'search constantly for ways
of celebrating boys' successes' (Bleach, 1998d: 53), giving boys more
responsibilities within the school, and also purposely displaying boys'
work 'even if it is not as neat or as well-presented as the girls''
(Bleach, 1998b: 29).

The problems with these arguments are very similar to those
associated with the need to make the curriculum more 'boy-friendly'.
First, there is simply no evidence to suggest that the lack of male
teachers in primary schools can be linked directly to boys' poorer
performance (Skelton, 2001, 2003). Indeed male classroom teachers
have always been under-represented in primary school settings and
particularly in the early years. It cannot therefore be used as an
explanation for the increase in boys' poor performance relative to
girls that is evident in the mid- to late 1980s (see Figure 1.2). Second,
such explanations tend, by implication, to blame female teachers
for boys' lack of achievement (Pickering, 1997). Rather, and as
highlighted above, there is a need to problematise boys themselves
and their dominant forms of masculinity. Third, and as Skelton
(2001, 2003) has argued, the 'solution' of simply increasing the
numbers of male teachers in primary schools ignores the issue of

what type of men and what kind of role models do we wish them to provide. A number of studies of primary schools, for example, have shown that male teachers can play a key role in encouraging and reinforcing competitive and at times aggressive forms of masculinity among boys (Connolly, 1998a; Skelton, 2001).

Overall, the range of explanations contained within the 'feminine schools' camp – whether they relate to the lack of a 'boy-friendly' curriculum or the feminisation of schools more generally – tend to construct a 'zero-sum' game where it is believed that the achievements of boys and girls are inextricably linked such that one group cannot succeed unless at the expense of the other (Epstein *et al.*, 1998b; Arnot *et al.*, 1999; Francis, 2000). As can be seen, the result is a plethora of advice and guidance that tends to unashamedly pander to boys' immediate needs and interests. These, in turn, are justified on the basis of 'equality of opportunity' and the need to 'redress the balance' of what is now believed to be a schooling system biased in favour of girls. Moreover, in working with stereotypical and taken-for-granted beliefs about boys' and girls' behaviour and learning styles, a logic is created where strategies aimed at addressing boys' poorer educational performance inevitably focus on meeting the interests of boys at the expense of girls.[2] In contrast, and as has been argued, rather than simply taking such stereotypical gender differences for granted, there is a need in relation to boys to problematise the notion of masculinity and to encourage boys to begin to question the dominant forms of masculinity that prevail within their peer cultures. It is only through such a means that boys will be encouraged to question their existing attitudes to education and, possibly, to develop alternative and more positive orientations to learning.

Failing schools

In reading through some of the materials produced by those within the 'feminine schools' camp as outlined above, it is interesting to note that some of the suggestions made for dealing with boys' poor performance tend not to be gender-specific but to be about little more than good teaching practice. These include, for example: advising teachers to provide children with a clear outline of the purpose of the lesson at the beginning of each session (Hannan, 1999); encouraging group work where appropriate to facilitate children's skills in cooperation and communication (Hannan, 1999; Noble and Bradford, 2000); taking care in marking children's work and ensuring that there are plenty of constructive and positive comments (Bleach, 1998d; Hannan, 1999); and developing more diverse and exciting tasks for homework (Bleach, 1998d). Indeed, more recently it does appear that there has been a shift in emphasis from explanations associated with the 'feminine schools' perspective towards this broader one based around standards and teaching practice – what can be termed, after Epstein *et al.* (1998b), the 'failing schools' perspective. It is difficult to identify the precise reasons for this shift in emphasis. However, the strong and effective critique of the 'feminine schools' approach by feminist researchers and many others may certainly have had a key role to play in moving the debates on (see, for example, Yates, 1997; Epstein *et al.*, 1998a; Arnot *et al.*, 1999; Raphael Reed, 1999; Francis, 2000; Skelton, 2001).

Overall, the increasing ascendancy of this 'failing schools' discourse has been heralded by the recent publication of two reports by Ofsted (2003a, 2003b) – *Boys' Achievement in Secondary Schools* and *Yes He Can: Schools Where Boys Write Well*. Gone, for the most part, are the types of strategy that tend to pander to boys' masculinities as with the 'feminine schools' perspective. In its place is the apparently 'gender-neutral' message that the key factor required for improving boys' performance is simply 'good teaching'. As the first of the two reports states in its introduction:

> Improving the achievement of boys is a complex matter in which interlinked factors play important parts. They include a positive learning ethos, good teaching and classroom management, close monitoring of individuals and effective support for learning. These factors are significant in all schools, whether mixed or single-sex, maintained or independent, and are relevant to girls as well as boys.
>
> (Ofsted, 2003a: 3)

A very similar point is also made in the introduction to the second report that is focused on the results of inspections of schools where the gap between boys and girls was found to be much smaller than average (Ofsted, 2003b). This report sets itself the task of identifying those factors that appear to have contributed to boys' increased performance in English specifically. It reinforces the apparently 'gender-neutral' message in terms of what constitutes good practice by arguing that: 'many of the factors that promote the success of schools in achieving good standards of boys' writing ought to have an equally strong effect on the performance of girls' (p. 3). For the authors of this report, the problem of boys' poor educational performance tends to lie in poor quality teaching. As they go on to argue: 'boys may be disproportionately affected in their attitude to learning and their performance in writing by mediocre or poor teaching and assessment' (Ofsted, 2003b: 3).

Such a discourse is not only confined to Britain, however, but seems to be assuming increasing prominence in other countries as well. Martino and Berrill (2003), for example, provide a quote from a recent Australian government report published in 2002 entitled 'Boys: Getting it Right' that adopts a similar argument:

> Of course having a relevant and interesting curriculum that is taught well is just as important for girls as it is for boys. However, boys are more likely than girls to respond to dull subject matter or uninspiring teaching in an overt and challenging way that will disrupt their own and others' learning.
>
> (quoted in Martino and Berrill, 2003: 104)

Overall there are three points to make concerning these arguments. The first is simply that there is no evidence, to date, to support the idea that poor or mediocre teaching is the cause of boys' poor performance. In fact there is some evidence to suggest the precise opposite – that as standards have increased in schools so have boys' lower levels of achievement compared to girls. This can be illustrated by Figure 2.1. As usual, the gender gap is shown on the vertical axis in terms of the number of boys per 100 girls gaining five or more GCSEs grades A*–C in England. An overall measure of educational 'standards' is provided by the horizontal axis which simply represents the overall proportions of school leavers gaining five or more GCSEs grades A*–C in England. It is accepted that this is a rather crude measure of educational standards. However, as it is the one that the government most commonly uses, it will suffice for the purposes of re-assessing the arguments of Ofsted (2003a, 2003b), which is a government-appointed body.

As can be seen, each year between 1974/5 and 2001/2 has been plotted on the graph in terms of the overall levels of achievement that year and then the gender differences in achievement that exist for that year. What the graph clearly shows is that as school standards increase, at least according to the government's measure, the achievements of boys compared to girls decreases. This is certainly

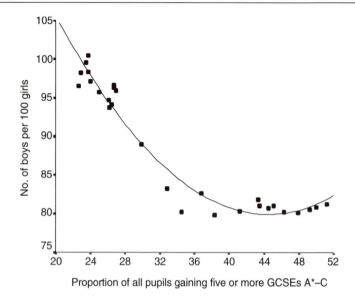

Figure 2.1   Relationship between the number of boys per 100 girls gaining five
or more GCSEs grades A*–C or their equivalent and overall levels of
achievement in England for each year between 1974/5 and 2001/2

Source: Based upon a secondary analysis of data supplied by DfES.

contrary to the 'failing schools' discourse that would suggest that as
school standards increase and thus schools become more effective
(measured by increasing examination achievements) then the gender
gap should reduce.

Alongside this lack of evidence (and in fact the possible existence
of some evidence to the contrary), the second point to make
regarding the 'failing schools' discourse is that rather than being
'gender neutral' it has a number of strongly gendered messages
regarding boys and girls. The most obvious and patronising one is
that while poor teaching cannot be tolerated for boys, it presumably
can for girls. There is a real danger that, as this new discourse begins
to take hold, educational resources will continue to be channelled
at developing effective teaching for boys. Such a mode of thinking
is already evident in the work of Noble and Bradford (2000: 101),
for example, who argue that: 'Lesson plans which work for boys
have got to be good. Lesson plans which work for girls can be much
looser, as experience and research suggest that girls are still willing

to work despite poor teaching'. As with the 'feminine schools' discourse, therefore, while the content of the arguments may have changed, the effects are still the same in continuing to justify the privileging of boys' needs over girls'.

The third and final point to make is that this discourse, just like the 'feminine schools' one, fails to address the issue of masculinity directly and thus essentially leaves it intact (Epstein *et al.*, 1998b). This is not to say that there is no merit to the types of suggestions emerging from this 'failing schools' discourse. In fact, as already stated, much of it can be seen simply as good practice in the classroom (so long as it is not felt that it only needs to be applied to boys!). Moreover, there are some good, practical suggestions that could provide elements of a framework within which effective, critical work with boys and girls can be developed. These include, for example, group work, the development of partnerships with parents and the need to develop a more sensitive approach to discipline (Ofsted, 2003a). This last point is particularly important given that there is a tendency, as Martino and Pallotta-Chiarolli (2003) have pointed out, for boys to receive harsher and more public chastisement than girls and for this to simply tend to reinforce resentment and male resistance to schooling (see also Pickering, 1997; Francis, 2000; Lynch and Lodge, 2002).

The overall point is that, notwithstanding the patronising construction of girls, there are a number of positive suggestions to emerge from this 'failing schools' discourse. However, so long as it fails to critically address the problem of masculinity, such a discourse is unlikely to address the key issue of boys' lower levels of attainment in relation to girls.

The crisis of masculinity

Alongside this focus on schools, whether feminine or failing, there exists an additional range of arguments used to explain boys' poor educational performance that tend to focus more broadly on changes in society and how these are adversely affecting young men. Such arguments have certainly gained much prominence over recent years witnessed, for example, by Jack Straw, the then Home Secretary, claiming in 1999 that the main 'social issue of our time' is that relating to the behaviour and role of young men (O'Donnell and Sharpe, 2000: 1). It was at this time that Stephen Byers, the then Schools Minister, also drew attention to the over-representation of boys among those permanently excluded from school and blamed this on a 'laddish, anti-learning culture' (Head, 1999; Francis, 2000). A flavour of the discourse concerning what has been labelled the 'crisis of maculinity' is summarised by O'Donnell and Sharpe:

> On the face of it there certainly seems to be a 'boys' problem'. Boys are now under-performing compared to girls in nearly all subjects at GCSE; the less well qualified can be difficult to employ and as a result often struggle to construct stable and fulfilling lives; boys commit about three times as much crime as girls; and they are generally perceived as far more anti-social in their general conduct than girls. Much of the damage they do is to themselves. Boys are far more likely to attack each other than to attack girls, and the suicide rate for young men between the ages of 15 and 24 has almost doubled since 1976 and is far higher than the corresponding figure for young women.
>
> (O'Donnell and Sharpe, 2000: 1)

What we see here is a good depiction of some of the problems associated with masculinity and this serves, if nothing else, to help us begin to understand that boys' poor performance is but one element of a much more deeply-rooted male malaise. However, there are two points worth making about this discourse. First, while it quite rightly highlights the damaging effects of masculinity on men, very little is said about the more damaging effects of masculinity on women. In this sense, alongside issues of sexual harassment and domestic violence, there is also the key factor of male power and its consequences in terms of women's subordination and the continuing barriers they face in relation to employment and career opportunities. There is a danger, therefore, that this discourse simply constructs men as the main victims of masculinity and forgets women and girls altogether (Skelton, 1998).

The second point to draw out is that there is a clear implication that what we are witnessing is a *growing* problem. Indeed it is precisely this point that is used to explain why boys are apparently falling further behind girls in school. Most commonly, the growing crisis is linked to broader changes in society, particularly in terms of the family and work, that have tended to undermine the traditional role occupied by men (Arnot *et al.*, 1999; Head, 1999). Thus, in terms of the family, the traditional model of male as breadwinner and head of the household is now giving way to an increasingly complex range of family forms including cohabitation and reconstituted families where women are also becoming as equally likely to work as men. Alongside this, there has been major economic restructuring characterised by higher levels of unemployment and the decline of the (largely male-dominated) manufacturing sector and rise of the (often female-dominated) service sector. The days where young men were guaranteed a job after leaving school have therefore long gone. Moreover, the types of jobs that are available are often insecure, part-time and/or poorly-paid.

The key point arising from this is that men are now seen as in crisis. The traditional ways in which they gained a sense of purpose and identity, namely through their work and position within the family, have been systematically eroded over the last two decades. The consequence for some, it is argued, is simply to withdraw. As Bleach (1998c: 11) contends, for example, 'When they see what has happened to their fathers, their brothers and their extended families, it undoubtedly contributes to a reduction of motivation and self-respect in some of them'. For other boys, they tend to compensate for these changes by seeking out alternative forms of status and identity, often through the construction of exaggerated forms of masculinity based around violence, sport and sexual prowess (Canaan, 1996; Nayak, 2003).

The problem with this notion of a crisis is that it tends to exaggerate the extent of the current problem facing boys and men and also to deny important continuities with the past. It is thus not all boys who are being adversely affected by these broader social changes. For example, it is hard to see how white, middle class boys can be characterised as being in a 'state of crisis'. Moreover, if we return to the actual evidence regarding trends in boys' educational performance then we can see that boys, as a whole, are far from being 'in crisis'. As we saw in Figure 1.2, the key drop in boys' relative levels of achievement compared to girls occurred in the mid- to late 1980s. And yet, if we look at Figure 1.1 and the changing nature of boys' absolute levels of achievement, then this time also represented their most sustained period of improvement in performance compared to any other. If boys as a whole were becoming significantly more disillusioned with education during this period then it is hard to reconcile this with such high rates of improvement in examination performance. The point is, then, that these changes associated with economic restructuring and the family are not impacting evenly on all boys as a whole but tend to have a much greater impact upon particular groups of boys, especially working class boys, living in specific regions. Clearly there are many other boys who remain able to significantly improve their educational performance year-on-year throughout this period.

In addition, this tendency to focus on the current problems posed by a 'crisis of masculinity' also has the effect of denying the continuities with the past. Thus, while it is true that these broader social and economic changes are requiring certain groups of boys to have to reconsider their future place and role within society and thus to develop differing forms of masculinity in response, this is nothing new. Boys and men have always been required to do this. The history of masculinity is therefore one of evolution and continual redevelopment as boys and men actively seek to renegotiate their positions of power and authority in the shadow of broader social change. However, while the particular configurations of masculinity continue to evolve and change, there has always been a tendency, as Francis (2000) has argued, for boys to be violent, to harass and dominate women and to be excluded from school. Moreover, and in relation to the focus of this present book, boys have also always tended to perform less well in education compared to girls (Cohen, 1998).

Thus while such economic and social changes are significant, it is important that we do not exaggerate their significance nor overlook the central role that masculinity has always tended to play in the poor educational performance of boys. This leads to two final points. First, there is still a need to develop an adequate understanding of the nature and role of masculinity itself in boys' lives. This is something that will be addressed shortly. Second, while masculinity is able to explain the general tendency for boys to perform less well in education compared to girls, there remains the need to explain the specific 'surge' in the gap between boys and girls that occurred in the mid- to late 1980s (see Figure 1.2). The broader changes that have occurred in relation to economic restructuring and the family may be able to partly explain why the relative performance of particular groups of boys may have declined further. However, we have seen that these changes are not able to account for the overall patterns of differential achievement between boys and girls that occurred during the late 1980s. Before looking a little more closely at the notion of masculinity, therefore, it is useful to briefly examine what could have caused this specific pattern of achievement during this period.

Feminism and girls' aspirations

The period of the mid- to late 1980s is one where the differences in achievement between boys and girls grew significantly. It will be remembered from the previous chapter that before this time there was relative stability with about 95 boys to every 100 girls gaining five or more GCSEs grades A*–C, or their earlier equivalent. During the second half of the 1980s this dropped significantly so that, by the end of the decade, there were on average around 80 boys to every 100 girls achieving the same. As also seen, this difference has since been relatively stable during the 1990s and to the present day. So far, we have examined arguments for these patterns that have tended to focus on boys themselves in one form or another. However, to understand this particular change, we need to refocus our attention away from factors affecting boys and onto those affecting girls. In essence, the increase in the gap that emerged during this time was not the result of boys tending to fall further behind but rather the result of girls simply realising their potential. As Boaler (1998: 119–20) explains very clearly:

> The heightened position that girls now occupy with regard to general GCSE achievement is no more than they deserve. This … is because the superior position that boys traditionally held was caused by the systematic barriers that were placed in the paths of girls; now that these barriers are, in some places, being removed, the attainment of girls is a more accurate reflection of their interest, motivation, and ability … [G]ender patterns are shifting, not because of a climate of boy-disadvantage, but because of a climate that is moving closer to equality of opportunity, in which girls are being *allowed* to achieve.
>
> (Boaler, 1998, quoted in
> Epstein *et al.*, 1998a: 106, original emphasis)

From this perspective, while boys have always performed less well than girls, the real extent of the gap has been obscured by the fact that girls have historically tended to be held back in relation to education and schooling. However, a number of changes have taken place during the 1980s in particular that have, as Boaler argues, allowed girls to begin to achieve their full potential. This, in turn, has also brought to light the realities of boys' poor educational performance.

At the heart of these changes is the increasing impact that feminism has had on debates concerning education and schooling. During the 1970s and early 1980s a number of important studies were published by feminist researchers that highlighted the inequalities that girls experienced in school in relation to: low teacher expectations of girls and the lack of attention they gave them; the tendency for girls to be channelled away from science and technology subjects; and the tendency for boys to dominate classroom activities and to routinely harass girls (Stanworth, 1981; Spender, 1982; Arnot and Weiner, 1987; Weiner and Arnot, 1987; Skelton, 1989). Such work had a number of consequences. First, as Arnot *et al.* (1999: 151) have pointed out, it increased the awareness of schools and teachers of the problems and inequalities faced by girls. This, in turn, helped encourage equal opportunities by individual teachers in schools committed to reform as well as the establishment of a range of broader initiatives in the early 1980s such as the *Girls and Technology Education Project* (GATE), the *Girls into Science and Technology Project* (GIST) and *Girls into Mathematics* (GAMMA) – all of which aimed to work with schools and teachers to address gender stereotypes and to encourage girls into traditionally male-dominated areas of the curriculum (Arnot *et al.*, 1999).

Second, at about the same time, the government established the *Technical and Vocational Education Initiative* (TVEI) aimed at stimulating curriculum development in technical and vocational subjects for children aged 14–18. Of most significance was the fact that the initiative included a requirement for schools to make efforts to address gender stereotyping in its work and this was later seen, by many schools, as an important impetus for them to engage in gender equality work (Arnot *et al.*, 1998). Third, not only was feminism having an effect upon girls indirectly through these various programmes and activities but it was also impacting upon girls directly through its ability to increase girls' awareness and aspirations generally. Throughout the 1980s and into the 1990s studies have shown that girls, generally, have become more confident and self-assured in their academic abilities and are much more likely than before to have aspirations that include successful careers (Arnot *et al.*, 1998, 1999; Francis, 2000). Fourth, and finally, a number of other factors have been cited in relation to their effects in increasing girls' opportunities. These include the passing of the Sex Discrimination Act 1975 that covered educational provision, the inclusion of a focus on equal opportunities policies in Ofsted school inspections and also the introduction of GCSEs in 1985 and later the National Curriculum that all opened up greater opportunities for girls to study a more diverse range of subjects.

Overall, therefore, it would appear that the actual increase in the gender gap that has occurred in the mid- to late 1980s was not due to particular problems faced by boys (whether these be feminine schools, poor teaching or wider social and economic changes resulting in a broader crisis of masculinity), but due simply to girls being able for the first time to begin to achieve their full potential because of the removal of the barriers that had previously held them back. The progress of girls, therefore, has occurred in its own right and has not been at the expense of boys.

What this suggests, in turn, is that the apparent 'dive' in boys' educational achievements in the late 1980s is likely to be a distraction in relation to attempts to explain their overall levels of achievement. Rather, it is likely that boys have always achieved to a similar extent and that, with the increased opportunities open to girls, all that has happened is that we now have a fuller picture of the extent of that poor performance. The particular events and changes faced by girls, as described above, certainly help to explain the shape of the trend line shown in Figure 1.2. What they do not do, however, is explain why boys have lagged behind in the first place. To understand this we need to look at the issue of masculinity itself.

Laddish behaviour

In terms of popular debates, the most common way in which masculinity has been discussed in relation to its effects on educational achievement has been through reference to 'laddish' behaviour. In her extensive interviews with boys and girls in three London secondary schools, Francis (2000) identifies the boys' laddish behaviour as the key factor impacting not only on their achievement but also on that of the girls as well. According to Francis, it was the 'laddish persona' that encompassed more of the traits that have been traditionally associated with masculinity than any other. In this sense she describes laddism as including:

> Interest in masculine-typed activities such as football, the objectification of and sexual activity with females, an irreverent and rebellious attitude to authority, physical strength, boisterousness, bravery, daring, camaraderie and 'having a laugh'.
>
> (Francis, 2000: 124)

Mac an Ghaill (1994) describes this overall culture as the '3Fs' – 'fighting, football and fucking'. The main problem with this type of laddish culture is that it is simply incompatible with what Francis (2000) identifies as two of the traits required of pupils in classrooms – obedience and diligence. It is therefore not 'cool' to be seen as conformist and hard-working in class and, moreover, it may be dangerous given that it could attract the derision of other boys. The effects of male peer pressure are therefore strong and have led, as Warrington *et al.* (2000) found in their own school research, to some boys having to pretend that they are not doing as much work as they actually are in class (see also Frosh *et al.*, 2002). Moreover, and as Frosh *et al.* (2002) have also found, not only did few of the (working class) boys in their study manage to be popular among their peers while being overtly academically successful but popular boys were also expected to 'backchat' their teachers. Overall, there is little doubt that this type of laddish, anti-school sub-culture evident among particular groups of boys has a significant role to play in limiting their educational achievement and, equally importantly, that of those around them (see, for example, Willis, 1977; Corrigan, 1979; Jenkins, 1983; Brown, 1987; Mac an Ghaill, 1994).

There are two problems with this argument concerning laddism, however. The first is that it can only partially account for boys' lower levels of attainment compared to girls. The reason for this is that laddism represents a particular form of masculinity most associated with certain groups of working class boys. This is evident in the fact, for example, that nearly all of the studies listed above – including Francis's (2000) – are of working class boys. This is not a criticism as such but merely to point out that we need to be extremely careful not to apply the findings of one particular section of boys to all boys in our attempts to explain boys' poor educational performance. In Frosh *et al.*'s (2002) study, for example, they found that boys in private schools, in particular, were actually able to maintain popularity among their peers while also working hard and doing well at school. More generally, and as Lucey and Walkerdine (2000) point out in response to the appropriation of the notion of laddism by government:

> Government refers to the need for strategies to tackle anti-school 'laddish' cultures which are held responsible for boys' poor performance. Once again class differences are simply glazed over, as if all boys are doing badly, as if all 'laddish' cultures have the

same genesis or, crucially, the same effects and consequences for all boys.

(Lucey and Walkerdine, 2000: 40)

Overall, it is clear from the evidence presented in the previous chapter that boys' poor performance is not just a problem for particular (working class and Black) boys. In all major social class and ethnic groups, boys are performing less well than girls. This is not to say that all boys are performing equally poorly. As is also evident, for example, there are clear and significant differences between boys from different social class and ethnic backgrounds. Moreover, those boys from social class and ethnic groups that are already doing the least well in education are also the ones most likely to be the furthest behind the girls in their respective groups. The point is simply that low educational attainment is not confined to certain groups of boys and that this, in turn, draws attention to the need to problematise masculinity more generally and learn more about the differing ways it is constructed among differing groups of boys and the particular impacts these diverse forms of masculinity have on their education and learning.

The second problem with this notion of laddism is that it can imply at times that masculinity is almost a lifestyle that can be worn or discarded at will. This perception is certainly encouraged by those studies that tend simply to describe the main characteristics of boys' laddish behaviour with little attempt to explain or help understand where they have come from. It is therefore also important to develop an approach to the study of masculinity that aims to ground any analysis within the context of broader social processes and structures. With these two points in mind, it is worth setting out, in the final section of this chapter, an overall framework for understanding masculinity that will inform the two qualitative case studies of young boys to follow in Part III.

Theorising masculinities

Current theories of masculinity can be understood in part as a response to the problems associated with traditional sex-role theory. Sex-role theory certainly dominated the literature on gender and education during the late 1970s and for much of the 1980s and, for educational practitioners and the public, probably remains the main way of understanding the influence of gender on children's development today. It is based upon the distinction made by Oakley (1972) and others between the categories 'sex' and 'gender' (see Lindsey, 1990). Such a distinction was made as a way of countering crude biological explanations for the differences between males and females. Rather, while sex is fixed and represents the biological (usually anatomical) differences between men and women, gender is socially constructed and reflects the differing forms of behaviour that men and women are socialised into and which they come to internalise from a very early age. Thus, the differences in behaviour found among males and females are not natural but a product of the influences of society. Much of the research on sex-role theory that has emerged from this basic starting point has tended to focus on the complex ways in which infants and young children are socialised into their respective identities of being masculine for boys or feminine for girls (see, for example, Chetwynd and Hartnett, 1978; Clarricoates, 1978; Deem, 1980; Delamont, 1980).

Overall, the contribution that sex-role theory has made should not be underestimated. As Edley and Wetherell (1995) point out, for example, it was the first systematic attempt to present a genuinely social account of gender differences. The distinction made by early feminists between sex and gender has certainly played a crucial role in problematising gender differences and thus the relations and structures of inequality upon which they are based. Moreover, the use of sex-role theory in early research has also played an extremely important role in drawing attention to the significance of gender in the experiences and development of children. By the late 1980s, however, criticisms were beginning to emerge regarding this theoretical framework, much of which from feminist and pro-feminist writers. Three of the key problems will be mentioned briefly here. First, it was argued that sex-role theory tends to construct boys and girls as passive receptacles of the socialisation of others (Mac an Ghaill, 1996b; Skelton, 2001). Not only does this tend to paint a negative view of girls as victims, as Arnot (1991) has pointed out, but it also, to coin a phrase, 'lets boys off the hook'. As Salisbury and Jackson (1996: 6) have argued, 'all this talk of "internalising dominant stereotypes" doesn't give any critical purchase on questions of boys' resistance … It doesn't analyse boys and masculinities in such a way that allows them to accept active responsibility for their own changes'. There is a need, therefore, to move beyond this deterministic and 'over-socialised' view of gender identities and to recognise the agency of boys and girls and the central role they play in the development and expression of their masculine and feminine identities.

A second problem associated with sex-role theory is what Jackson (1998) refers to as 'gender absolutism'. In other words the theory constructs just two, monolithic identities – masculinity and femininity – and thus denies the fact that there are many forms of masculinity and femininity and that these are constantly evolving and changing as boys and girls renegotiate their identities within specific social contexts (Connell, 1995; Mac an Ghaill, 1996b; Martino and Pallotta-Chiarolli, 2003). This has certainly already been hinted at earlier in relation to the differing masculinities that tend to be developed between middle class and working class boys in school. As also seen in the previous chapter, the educational achievements of boys and girls tend to differ markedly in relation to their social class and ethnic backgrounds. A need exists, therefore, for these absolutist categories of masculinity and femininity to be broken down so as to reveal the complexity of boys' and girls' lives. A key part of this task, then, is to understand the ways in which factors such as social class and ethnicity interact with gender. As Connell (1995: 76) rightly points out: 'To understand gender ... we need to constantly go beyond gender'. It is precisely for this reason that social class plays such a key role in the analysis of young boys' masculinities provided through the case studies to follow.

Third, and finally, one of the key criticisms of sex-role theory has been its neglect of the issue of power, especially in relation to studies of masculinity (Carrigan *et al.*, 1985; Brittan, 1989; Connell, 1987, 1995; Mac an Ghaill, 1996a). This is evident in at least two senses. One has been the tendency to focus on how boys and girls are socialised into their respective masculine and feminine identities with little attention being paid to the relations of power and control that are not only established between boys and girls but also between differing groups of boys and differing groups of girls. The way in which particular expressions of masculinity tend to involve the domination and harassment of girls has already been touched upon above. However, in relation to masculinity, for example, there is also a need to study the hierarchies of power that exist and which locate particular forms of masculinity in relations of domination and subordination to one another (Mac an Ghaill, 1994; Connell, 1995; Martino and Pallotta-Chiarolli, 2003). The second aspect of power that has been neglected is its institutional basis. In other words, masculinity is not just something embodied and expressed by individual boys and men but it is also something embedded within the routines, structures and ethos of key institutions (Connell, 1993, 1995). As Skelton (2001) has shown in relation to primary schools, for example, there are particular and distinct forms of masculinity that can predominate not just in terms of the overall culture and ethos of the school but also through its routine practices in relation to classroom organisation and modes of discipline. In this sense Skelton (2001) argues that there is a need to understand what Kessler *et al.* (1985) have termed the particular 'gender regime' that is in operation in any particular school and the role it plays in the formation of dominant modes of masculinity and femininity and, consequently, how these are hierarchically related.

In response to these concerns, there is now emerging a significant body of research on masculinities (Mac an Ghaill, 1996a; Hearn and Morgan, 1990; Segal, 1990; Connell, 1987, 1995; O'Donnell and Sharpe, 2000; Skelton, 2001; Martino and Pallotta-Chiarolli, 2003). Perhaps the most theoretically developed and widely-used account of masculinities is that provided by Connell and his colleagues and summarised in Connell (1995). With the concerns relating to sex-role theory as outlined above very much in mind, Connell has suggested that we need to develop a dynamic understanding of masculinity and femininity as *gender projects*, reflecting the active and unfinished role that people play in constantly struggling to develop and redevelop their gender identities in response to specific and forever-changing social contexts. Such gender projects operate at a range of levels, most notably in relation to the individual level, the broader cultural/ideological level and the structural/ institutional level. The key requirement for Connell (1995) is that particular forms of masculinity can only be understood in relation to how they are generated and reproduced across these three levels. Practically, and in relation to the case studies to follow, this means not only focusing on the appropriation, management and expression of masculinity by the young boys themselves but also locating all of this within the broader context of the influence of dominant cultures of masculinity as evident in the local neighbourhood and more broadly in the media. It also means including an appreciation of the context provided by the school and the way it, as an institution, also tends to embody and reproduce particular forms of masculinity.

Within this overall approach, one of the most important contributions that Connell (1995) has made is in his focus on power and the way that different forms of masculinity are hierarchically structured in relations of domination and subordination. While there are many different forms of masculinity in practice, Connell (1995) suggests that these can be grouped into four main types that reflect the overall 'gender order' and its related 'configurations of practice'. These are: hegemonic, subordinate, marginalised and complicit masculinities. In brief, *hegemonic masculinity* is the dominant form of masculinity that achieves the highest status and the greatest influence and rewards. It is expressed and reproduced particularly through the corporate structures of 'top levels of business, the military and government' (Connell, 1995: 77). Hegemonic masculinity is not static and fixed, however, but forever evolving and reinventing itself through time and may also take slightly different forms in differing contexts. As Kenway and Fitzclarence (1997: 121) summarise:

> At this stage of Western history, hegemonic masculinity mobilizes around physical strength, adventurousness, emotional neutrality, certainty, control, assertiveness, self-reliance, individuality, competitiveness, instrumental skills, public knowledge, discipline, reason, objectivity and rationality.
>
> (quoted in Skelton, 2001: 50)

The other three types of masculinity stand in relation to this dominant, hegemonic form. *Subordinate masculinities* represent those that directly conflict with some of the key features of hegemonic masculinity and thus tend to be actively repressed. The most obvious example of a subordinate masculinity, according to Connell, are gay masculinities that are not only culturally stigmatised by hegemonic masculinity but are also materially repressed through systematic social, legal and economic discrimination. In contrast, *marginalised masculinities* reflect the differing positioning of men resulting from the interplay of social class and ethnicity. Thus while working class and/or Black masculinities may incorporate and attempt to reproduce some of the key features of hegemonic masculinity, their class position and ethnic background still act to marginalise them in relation to the dominant form of hegemonic masculinity. Finally, Connell (1995) uses the term *complicit masculinities* to refer to those men who, even though they may attempt to distance themselves from or even be in opposition to hegemonic masculinity, still benefit indirectly from it. Thus there may be men who purposely distance themselves from the aggressive and sexist nature of dominant forms of masculinity. However, they will still benefit from being men in a male-dominated society. As

Connell (1995: 79) argues: 'masculinities constructed in ways that realize the patriarchal dividend, without the tensions or risks of being the frontline troops of patriarchy, are complicit in this sense'.

Overall, this way of thinking about masculinity is certainly useful and helps to address the three key problems mentioned earlier. In fact the different types of masculinity and their relationships to one another as outlined above, together with the need to understand all of these within broader social structural contexts, will inform much of the case studies to follow.

Conclusions

This chapter has provided a detailed summary and re-evaluation of the key explanations that have been proposed for boys' poor educational performance in light of the statistical evidence outlined in Chapter 1. It will be remembered from the previous chapter that boys have always tended to perform less well than girls. In relation to older boys and as shown in Figure 1.2, up until the mid-1980s there were about 95 boys to every 100 girls achieving five or more GCSEs grades A*–C. However, from the mid- to the late 1980s the gap widened significantly so that by the early 1990s there were only about 80 boys to every 100 girls achieving the same. This gap seems to have stabilised ever since. From the discussion above, we can draw out two key factors that taken together can explain much of this pattern.

First, the general tendency for boys to perform less well than girls can be explained by the dominant forms of masculinity that exist among boys in school. At a general level, it tends to provide the basis for sub-cultures to develop among boys that frown upon working hard and doing well at school. However, there is not one form of masculinity but many different masculinities that are created by boys in response to their specific social contexts. For those who are already doing badly at school then it can significantly exacerbate this situation through the development of an explicit anti-school culture. This tends to be found, in particular, among working class boys and/or boys from particular minority ethnic groups. For some, the development of exaggerated masculine identities may have increased over the last decade or so as they attempt to compensate for broader changes in society, particularly changes in the family and economic restructuring that have all tended to remove the traditional ways in which these boys would have gained a strong sense of masculine identity.

For other (mainly middle class) boys, however, who tend to be in an environment where academic success is the norm, while they are still held back to a certain extent by this reluctance to be seen to work hard, this is counter-balanced somewhat by an emphasis on academic competition and the need to be successful. Thus, overall, while masculinity can explain boys' poorer levels of educational attainment compared to girls, its particular manifestations do tend to either exacerbate further or reduce the size of the gender gap to a certain extent as illustrated by Figure 1.5 in the last chapter.

Second, the increase in the gap between the performance of boys and girls during the specific period in the mid- to late 1980s can largely be explained by the removal of previous barriers faced by girls in schools together with a general increase in their educational and career aspirations. In this sense, it was not that boys were falling behind girls but simply that girls were being allowed to reach their full potential for the first time. It is probably the case, therefore, that the wider gap that now exists between boys and girls is a more accurate reflection of the overall differences in the attitudes and motivations of boys and girls. The only difference between now and the 1970s is that the size of this gap had previously tended to be partly concealed because girls were being held back.

As regards the present book, what all of this shows is that the key factor to address in terms of boys' poor educational performance is masculinity itself. It is with this in mind that the final part of this chapter introduced some of the major theoretical issues associated with the concept of masculinity. As was argued, there is a need to recognise that there are masculinities and not just one masculinity and that these need to be understood in terms of the specific social and structural contexts within which they are developed. It is this that provides the rationale for the two case studies to follow in Part III that focus on young boys in two very different schools – one located in an affluent middle class area and the other in a poor, socially deprived working class area. The aim of these case studies will be to assess whether the arguments concerning the differing forms of masculinity that exist and their differential impacts upon boys' dispositions towards education, as outlined above, are applicable to boys in the early years. Moreover, and if so, the case studies will also aim to identify what the dominant forms of masculinity among working class and middle class boys are at this young age and how they tend to influence the boys' attitudes towards schooling.

Part II

Theorising boys and masculinities in the early years

Chapter 3

Vygotsky, Bourdieu and the social contexts of young children's development

Introduction

Traditional models of child development continue to represent a powerful obstacle in the way of those wishing to undertake work with young children around issues of gender (Walkerdine, 1984, 1990; MacNaughton, 1997, 2000). Consider, for example, some of the common arguments put forward against work aimed at encouraging young children to reflect upon what it means to be 'a boy' or 'a girl' and challenging common stereotypes that they may have around such identities:

- 'Children of that age are just too young to recognise gender differences – certainly in terms of anything beyond simply being able to distinguish between boys and girls'.
- 'Even if young boys and girls are beginning to learn what it means to be masculine and feminine they are just not "ready" at this age to verbalise their views, let alone reflect upon them'.
- 'We shouldn't be interfering with young children's development like this in any case. We strongly believe in the importance of play and "child-centred" learning'.

All of these arguments are underpinned by a particular theory of child development – namely that based upon the influential work of Piaget (1962, 1965, 1977). As can be seen, the problem is that unless these arguments are effectively dealt with then many teachers and early years practitioners will remain reluctant to begin addressing issues of gender among young children. This, then, is the purpose of the present chapter. It will begin with a necessarily detailed outline and critique of Piaget's model of child development before then proposing an alternative framework for understanding how young children learn and develop, based upon the work of Vygotsky. This, in turn, will provide the framework within which the case studies to follow in Part III of the book will be analysed and understood.

One of the key problems that will be raised in relation to Piaget's account, as Burman (1994) has suggested, is the way Piaget has viewed children's development from the 'inside out'. In other words, children are viewed as independent entities whose cognitive development occurs naturally within their individual minds only to then find expression 'on the outside' through more complex forms of activity and behaviour. This, in turn, leads to a universal model of development where children all tend to pass through the same set of stages and thus where the course of their development remains largely unaffected by the social contexts within which they are located. Such an account therefore allows no space for considering how wider social relations and processes, such as gender and social class, can possibly influence both the rate and direction of particular children's development.

To counter this problem, there is a need to turn Piaget's approach on its head and to therefore focus on how development takes place from the 'outside in'. In this sense, we need to find ways of understanding how broader social relationships – reflecting dominant forms of masculinity and social class relations – come to be internalised by young children and thus influence and shape their cognitive development. It is precisely this approach to development from the 'outside in' that is at the heart of Vygotsky's (1978) work, as will be discussed following the outline and critique of Piaget's theoretical approach. In discussing Vygotsky's work, however, it will be pointed out that there has been a tendency in Vygotskian research not to deal adequately with the complexity of the social relations within which young children are located and thus which they then internalise. With this in mind, the chapter will conclude by suggesting that Vygotsky's overall approach can be usefully supplemented with the two sociological concepts of 'habitus' (Bourdieu, 1977, 1990) and 'figuration' (Elias, 1978, 1994).

Piaget and traditional models of child development

It is not an exaggeration to say that the work of Piaget (1962, 1965, 1977) has, since the 1960s, largely set the agenda regarding early years theory and practice not only in the UK but in most industrialised nations around the world (Burman, 1994; Smith *et al.*, 1998; Wood, 1998). Within the UK, his theories of child development, with their emphasis on child-centred learning, underpinned the findings and recommendations of the Plowden Report (1967) – *Children and their Primary Schools* – that largely redefined the nature of primary schooling at that time (Galton *et al.*, 1980).

Moreover, while much of the detail of what Piaget had to say about the precise nature of children's development has since been challenged, his overall framework – of viewing children's learning in terms of universal stages of development and also emphasising the centrality of children's self-directed play – remains hugely influential in early years settings. It is with this in mind that it is useful here to offer a rather detailed overview and critique of Piaget's work. This will not only help us to think again about some of the thinking and practices we tend to take for granted in the early years (based around the view of development from the 'inside out') but will also provide the context and rationale for the construction of an alternative theory of how children learn and develop, from the 'outside in', found in the work of Vygotsky.

As we will see shortly, while there are a number of significant problems relating to Piaget's theories, it is important to state at the outset that these should not prevent us from recognising the extremely important contribution his work made at the time in challenging the then dominant behaviourist models of learning, exemplified by the research of Skinner (1938, 1968). Such models set about establishing a science of learning based upon literally thousands of behavioural experiments and tests conducted with many different species of animal and with humans. Inspired by Pavlov's studies of dogs in 1927, they were underpinned by a belief that animals and humans learn in essentially similar ways, through observing and imitating the behaviour of others as well as through conditioning by a wide range of external rewards and reinforcements (Wood, 1998). Within this behaviourist approach children played an essentially passive role, simply responding automatically to the systems of stimuli and reinforcements presented to them.

In stark contrast to this, Piaget proposed a radically different view of children centred around the active role they play in their own learning and development. This view is summarised in Figure 3.1 and illustrates how children's activity and the way they explore and experiment with the things around them lies at the heart of their cognitive development. Through self-directed exploration and

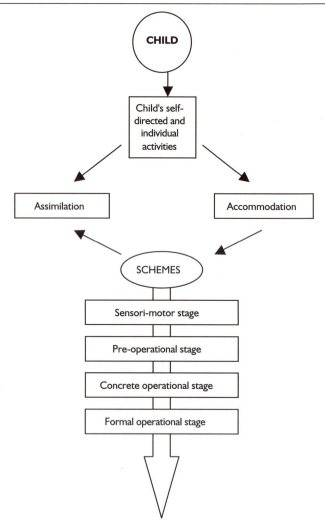

Figure 3.1   Piaget's theory of children's development

play, children are forever developing ever-more complex mental structures – or schemes – to help them make sense of their environment and to guide their actions. Each scheme is not composed simply of a set of thoughts or memories but also of related actions and strategies. Schemes therefore not only help children to make sense of a particular object or event but also to guide them in terms of how they should behave towards it.

Piaget explained this process whereby children refine and develop their cognitive schemes with the two inter-related concepts of *assimilation* and *accommodation*. Through self-directed activity, children are forever encountering new experiences. These new experiences can either be made sense of and thus categorised within their existing schemes (i.e. be assimilated) or will require them to refine their existing schemes to incorporate and make sense of this new experience (i.e. to accommodate this new and different experience within a revised scheme). As the arrows in Figure 3.1 are intended to illustrate, existing schemes therefore tend not only to inform the way that children make sense of familiar experiences (i.e. assimilate them) but schemes are also revised and changed through children's exposure to unfamiliar experiences (i.e. accommodation). At the heart of all of this, however, is the child working independently and under their own motivation. As mentioned earlier, it is therefore a view of development from the 'inside out' – being instigated by the child's own natural and internal curiosity and only consequently being manifest on the outside as they develop and engage in more complex forms of behaviour as a result.

This view of development from the 'inside out', with its neglect of the influence of broader social and cultural factors, allowed Piaget to argue that a universal developmental path can be identified along which all children travel. Such a path consists of four key stages through which all children are expected to progress and that mark the most fundamental accommodations that children will be required to make to their schemes. Moreover, given the way in which children's learning is viewed in such a sequential way, with each stage being built on the achievements gained in the previous ones, Piaget argued that these stages are invariant. In other words, children could not 'skip' a particular stage but had to pass through each stage in turn. The four key stages are illustrated in Figure 3.1. Given that these stages have been (and remain) highly influential in early years thinking and practice, it is worth briefly outlining their key characteristics here.

Piaget termed the first stage of development the *sensori-motor stage*, typical of children aged 0–2. During this stage, children initially respond to their environment with simple reflexes. Over time they begin to develop the ability to use symbols to represent their environment and help them to think about it. This was evident, for Piaget, by their development of 'object permanence' towards the end of this stage that represents young children's recognition that objects continue to exist even when out of their sight. This development of symbolic thought provides the basis for the second stage – the *pre-operational stage* – that Piaget argued is typically found among children aged 2–7. During this stage children make significant progress in relation to symbolic thought and begin to learn and make use of a range of representational schemes including language, writing, numbers and pictorial and spatial representations.

However, children are limited at this stage by their inability to employ logical mental operations. They therefore tend to be egocentric and unable to empathise with others; cannot attend to more than one task at a time (a limitation known as centration); and cannot comprehend such mental operations as conservation and reversibility. To take the example of conservation, this represents the child's ability to understand that while the appearance of a substance may change, its underlying physical properties will remain the same. One way in which Piaget demonstrated this was through his conservation of number test. In this test he arranged two rows of sweets, with equal numbers and forming parallel lines of equal length. In front of the children he then re-arranged one of the rows so that the sweets were more spread out and thus created a longer line. When the children were then asked to compare the two rows of sweets, children below the age of seven were likely to say that the longer line had more sweets in it. In other words, they could not grasp the notion of conservation – that although the appearance of the line had changed, its physical properties (i.e. the number of sweets within it) had remained the same.

By the end of this stage, however, children are beginning to develop the ability to employ logical mental operations and this marks their transition into the third stage – the *concrete operational stage* – that typically relates to children aged 7–12. During this third stage children are now able to understand notions such as conservation and also that of reversibility – the ability to observe a sequence of events and to appreciate the fact that these events can be repeated in reverse order to 'undo' the changes that have been made. Children are also able to order and classify objects and to think beyond themselves and begin to appreciate the perspectives of others. However, during this stage children are still largely constrained to employing their newly-acquired logical thinking to concrete and immediate events. It is only when they are able to begin to apply these types of mental operations to more abstract and hypothetical situations that they are regarded by Piaget as moving into the final stage of development – the *formal operational stage* – that typically occurs at about the age of 12. It is at this point that children have acquired the ability to use and employ the highest levels of cognitive thinking, known as hypothetico-deductive reasoning. They are now able to think rationally and reason deductively while also being able to develop and test hypotheses.

Overall, as mentioned earlier, Piaget's work has been hugely influential. His stress on the child and the active role s/he plays in her/his own development certainly provided the basis for one of the key elements of current early years practice, that of child-centred learning. The basic idea here is that children should be encouraged to engage in self-directed activities to allow them the space to learn and develop 'naturally', each at their own pace. The role of the early years practitioner is therefore restricted mainly to one of providing children with a rich and diverse environment for them to explore and experiment with. This emphasis was clearly evident in the Plowden Report (1967) when it set out what it felt should be the aims of primary education:

> The school sets out deliberately to devise the right environment for children, to allow them to be themselves and to develop in the way and at the pace appropriate to them. ... It lays special stress on individual discovery, on first hand experience and on opportunities for creative work. It insists that knowledge does not fall into neatly separate compartments and that work and play are not opposite but complementary.
>
> (Plowden Report, 1967: 187)

The other key implication arising from Piaget's work has been the notion of 'readiness'. Given the way in which children are thought to develop sequentially, through a range of well-defined stages, Piaget argued that children should only be encouraged to learn particular forms of knowledge or concepts when they are 'ready', i.e. when they have acquired the cognitive schemes to be able to accommodate this knowledge. This has led to the wide-spread notion of 'developmentally-appropriate' learning for children of differing ages.

Overall, this developmental perspective offered by Piaget has been the subject of extensive critique both from within psychology and from those working within the emerging area of the sociology of childhood (Donaldson, 1978; Henriques *et al.*, 1984; Broughton, 1987; Bradley, 1989; Morss, 1996; Prout and James, 1997; James *et al.*, 1998). There are four key points that are particularly worth highlighting here. The first point raised regarding Piaget's work is its tendency to significantly under-emphasise the competence and cognitive abilities of young children. There is now a substantial body of research that has attempted to both replicate Piaget's own experiments and also repeat them in differing formats (for summaries see Smith *et al.*, 1998; Wood, 1998; Keenan, 2002). What they have consistently shown is that many of the key findings of Piaget's research are more a product of the artificial nature of the experiments and tests used than an accurate reflection of the children's abilities at a particular age. This is evident if we return to Piaget's conservation of number test described briefly above. McGarrigle and Donaldson (1974) repeated this experiment but used a character called 'naughty teddy' to lengthen one of the rows of sweets by accident. This time when the children were asked to compare the two lines many more 4–6-year-olds were able to recognise that the rows still contained equal numbers of sweets, thus demonstrating their ability to appreciate the notion of conservation. Donaldson (1978) has suggested that the reason why many more children were able to successfully complete this second experiment was that it made more sense to them. In the original experiment, Donaldson argued that the children's answers were likely to represent their attempts to make sense of an unusual situation. In this way when the experimenter altered the rows of sweets and asked the children to compare them, it was probably quite logical for them to assume that a change must have taken place, otherwise why would the experimenter be asking the children to compare them? Overall, what this and many other follow-up experiments have shown is Piaget's failure to recognise the social competence of young children and their ability to interpret situations in differing ways and to respond accordingly. Rather than just reacting mechanically, children tend to be actively involved in trying to make sense of the actions of the experimenter and to provide them with answers that they feel are expected.

A second, related criticism of the type of developmentalist approach offered by Piaget is its preoccupation with end-points. In this sense, children are not studied in their own terms but simply against the ultimate yardstick of abstract, hypothetical reasoning epitomised by the formal operational stage (James and Prout, 1997; James *et al.*, 1998). The problem with this is that it tends to result in a partial and distorted account of children's lives that further acts to underestimate their social competence. As Corsaro (1997) explains, for example, in relation to research on children's friendships:

> The focus of nearly all of the research is on identifying stages in the child's abstract conceptions of friendship. These conceptions are elicited through clinical interviews, and their underdeveloped conceptions are compared to those of the competent adult. ... Yet few psychologists study what it is like to be or to have a friend in children's social worlds, or how developing conceptions of friendships are embedded in children's interactions in peer culture.
>
> (Corsaro, 1997: 17)

The key methodological implication to arise from these first two criticisms is the need to study children in a more naturalistic manner and to provide them with the space to raise and explore their own experiences and perspectives. This, in turn, requires researchers to focus more on the study of children in their natural social settings rather than through the use of contrived and artificial experimental methods. It also means resisting the temptation to impose adult frameworks, concerns and priorities onto children and, rather, studying children in and of themselves as well as being sensitive to the differing ways in which they experience and make sense of the world (Connolly, 1997; Christensen and James, 2000). This is a point that will be returned to in the next chapter when outlining the methodology for the case studies that follow.

The third key problem with Piaget's account is his claim that his stages of development are universal and invariant. This, in turn, reflects his view of development naturally occurring from the 'inside out' and thus essentially untouched by the effects of broader social contexts and cultures. However, and as a wide range of studies have consequently shown, these key stages of development are not applicable to all children and neither is children's progress as orderly and clear-cut as Piaget has suggested (Smith et al., 1998; Wood, 1998; Keenan, 2002). The key problem here is Piaget's tendency to generalise from research that usually involved White, Western middle class children. The developmental pathway that Piaget has suggested that children follow, leading to the development of rational scientific thinking, is actually a specifically Western (and middle class) phenomenon (Walkerdine, 1984; Corsaro, 1997; James et al., 1998) and, as research has shown, is neither characteristic of all societies nor even of all social groups within a particular society (Rogoff, 1990; Rogoff *et al.*, 1993; Woodhead *et al.*, 1998; Valsiner, 2000). There is thus a need to develop an understanding of the diverse ways in which children learn and locate these within particular cultural, material and economic contexts (Walkerdine and Lucey, 1989). As will be seen in the next section, this approach to understanding development from the 'outside in' is the starting point for Vygotsky's (1978) work and provides the basis for the two case studies to follow.

The fourth and final main point to raise here relates to the gender implications of Piaget's theories of child development as they are applied in practice. Not only do they tend to discourage gender equity work in the early years but they also tend to privilege the needs and interests of boys (Walkerdine, 1983; Paechter, 1998; MacNaughton, 1996, 2000). The extract from the Plowden Report quoted earlier illustrates the type of practice encouraged by Piaget's developmental perspective. As MacNaughton (1997) has argued, it constructs a 'developmental gaze' among educationalists that interprets children's behaviour strictly on an individual basis against key developmental milestones. It is a gaze that is restricted in its focus to *how* children think rather than *what* they think. There is no room within this to question the gendered nature of the attitudes and perspectives that children learn or the ways in which gender impacts upon the children's relationships with others. Moreover, the strict reading of Piaget's work, with its emphasis on self-directed play, rules out any attempts to intervene in children's activities and undertake direct work with them around issues of gender (Burman, 1994). As MacNaughton (2000) has found, those who would like to adopt a more proactive approach to challenging existing gender stereotypes in play, for example, can often be left feeling that this is 'bad practice' and at odds with what is in the best interests of the child.

In addition, not only does this emphasis on children's self-directed learning tend to significantly limit the possibilities for gender equity work, it also actually tends to privilege the needs and interests of boys and thus deny and subjugate those of girls. At the heart of the model is the view of the child as a 'little scientist' – working autonomously and naturally inquisitive about their immediate social environment and forever exploring and experimenting with it. This construction of the child as active, assertive and confident reflects the stereotypical traits traditionally associated with males and masculinity (Walkerdine, 1983; Paechter, 1998). It also directly contradicts those associated with females and femininity of being dependent, passive and subservient. As such, it creates an environment in which boys' inquisitive and demanding behaviour tends to be accepted and rewarded whilst that same behaviour from girls is more likely to be regarded as a transgression and thus discouraged and punished (Belotti, 1975; Walkerdine, 1990; Francis, 1998).

Vygotsky and the social contexts of children's development

As can be seen, there is a need to develop an alternative understanding of the way children learn and develop – one which acknowledges the importance of wider social processes and contexts, including gender, in influencing and shaping their development and one that also focuses on the children's own experiences and perspectives. It is with this in mind that we will now examine the pioneering work of Vygotsky (1978). What I want to do in this and the next section is to propose an alternative theory for understanding children's development based upon the work of Vygotsky. This, in turn, will provide the theoretical framework for understanding the young boys in the two case studies to follow in Part III of the book. In relation to Vygotsky, it is interesting to note that while passing references have been made to the potential contained in his work to develop more radical accounts of children's development (i.e. Walkerdine, 1990; Burman, 1994; Morss, 1996), his theories have largely been overlooked in the critical accounts of developmentalism discussed above. Moreover, given the possibilities that Vygotsky opens up for social accounts of children's learning, it is a little surprising to note that his work is not even referenced in some of the key defining texts within the sociology of childhood in the UK (see, for example, Stainton Rogers and Stainton Rogers, 1992; Jenks, 1996; James and Prout, 1997; James et al., 1998).

As Resnick and Nelson-Le Gall (1997) point out, Vygotsky was the first modern developmental theorist to place social interaction at the heart of his analysis. While he shared Piaget's emphasis on the active role that children play in their own learning, he differed markedly from Piaget in his rejection of the view of children as essentially solitary figures working away in isolation on their own cognitive development (Keenan, 2002). If we look again at the summary of Piaget's theory in Figure 3.1, it can be noted that the child and their activities are free-standing. Adults tend to play no major role in children's development (other than, as we have seen, to ensure the child's safety and to provide a rich and diverse environment within which s/he can play and explore).

In contrast, Vygotsky's work provides a radical alternative to this view of development from the 'inside out' with its neglect of social context. Vygotsky's overall approach is summarised in Figure 3.2 and represents, as explained earlier, a model of development from the 'outside in'. As can be seen, the starting point for children's learning and development is the network of social relationships that they are engaged in. For Vygotsky, it is what goes on 'outside' – in terms of the wider culture and social relationships within which a child is located – that then structures what happens 'inside' (i.e. the child's subsequent cognitive development). As Vygotsky (1978: 88) argued: 'human learning presupposes a specific social nature and a process by which children grow into the intellectual life of those around them'.

A key concept Vygotsky (1978) uses to explain how this happens is that of *internalisation*. As illustrated in Figure 3.2, internalisation represents the process whereby children's mental schemes are constructed as a result of their involvement in wider social relations. As Vygotsky explains:

> Every function in the child's cultural development appears twice: first, on the social level, and later, on the individual level; first, *between* people (*interpsychological*), and then *inside* the child (*intrapsychological*). This applies equally to voluntary attention, to logical memory, and to the formation of concepts. All the higher functions originate as actual relations between human individuals.
>
> (Vygotsky, 1978: 57, original emphases)

Thus, through relationships with others, children are encouraged to engage in ever more complex forms of activity and behaviour (i.e. the social level). As they become accomplished at these they are then internalised in relation to specific cognitive schemes (i.e. the individual level). A simple example Vygotsky (1978) uses to illustrate this process of internalisation is the development of pointing among infants. At first, an infant's movement represents little more than a failed attempt to grasp an object out of their reach. Their arm remains outstretched and oriented towards that object. However, it is when

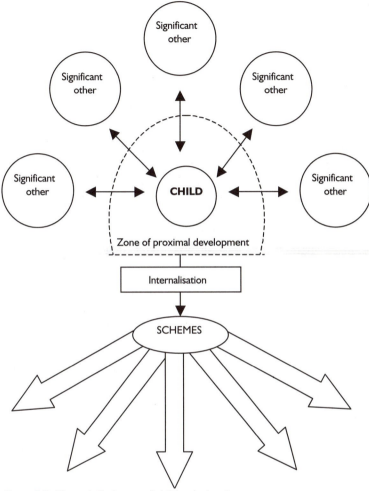

Figure 3.2 Vygotsky's theory of children's development

an adult responds to the child's movements that the situation changes. The infant's attempts to grasp the object tend to be interpreted by those around them as a gesture and lead them to fetch the object for the infant. Over time, the infant begins to reinterpret their own behaviour in the light of the interpretations and activities of those around them. Thus, what began as an unsuccessful attempt to grasp an object comes to be understood and used by the infant as a gesture actually directed at another person. The grasping movement therefore transforms into the essentially social act of pointing and, with time, the infant simplifies the action so that it readily becomes a proper gesture.

While this is a simple example, it does illustrate the emphasis Vygotsky gives to social activity in the development of children's thinking and learning. In this case, it can be seen that a particular mental scheme (i.e. pointing) first appears in interactions between the infant and those around them and then when it has been successfully learnt and accomplished it becomes internalised by the infant to form a mental scheme. It is this process that leads Vygotsky, as we have seen, to argue that all higher mental functions (i.e. other than purely reflexive, natural ones) have their roots in social relations. They first exist as social activities that the child is involved in and then, second, become internalised as mental schemes.

The other key notion that Vygotsky has introduced that follows on from this is the *zone of proximal development* (ZPD). The ZPD represents the difference between what a child can actually achieve unaided as a result of their current understanding and cognitive schemes and what they can achieve with the help and guidance of someone more experienced. As Vygotsky (1978: 86) explains, the ZPD is 'the distance between the actual development level as determined by independent problem solving and the level of potential development as determined through problem solving under adult guidance or in collaboration with more capable peers'. In essence, the ZPD represents the space within which children learn and develop. To explain this, it can be said that children will encounter one of three experiences through their interaction with others. The first will be experiences that they are familiar with and have therefore already internalised particular schemes to make sense of. In this case, the child simply draws upon these pre-existing schemes and thus learns nothing new from these particular experiences. The second will be experiences that are too far removed from their existing schemes and thus impossible for them to make sense of.

It is the third type of experience, in between these first two, that represents the ZPD. This type of experience involves the child engaging in activities with others that are new and which they could not achieve on their own. For example, suppose there is a young girl attempting to count her large collection of toy cars that she keeps in a box. For argument's sake, let us say there are over 100 of these cars. The girl is sitting on the floor attempting to count them all individually and is becoming increasingly frustrated each time she loses her concentration and forgets what she has counted so far. On noticing this, her older sister shows her how she can organise the cars into batches of ten and then how she can work out how many cars she has by counting the number of batches she has made. Through doing this with the help of her sister, the younger girl learns a new and more advanced counting scheme.

Overall, therefore, it is this third type of social experience – within the zone of proximal development – that underlies children's learning and development. As Figure 3.2 tries to convey, it is the activity engaged in within the ZPD that subsequently becomes internalised by the child into an ever more complex set of cognitive schemes. There are two key points to draw out from this overall approach to understanding children's development. First, and as Vygotsky (1978: 55) points out, it 'refutes the notion that development represents the mere unfolding of the child's organically predetermined system of activity'. Rather, there are no universal stages to children's learning and nothing is predetermined in relation to their development.[1] As he went on to argue:

> Our concept of development implies a rejection of the frequently held view that cognitive development results from the gradual accumulation of separate changes. We believe that child development is a complex dialectical process characterised by periodicity, unevenness in the development of different functions, metamorphosis or qualitative transformation of one form into another, intertwining of external and internal factors, and adaptive processes which overcome impediments that the child encounters.
>
> (Vygotsky, 1978: 55)

This is illustrated in Figure 3.2 by the diverse range of developmental paths that children can take as they progressively develop their cognitive schemes as a consequence of the very different sets of social relations that they are involved in. In fact there is now a growing body of work, inspired by Vygotsky, that has demonstrated the importance of social context and also the role played by significant others in relation to children's development (Heath, 1989; Newman et al., 1989; Rogoff, 1990; Lave and Wenger, 1991). One of the most notable of these is the work of Rogoff and her colleagues (Rogoff, 1990; Rogoff et al., 1993, 1998) and their attempts to show how diverse developmental goals and paths not only exist between different societies but also between different groups and communities within any one society (Rogoff *et al.*, 1993, 1998). For example, their comparative research involving four different communities certainly highlights the fact that the emphasis on verbal instruction and the adults' explicit structuring of children's learning does tend to be a middle class phenomenon. In the two working class communities they studied they found a much greater focus on non-verbal communication, an emphasis on children taking responsibility for their own learning and a greater participation of children in the activities and events of their families and community (Rogoff *et al.*, 1993).

The second key point to draw out from Vygotsky's work relates to the key role played by adults and significant others in children's learning and development. In contrast with Piaget's approach (see Figure 3.1), it can be seen from Figure 3.2 that children's relationships with significant others lie at the heart of their development. Simply through their engagement in activities with significant others, therefore, children will learn and develop. However, what Vygotsky's work does is to create space for adults to play a more direct and proactive role in children's learning. Just as illustrated earlier with the example of the older girl helping her younger sister to count her toy cars, it is quite possible for adults to use a range of activities to assist children in reaching their goals. This may include modelling a particular action, suggesting a strategy for solving a problem or breaking down an activity into manageable parts. The key to all of this is following the lead created by the child in terms of their own interests and experiences as well as being mindful of what they can reasonably learn (i.e. attempting to work within the child's zone of proximal development). This more proactive approach to encouraging children's learning and development was first introduced by Bruner and his colleagues and originally labelled *scaffolding* to emphasise the support that is given to facilitate children's growth and development (Wood *et al.*, 1976).

Overall, it can be seen that the key Vygotskian concepts of internalisation and the ZPD have gone a long way to address the concerns raised earlier in relation to traditional models of children's learning and development. More specifically, they provide a radical alternative to the universal and invariant stages of development model offered by Piaget. In its place, these concepts enable an understanding of children's development that is diverse and contingent and that is crucially related to the specific social, cultural and economic contexts within which children are located. These concepts also help to recognise the competence of young children and warn against the use of crude generalisations about children's age-specific social and cognitive abilities. Children are not tied to a universal developmental pathway but are only limited in terms of their learning and growth by the environments that surround them. It should therefore come as no surprise to find that some children will develop extremely high levels of competence in particular skills (whether academic, physical and/or social) reflecting the specific experiences and needs they are subject to within their own communities. Finally, while these concepts also tend to ignore gender by focusing on *how* rather than *what* children learn, they do at least open up the potential for more proactive and interventionist work with young children around issues of gender. Some of this has already been touched upon above when introducing the notion of scaffolding and the more direct role that adults can play in children's learning and development. These are ideas that will be developed more fully in the final part of the book (Chapter 9) as the basis for considering the most appropriate and effective ways of working with young boys.

Having said this, there are still some problems with this overall Vygotskian framework that need to be addressed. They are problems that relate to the fact that such work remains embedded in psychological ways of thinking and, as such, has a rather limited understanding of the social (Smith, 1996). This is evident in three main respects. First, there remains an emphasis on individual agency underpinning these accounts where, as Morss (1996: 7) explains: 'the individual person [is] treated as a free agent, detached from the social setting, and able to make voluntary decisions about such matters as social interaction'. In other words, there is a tendency to view each child as an individual, in full control of their ideas and thoughts. However, there is a need to develop a more sophisticated understanding within these accounts of the relationship between individuals and the social structures within which they are located (Henriques *et al.*, 1984). More specifically, there is a need to understand how children are not just free-thinking individual agents but how their actual thoughts and behaviour are influenced and shaped by the broader social and cultural contexts around them.

Second, there is a tendency to depict the social simply in terms of interpersonal relations. As Henriques *et al.* (1984) explain, much of the research that has been conducted in this area has tended to focus on relationships between mothers and their young children and to compare the different child-rearing practices that exist between different communities and cultures. This is depicted, for example, in Figure 3.2 by the simple and discrete two-way interactions between the child and specific individuals. What is lacking from such accounts is the way in which these individuals interact and also the influences of broader social structures (Wertsch, 1991; Morss, 1996; Skelton and Hall, 2001). Again, there is a need to make use of more socio-logical concepts to help understand the role that peer groups, institutions (particularly the family and the school) and the wider community play in influencing what children learn.

Finally, the type of Vygotskian approach outlined above tends to take culture itself for granted and provides little space for an analysis of conflict or power relations, either within families or within the community more generally, and the effects these have on children's learning and development (Urwin, 1984; Morss, 1996; Duveen, 1997). Rogoff *et al.* (1993: 3), for example, defined 'community' simple as 'a group of people having some common local organisation, values, and practices'. What this and other definitions lack is a recognition of the differential relations of power that exist and the way that some groups within a community are able to define their own knowledge and ways of being as the norm and impose these on others. There is also no recognition of the power struggles that may exist within the family, between a child and their mother for example, and the ways this impacts upon what the child learns and how they develop. As before, there is a need to draw upon some of the insights provided by sociology in order to add this dimension to the understanding currently provided by Vygotsky. It is to this that the chapter now turns.

Bourdieu, Elias and a little more on the social contexts of children's development

As we have seen, while the overall framework provided by Vygotsky represents a useful way of understanding children's learning and development, there is a need to pay a little more attention to the way in which the social contexts within which children are located can be theorised within this. In this section it will be suggested that the two inter-related concepts of *habitus*, as developed in the work of Bourdieu (1977, 1990), and *figuration*, as proposed by Elias (1978, 1994), help to address the three problems associated with current Vygotskian work as outlined above. Indeed, what will be suggested here is that the two concepts, when used together, provide a better way of understanding how children learn and develop through internalising the sets of social relations that they are engaged in. In this sense, and as illustrated in Figure 3.3, it will be argued below that the concepts of habitus and figuration can be directly mapped onto Vygotsky's existing theoretical framework. Rather than representing an alternative to and/or replacement of Vygotsky's work, these two concepts should therefore be seen simply as a more appropriate way of applying the key insights he has offered. With this in mind, we will now look at the concepts of habitus and figuration in turn and explain what they mean and also how, precisely, they map onto Vygotsky's existing framework, as shown in Figure 3.3.

Bourdieu's work and, particularly, his notion of habitus are now becoming increasingly popular in educational research (Grenfell *et al.*, 1998). In relation to the habitus many of its traits are actually already evident in the notion of schemes as used by both Piaget and Vygotsky. It will be remembered that schemes are mental structures that children construct in order to make sense of their environment and to guide their actions. Each scheme is not composed simply of a set of thoughts or memories but also of related actions and strategies that they have learnt to guide their responses to particular objects or events. As we saw, the difference between Piaget and Vygotsky was not so much in terms of their understanding of this notion of schemes but with how schemes are learnt and developed. For Piaget, schemes derive from the natural and individualistic activities of young children. In contrast Vygotsky argued that these schemes derive from a child's involvement in social relations and thus can be seen as the eventual internalisation of the social activities they have been engaged in.

The key point here is that once these schemes have been generated and internalised they tend to be represented as 'habits' – taken-for-granted ways of thinking about and acting upon the social world that unconsciously guide a child's actions and predispose them to think and act in particular ways. Moreover, in line with the work of Vygotsky, it can be seen that these habits reflect the ways of thinking and forms of behaviour that children have progressively come to internalise because of their location in particular social contexts. It is precisely this combination of habits as they are internalised within the individual child as a coherent set of schemes that are reflective of the broader social structures within which they are located, that forms the basis of the notion of the habitus. As Bourdieu (1993) has explained:

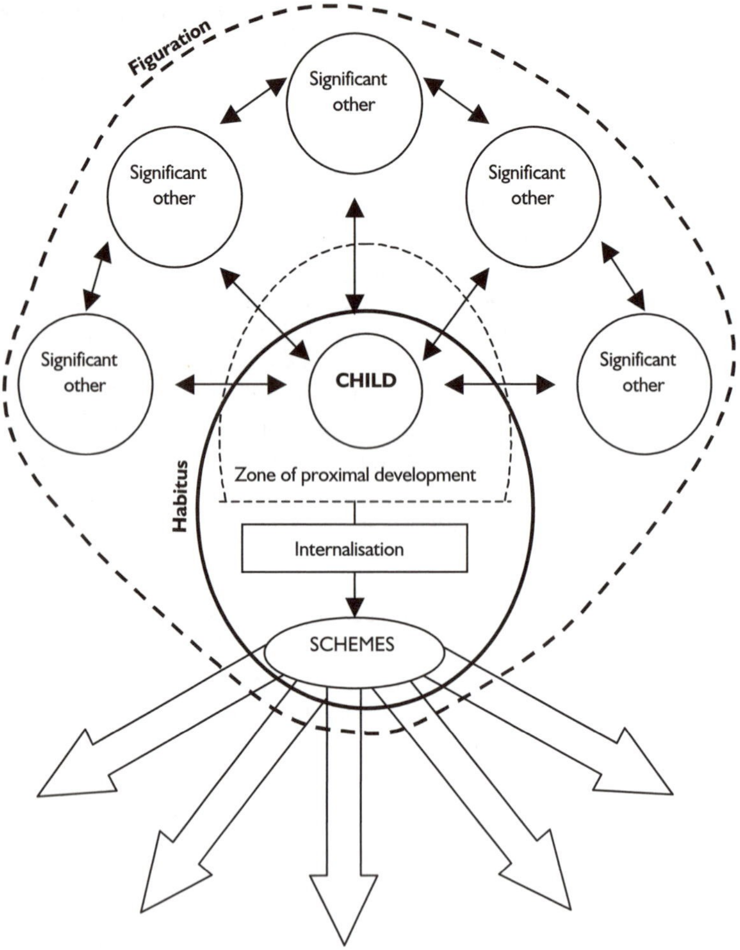

Figure 3.3 The relationship between habitus and figuration and Vygotsky's theory of children's development

The habitus, as the word implies, is that which one has acquired, but which has become durably incorporated in the body in the form of permanent dispositions. So the term constantly reminds us that it refers to something historical, linked to individual history, and that it belongs to a genetic mode of thought, as opposed to essentialist modes of thought.

(Bourdieu, 1993: 86)

For Bourdieu, then, our internalised modes of thought are not naturally-given (i.e. essentialist) but are socially constructed – developed and generated (i.e. genetic)[2] from our lived experience. However, Bourdieu was concerned to stress that the habitus means a little more than traditionally implied by the use of the term habit. Whereas habits tend to be seen simply as automatic, unthinking responses to situations, Bourdieu wanted to use the concept of habitus to stress its formative qualities – in other words the way it moulds and shapes our behaviour. As Bourdieu explains:

> But then why not say 'habit'? Habit is spontaneously regarded as repetitive, mechanical, automatic, reproductive rather than productive. I wanted to insist on the idea that the habitus is something powerfully generative. To put it briefly, the habitus is a product of conditionings which tend to reproduce the objective logic of those conditionings while transforming it. It's a kind of transforming machine that leads us to 'reproduce' the social conditions of our own production, but in a relatively unpredictable way, in such a way that one cannot move simply and mechanically from knowledge of the conditions of production to knowledge of the products.
>
> (Bourdieu, 1993: 87)

As can be seen, the habitus addresses the first of the three problems associated with current Vygotskian accounts outlined earlier in terms of their tendency to treat individuals as free agents, largely detached from their social settings and able to make rational choices regarding their actions. While individuals are free to make choices they can only do so within the parameters of 'what they know', i.e. the habitus they have internalised. In this sense, they are not separate from the social structures that surround them but are integrally shaped by them. To take a simple example, young working class children raised on socially-deprived housing estates may well not know of anyone who has stayed on at school and gone to university. Their experience gained through their local estate and of family and friends living there provides the parameters for their worldview. It tends to shape the way they think and forms the boundaries within which they make decisions. 'What they know', then, is that everyone leaves school at 16 and finds work locally or attempts to make a living in other ways. Staying on at school and aiming for university is just not part of their practical experience, of their habitus. While working class children are free to make choices, therefore, the range of choices available to them are constrained by their lived experience, by what they know. This use of the habitus as an alternative to the view of individuals as rational free agents is also stressed by Bourdieu:

> To speak of habitus is to assert that the individual, and even the personal, the subjective, is social, collective. Habitus is a socialised subjectivity. This is where I part, for instance, with Herbert Simon and his notion of 'bounded rationality'. Rationality is bounded not only because the available information is curtailed, and because the human mind is generically limited and does not have the means of fully figuring out all situations, especially in the urgency of action, but also because the human mind is *socially* bounded, socially structured. The individual is always, whether he likes it or not, trapped – save to the extent that he becomes aware of it – 'within the limits of his brain'.
>
> (Bourdieu and Wacquant, 1992: 126, original emphasis)

Overall, it can be seen that there are more than a few similarities between this notion of habitus and Vygotsky's original concept of internalisation. Both represent the way in which external social structures come to be internalised in the mental schemes or habits of individuals. Moreover, the way that Bourdieu describes the relationship between the habitus and these broader external social structures (what he terms 'fields' of relations) has more than a passing resemblance to Vygotsky's (1978: 57) explanation of how: 'every function in the child's cultural development appears twice: first, on the social level, and later, on the individual level'. Compare this with the following quote from Bourdieu:

> The relation between habitus and field operates in two ways. On one side, it is a relation of *conditioning*; the field structures the habitus ... On the other side, it is a relation of knowledge or *cognitive construction*. Habitus contributes to constituting the field as a meaningful world, a world endowed with sense and value ... Social reality exists, so to speak, twice, in things and in minds, in fields and in habitus, outside and inside of agents.
>
> (Bourdieu and Wacquant, 1992: 127, original emphasis)

The notion of habitus is preferable to that of internalisation for two reasons, however. First, it implies a more dynamic and dialectical relationship between the cognitive development of the individual and that of the social structures within which they are located. As the quote from Bourdieu outlines above, it is not just a one-way relationship with social structures (fields) determining the habitus. Rather the habitus also, in turn, plays a central role in the reproduction of these social structures through the way it influences and shapes the actions of individuals. Second, the habitus also goes beyond a limited focus on the learning of discrete mental schemes as implied in Vygotsky's notion of internalisation. It also incorporates a more holistic understanding of the broader dispositions that individuals come to embody and which unconsciously shape and guide not only the way they think and behave but also the particular investments they have in certain forms of knowledge and ways of acting. This was evident, for instance, in the example of young working class children and universities described above. As will be seen, it is these broader sets of dispositions (reflective of the child's social class and ethnic background as well as their gender) that provide the context within which these more discrete mental schemes are then learnt and internalised.

With all this in mind, and referring back to Figure 3.3, we can now see how the notion of habitus maps onto the existing theoretical framework offered by Vygotsky. In essence it can be seen as the collective term for all of the particular cognitive schemes that a child has internalised from their broader social environment. However, the habitus also incorporates the child as well – reflecting the fact that it is not possible to make an artificial distinction between the child and their cognitive schemes. Thus, the more the child begins to learn and internalise particular ways of thinking and behaving, the more these will inevitably become embodied in relation to their manner and physical appearance and the way they hold and present themselves.

The child, in terms of their physical body, is therefore simply the tangible expression of their mental schemes. This is easily illustrated with the example of masculinity. In this sense, a young boy will learn through interactions with others particular ways of thinking and behaving based around strength, sporting prowess and competitiveness. The more these are internalised as taken-for-granted habits or dispositions, the more the young boy's behaviour and identity will be unconsciously structured by them also. The young boy will therefore dress in a certain manner and stand and talk in particular ways to reflect these masculine characteristics. Moreover, the more he does this, the more he will physically come to embody these traits. This process has already been explained in the previous chapter in relation to the discussion of testosterone and brain structures. As was argued, it is not simply that a child's behaviour is determined by their biology but that their behaviour can also influence the way their bodies develop (including the production of hormones and the development of the brain). It is in this sense that the habitus, as indicated in Figure 3.3, encapsulates not just the cognitive schemes of a child (their taken-for-granted ways of thinking and behaving) but also their actual bodies – the ways in which their very beings have come to incorporate and express these schemes.

With this concept of habitus in place, the other main task is to develop a means of describing and understanding the broader social contexts within which the habitus is developed. As Figure 3.3 indicates, these social contexts represent little more than the particular networks of social relationships within which the child is based. What is being stressed here, more so than in the traditional Vygotskian approach (see Figure 3.2), is the complex interdependent nature of these networks (and hence the addition of the arrows connecting all of the significant others in Figure 3.3). Rogoff and her colleagues come closest to recognising this when they attempt to broaden the focus of research away from just studies of mothers and toddlers to the wider social and cultural networks within which the child is located (Rogoff, 1990; Rogoff *et al.*, 1993, 1998). As Rogoff explains:

> I mean to include not just parent-child relationships, but also the other social relationships inherent in families and communities, such as those involving children, parents, teachers, classmates and neighbours, organised not as dyads but as rich configurations of mutual involvement ... [C]hildren are involved with multiple companions and caregivers in organised, flexible webs of relationships that focus on shared cultural activities ... [which] provide children with opportunities to participate in diverse roles.
>
> (quoted in Wood, 1998: 101)

It is this view of an interdependent network of social relationships that Elias has attempted to capture with his notion of *figuration*.[3] As can be seen from Figure 3.3, a figuration is simply a term to describe all of the interdependent social relationships that the child is located within, and within which their habitus is formed. In this sense, and as illustrated in the diagram, the habitus does not exist outside of the figuration but is completely located within it. Individuals are therefore not distinct or closed entities but are inextricably linked into and can only be understood as members of interdependent networks or figurations. This is the starting point for Elias in his development of the concept of figurations. As he argued (Elias, 1994: 213–14), there is a need to develop an image of the individual as:

> an 'open personality' who possesses a greater or lesser degree of relative (but never absolute and total) autonomy vis-à-vis other people and who is, in fact, fundamentally oriented toward and dependent on other people throughout his life. The network of interdependencies among human beings is what binds them together. Such interdependencies are the nexus of what is here called the figuration, a structure of mutually oriented and dependent people. Since people are more or less dependent on each other first by nature and then through social learning, through education, socialisation, and socially generated reciprocal needs, they exist, one might venture to say, only as pluralities, only in figurations.
>
> (quoted in van Krieken, 1998: 56)

Elias uses this notion of figuration to move beyond the tendency to treat concepts such as the 'family', 'school' or 'community' as if they were things or objects in their own right. Such ways of thinking tend to create artificial distinctions between individuals and these broader social structures. Rather, as Elias argues, they are all nothing more than particular figurations – composed ultimately of little more than interdependent networks of individuals. In this sense, 'society' is not something separate from individuals but is made up of a vast array of figurations that are, themselves, related to one another through chains of interdependence. According to Elias the concept of figuration can be:

> applied to relatively small groups just as well as to societies made up of thousands or millions of interdependent people. Teachers and pupils in class, doctor and patients in a therapeutic group, regular customers at a pub, children at a nursery school – they all make up relatively comprehensible figurations with

each other. But the inhabitants of a village, a city or a nation also form figurations, although in this instance the figurations cannot be perceived directly because the chains of interdependence which link people together are longer and more differentiated. Such complex configurations must therefore be approached indirectly, and understood by analysing the chains of interdependence.

(Elias, 1978: 131)

The point here, then, is that there are no pre-given and fixed figurations that can be objectively defined. The concept of figuration is simply an analytical tool to be used flexibly to help understand particular social phenomena. It is therefore up to the researcher to decide which figuration(s) to define and study and at what levels. In a school, for example, there are specific figurations formed by children in terms of peer groups, other figurations corresponding to relations between children and teachers in the classroom and still more figurations reflecting relations between the headteacher and staff. Beyond this there are figurations corresponding to local communities, to the city in which the school and community is located and, moreover, to the regional and national government and economy.

One key implication arising from this view of the existence of an array of differing figurations is that there is not just one habitus for each individual but a number of different habituses relating to the different social networks or figurations they inhabit. Thus a child will develop a taken-for-granted way of thinking and behaving when in the classroom that will be different from the predispositions they have learnt and internalised and which guide their behaviour when with their peers in the playground or when at home with their parents. Children, therefore, can be seen to have multiple habituses that reflect the complex range of social networks that they are involved in. In this sense there is no one, 'true' identity that each child has as manifest through their habitus but rather multiple identities and ways of being that are contingent and context-specific and that can often be contradictory. The taken-for-granted behaviour that a child engages in when relating to their teacher, for example, may well be very different if not diametrically opposed to the behaviour they have internalised and which they engage in when with their peers. What all this shows, therefore, is that the habitus can only be understood in relation to a specific social context or figuration.

The choice of particular figuration(s) to study (and thus the specific forms of habitus that arise from these) will reflect the research questions being asked. To be manageable, however, the analysis of particular figurations will always involve 'bracketing off' others. For example, if the focus is to be relations between teaching staff in a school then the particular sets of interdependent relations between teachers would form the basis of the study. What we would be interested in, in this case, would be the specific nature of interdependent relationships that existed between the teaching staff and how this has led to the development of particular forms of habitus among different staff. Obviously, however, such a figuration does not sit in isolation but will, itself, be related to and influenced by other figurations involving the children, the parents, the local education authority, the national economy and so forth. As Elias argues in the quote earlier, it is impossible to study each of these figurations in the same detail as that of the teaching staff. Rather, the internal dynamics of these figurations need to be 'bracketed off' and the analysis restricted to the overall influences that each of these other figurations has on the figuration of teachers (i.e. analysing the chains of interdependence).

Finally, having established broadly what a figuration is and how it relates to the habitus, it is important to sketch out some of the key defining characteristics of a figuration. Elias identifies three that will be briefly outlined in turn. The first, as already touched upon, is the interdependent nature of the relationships within the figuration. As Elias (1978: 134) contends: 'the concept of figuration puts the problem of human interdependencies into the very heart of sociological theory'. He attempts to explain the nature of these types of interdependent relationships through the use of a range of increasingly complex game models (see Elias, 1978: 80–103) that are summarised a little more fully for those interested in the notes to this chapter.[4] In essence, however, what Elias is keen to do is to stress the fact that none of us is completely free to do as we choose but that, rather, our actions always depend upon and are influenced by those of others. The choices we make and the options open to us at any particular time are therefore dependent upon the actions and behaviour of those around us. In this sense we are never fully in control of the path that our lives take. The dialectical nature of the unfolding interdependent relationships that exist ensure that they tend to develop a logic of their own. The more complex the sets of relations (figurations) we are involved in become, the less control we individually have over our life course. The actual nature of these interdependent relationships will become more apparent through the two case studies to follow.

The second key characteristic that Elias stresses in relation to figurations follows on from this emphasis on interdependence. According to Elias, power lies at the heart of all relationships and thus figurations. However, rather than viewing power in absolute terms – where some individuals possess power and others do not – this emphasis on interdependence requires us to think more in terms of *balances of power* and of *power ratios*. As Elias explains:

> Balances of power ... form an integral element of all human relationships. ... From the day of his birth, a baby has power over its parents, not just the parents over the baby. At the very least, the baby has power over them as long as they attach any kind of value to it. ... Equally bi-polar is the balance of power between a slave and his master. The master has power over his slave, but the slave also has power over his master, in proportion to his function for his master – his master's dependence on him. In relationships between parents and infants, master and slave, power chances are distributed very unevenly. But whether the power differentials are large or small, balances of power are always present wherever there is functional interdependence between people. In this respect, simply to use the word 'power' is likely to mislead. We say that a person possesses great power, as if power were a thing he carried about in his pocket. This use of the word is a relic of magico-mythical ideas. Power is not an amulet possessed by one person and not by another; it is a structural characteristic of human relationships – of *all* human relationships.
>
> (Elias, 1978: 74, original emphasis)

The task for those researching particular figurations is therefore to understand the specific balances of power that exist – what Elias also termed the power ratios – and that are characteristic of all interdependent relationships. As will be seen, this is a particularly useful way of understanding gender relations, especially given their physical and emotional nature and the way in which boys need girls to successfully construct dominant forms of masculinity (and vice versa for girls needing boys in terms of their successful demonstrations of femininity). It also helps us move beyond the rather absolutist understandings of power associated with earlier theories of patriarchy where men were seen to have power and women to be without it (Connell, 1995; Jackson, 1998). The third and final key characteristic associated with figurations that Elias has stressed is their dynamic nature. All too often, he has argued, structures such as the family or the community are treated as fixed and static objects rather than as entities that are undergoing change, that are part of a longer-term historical process. As Elias (1987: xvi) contends: 'present social conditions represent an instant of a continuous process which, coming from the past, moves on through present times towards a future as yet unknown'. This recognition has, in turn, provided the tendency for Elias to engage in detailed historical analysis – most notably in relation to his defining work regarding *The Civilising Process* (Elias, 1994). However, it is also of importance for studies of contemporary figurations such as the ones that form the case studies to follow. In this sense, this emphasis on process stands as a reminder that all social conditions and specific sets of relations are not static and fixed but historically constructed. In the study of contemporary masculinities, for example, this requires us to recognise their changing and evolving forms and to explain their present nature by reference to broader social changes. This need to locate particular figurations within broader processes of social change is also as relevant to studies of specific schools and communities. Moreover, it is equally applicable to the study of individuals. As Elias (1978: 118) argues, rather than having a fixed identity, individuals are:

> Born as infants, have to be fed and protected for many years by their parents or other adults, who slowly grow up, who then provide for themselves in this or that social position, who may marry and have children of their own, and who finally die. So an individual may justifiably be seen as a self-transforming person who, as it is sometimes put, goes through a process. ... Although it runs counter to our usual habits of speech and thought, it would be much more appropriate to say a person is constantly in movement; he not only goes through a process, he *is* a process.
> (Elias, 1978: 118, original emphasis)

Overall, it is this notion of figurations with its emphasis on interdependent relations, balances of power and on historical process that helps to address the second and third problems outlined earlier in relation to current Vygotskian work. As has been argued, figurational analysis helps us move beyond the tendency in Vygotskian research to focus mainly on interpersonal relations and, instead, encourages us to focus on the influence of broader social structures on children's learning and development. Moreover, a figurational approach also places the issues of power and conflict at the heart of the analysis and enables an understanding of how this also impacts upon the way that children learn and develop (through the development and reproduction of their habitus).

Conclusions and summary of the theoretical framework

Overall, through a detailed consideration and critique of Piaget's work each of the arguments listed at the beginning of this chapter in relation to doing gender work with young children has been addressed. As has been shown, young children are far more socially competent than we often give them credit for. As will be shown through the case studies to follow in Part III of the book, the young boys are certainly able to actively appropriate and re-work popular ideas concerning gender in the construction of their own masculine identities. The case studies also demonstrate how it is possible to encourage them to reflect upon their identities and the popular gender stereotypes that they often draw upon. Moreover, through the theories of Vygotsky it is possible to devise appropriate ways of undertaking such work with young boys that is sensitive to where they are at.

Given the range of ideas and arguments covered in this chapter it is useful to conclude with an overall summary of the alternative theoretical framework adopted for the case studies to follow and especially an outline of the key concepts to be used and how they relate to one another. As stated in the introduction to this chapter, the key objective in developing this theoretical framework has been to provide the conceptual tools necessary to understand the nature of masculinity as it is manifest in young boys' lives and how this impacts upon their dispositions to learning. From the discussion of masculinity in the previous chapter, it was argued that this requires a theoretical framework that focuses not only on how boys come to learn and internalise particular forms of masculinity but also on the broader social contexts within which this takes place – most notably the family, local community and the school.

With this in mind, the starting point for the construction of an appropriate theoretical framework has been the pioneering work of

Vygotsky and his stress on the social contexts of learning. The key concept is that of *internalisation* with its emphasis on how children's development is essentially characterised by the internalisation of the social relations that they are engaged in. Vygotsky's other concept of the *zone of proximal development* (ZPD) reinforces this key point by marking out the space in which children are actively learning at any point in time. In this sense, as we have seen, the ZPD is the distance between what a child can already achieve under their own initiative and what they can potentially achieve with the help and support of a more experienced person. It is through a child's relationships with adults and more experienced others that they learn how to achieve more complex tasks and it is this understanding that then becomes internalised.

However, it has been argued that underlying all of this work to date has been a failure to fully understand the nature of the social contexts that children come to internalise through their development. It is with this in mind that the chapter has suggested an alternative way of thinking about Vygotsky's notion of internalisation through the use of the two sociological concepts of *habitus* and *figuration*. In this respect, each child is located within a number of different sets of social relations – referred to as figurations. For each figuration, the child is engaged in a number of complex interdependent relationships characterised by differing balances of power and undergoing processes of change. Their routine experiences of these relationships will slowly become internalised as a set of taken-for-granted predispositions to thinking and acting in certain ways. These particular predispositions – known collectively as the habitus – become second nature and unconsciously structure the child's thought processes and guide their behaviour. In this way, the habitus provides a more comprehensive account of children's development – one which includes not only the acquisition of particular 'higher mental functions' as Vygotsky termed them but also, equally importantly, the broader sets of predispositions to learning that they acquire as a consequence of their social location.

Part III

Case studies of young boys and schooling

Chapter 4

Worlds apart

Introducing South Park and North Parade

Introduction

This part of the book provides the case studies of two groups of 5–6-year-old boys in Northern Ireland – those attending South Park Primary School,[1] located in an affluent, middle class area, and those attending North Parade Primary School, situated in a socially isolated and economically-deprived area that continues to experience relatively high levels of sectarian tensions and violence. The two groups of boys have been chosen to illustrate the fact, as stressed in the previous parts of the book, that not all boys are the same and that their masculine identities and thus their dispositions towards education differ in very significant ways according to a range of factors including, in this case, social class. In studying the boys' experiences and perspectives and locating these within the broader contexts provided by the local area, the home and the school, the case studies aim to demonstrate the dangers of working with sweeping generalisations and the need, instead, to understand boys within their particular social contexts.

More specifically, it has been decided to select two groups of boys who can be located towards opposite ends of the social class spectrum and to place their lives side-by-side in order to draw attention to the different social processes and practices that can be associated with the education of middle class and working class boys respectively. Many teachers and early years practitioners reading these two case studies may well find that the boys in their class or setting tend to fit somewhere in-between the types of processes to be outlined in the following chapters. In reality, of course, life is a little more complex. Moreover, it is not that easy to define and differentiate between what is actually meant by 'middle class' and 'working class'. For the following two case studies I will be using the two terms in line with the principles underpinning the official way in which occupational groups are now classified through the National Statistics Socio-Economic Classification (NS-SEC).[2] In essence, NS-SEC seeks to distinguish between a range of different occupational groups in terms of both their *labour market situation* and their *work situation*. Their labour market situation refers to their level and source of income, extent of job security and future career opportunities. Their work situation reflects more the actual conditions of their work in terms of the level of responsibility they have and also the degree of authority and control they have over their own working environment.

Clearly, a wide range of subtle distinctions can be made between a wide variety of occupational groups. However, for the purposes of this book the terms 'middle class' and 'working class' will be used to describe the two overall tendencies in relation to a person's labour market and work situations. Thus, middle class will be used to refer to those who have higher levels of income, good job security and future career opportunities as well as significant control over their own working environments and possibly responsibility and authority over others. By contrast, working class will be used to refer to those who have lower levels of income or no income at all. For those in work, it will be used to refer to a situation characterised by less security and fewer career opportunities as well as little control or authority over their own working environment. As will be seen, the two areas – South Park and North Parade – have been chosen to ensure that the families in these areas are differentiated quite clearly in this sense as middle class and working class respectively.

This chapter then provides an introduction to the case studies. It begins with a brief discussion of the methods used and the approach taken to analysing and interpreting the findings from the two case studies. The chapter then moves on to compare and contrast the two areas in relation to their differing socio-economic characteristics, their very different experiences of the violence in Northern Ireland and the differences found in relation to educational performance and provision generally and then within the two schools more specifically.

Methodology

As explained, the two schools were chosen because of their location towards the two ends of the social class spectrum within Northern

Ireland. Of course, the vast majority (some 96 per cent) of schools in Northern Ireland are also fundamentally divided between those that are Protestant and those that are Catholic in their orientation. To help simplify the comparative nature of this study, both primary schools chosen are Protestant. The precise nature of the schools and the local areas they are situated in will be described in much more detail shortly. In order to maintain anonymity, however, their names have been changed and precise details concerning their locations within Northern Ireland have been omitted. Moreover, some minor descriptive details have either been obscured or altered.[3]

The fieldwork took place during the 2001/2 school year. Between October 2001 and June 2002 I spent about a day per week in each of the two classes, ensuring that I attended on different days within the week to gain an overall impression of the young boys' schooling experiences. During this time I followed the boys through their school day, observing them in class and in the playground. While I would occasionally help out in class (i.e. by listening to children read or sitting with a group of children at a particular table), my main role in both schools was largely one of an observer. In addition to observations, I interviewed boys and girls from the two classes in small groups of three. Written parental consent was gained prior to the children being interviewed. Also, it was explained to children that they were free to leave the interview at any time if they wished to, although none did.

The groups were generally single-sex and reflected friendship groupings. Most children were interviewed on at least three occasions during the year. This, together with the time I spent talking with the children in the classroom and playground, ensured that I built up a good rapport with them. The interviews in both schools took place around a small table in a different part of the school building, in full view of other staff who would pass by occasionally. The children usually brought some class work with them that they nominally worked on when sitting at the table. The interviews were largely unstructured and consisted mainly of conversations where I would simply begin by asking some general, non-directive questions about what the children were doing in the playground or what they liked to play at home. This would usually be enough for the children to then continue their conversations under their own momentum. The key aim of the interviews was to provide the children with the space to raise and discuss those issues that were important to them. Combined with the observations gained from the classroom and playground, this helped to provide an account of the boys' lives that was more grounded in their own experiences and perspectives. Such a method does raise a number of ethical and methodological issues and these have been discussed in more detail elsewhere (see Connolly, 1996, 1997).

Alongside the observations and interviews with the children, data were also collected on the children's basic reading and arithmetic skills and a range of secondary source data was also analysed, including baseline assessments and school reports. In addition, semi-structured interviews were also conducted with the two class teachers and principals from both schools and also with parents.[4] In total, eight parents were interviewed from North Parade Primary School and ten from South Park Primary School. These interviews, together with statistical data (mainly from the 2001 Census) helped to build up a comprehensive picture of the local communities and family lives within which the boys were being raised.

Finally, there is a need to explain briefly the particular approach taken to analysing and writing up the two case studies. As discussed in the previous chapter in relation to the study of figurations, there is a need to decide upon the precise focus of the research and to 'bracket off' particular sets of relationships and figurations that are not of central importance. What I would like to have done in this particular study is to focus on the different forms of masculinity that are appropriated and expressed by the working class and middle class boys respectively and the differing ways in which these impact upon their experiences of and dispositions towards education. However, given the need to incorporate an analysis of the broader social contexts within which the boys are located (i.e. the school, family and local community), limits of space mean that it is not possible to describe and account for all of the different forms of masculinity that exist both within and between each of the two groups of boys. Rather, and for the sake of clarity, it is more appropriate at this stage to offer an outline of the broader factors and processes that tend to affect the two groups of working class and middle class boys respectively overall. This, in turn, will mark out the parameters of the range of experiences that young boys have of schooling as mediated by social class.

In this sense, therefore, the case studies to follow will focus on the way that the broader figurations represented by the two local communities and schools vary and thus how they impact differentially upon the two groups of boys in general. What is thus effectively being 'bracketed off' in this instance are the individual differences and variations that exist within each of the two groups of boys in terms of the diverse forms of masculinity that are produced and the differences that therefore follow, within this, in terms of the boys' dispositions towards education and formal schooling. The general outlines of working class and middle class boys' masculinities that will be offered respectively in the chapters to follow should therefore not be read as being applicable to all boys equally. Rather, the general experiences and social processes to be identified should be seen as simply providing the overarching backdrop against which individual working class and middle class boys are left to negotiate their own identities. Why and how particular boys come to either conform to or resist these more general processes will have to be the subject of another study.

Finally, in painting these broader pictures of working class and middle class boys' experiences of and dispositions towards schooling respectively, it is important to be clear about the nature of the findings to be reported and what claims can and cannot be made from them. As outlined above, these are qualitative, ethnographic case studies focusing on just two schools. It is simply not possible to attempt to make generalisations from the findings of these two case studies about working class and middle class boys respectively. In fact we already know, from the evidence presented in Chapter 1, what the general picture is. What we do not know is *why* these gender and social class differences exist at this young age. To address this question we need to get beneath the surface of the statistical findings to examine what is actually going on for particular boys in school – what are their experiences and perspectives and what are the specific processes that exist that can help us understand their differing dispositions towards education?

These types of question can only be answered by careful, in-depth analysis of the young boys and their lives and social worlds. What the two case studies will do, therefore, is to help identify *some* of the reasons why working class and middle class boys differ in their experiences of and attitudes towards education. What we cannot and should not then do is to assume that these reasons apply to all working class or middle class boys. Rather, and as I have argued elsewhere (Connolly, 1998b), the role of the two case studies is simply to help early years practitioners understand what *could possibly* be happening for the working class or middle class boys in their particular classes or settings. However, it is then up to the particular individual concerned to assess which particular processes found in these two case studies are actually applicable to her/his boys and which are not. In this sense, therefore, the aim of the case studies to follow is to raise teachers' and early years practitioners' awareness of some of the processes that underlie working class and middle class boys' experiences of schooling and to provide a 'checklist' (albeit a necessarily incomplete one) against which they can then assess the boys in their own class.

This approach has important implications for how the findings from the data are actually described and written up. Most significantly there remains a temptation in qualitative research to quantify particular social processes that are uncovered. For example, let us say that we find three reasons why there is a tendency for the working class boys in our case study school not to like reading as much as the middle class boys – Reasons A, B and C. The temptation of, and moreover the pressure on, researchers is to then report these as 'accurately' as possible. Thus it could be stated that Reason A applied to 70 per cent of the boys, Reason B to 45 per cent and Reason C to only 10 per cent of the boys. The key question is whether such detailed description is actually of any practical use. If we were simply concerned with the boys in that particular working class school then it may be. However, the aim is not to accurately describe the boys in just this one school but, in this particular example, to use the study to identify some of the broader reasons that tend to adversely affect working class boys' interest in reading. The problem with quantifying the reasons found in this particular school is that it wrongly encourages the reader to generalise about the relative significance of each one. Yet there is no way of knowing how representative the school is of working class schools more generally. It could therefore be the case that the relative importance of these three reasons is not representative of other similar schools but simply reflects the particular characteristics of this specific school and its community. A follow-up survey of a much larger number of randomly-selected schools, for example, may find that it is actually Reason C that is the most significant and that Reason A is the least important.

It is with this in mind, therefore, that no attempts will be made to quantify the particular processes that are identified and that impact upon the boys' experiences of and dispositions towards education in the case studies to follow. Reference will be made, instead, simply to the existence of 'a tendency' for 'some' working class or middle class parents or boys to have a particular experience or to think or behave in a certain way. In this sense the case studies will focus more specifically on drawing attention to those processes in relation to the two groups of boys that can help explain some of the reasons for the educational differences between them. In narrowing the focus in this way, the two case studies share a passing similarity with, but are not the same as, Weber's (1949) methodological use of 'ideal types'.[5] Overall, therefore, it is worth emphasising that *the two case studies are neither an attempt to generalise about all working class and middle class young boys nor, indeed, even about the young boys in the two schools.* Given the tendency for research to remain dominated by positivist modes of thinking with their need to produce generalisations and to assess findings in terms of how representative they are then this final point needs to be kept firmly in mind as we now move on to the two case studies.

South Park and North Parade

The remainder of this chapter will now compare and contrast South Park and North Parade and thus set out the broader social contexts within which the two groups of young boys are located. The contexts to be discussed here include the broader local areas in which the boys live and their families and respective schools. It may be tempting to ignore these broader contexts and launch instead straight into a detailed study of the boys themselves. However, this is dangerous for three main reasons. First, and as we have seen in the previous chapter, the way young children learn and develop cannot be properly understood without an appreciation of the social contexts and relationships within which they are located. Not all children are the same and they certainly do not follow a universal developmental pathway. Rather, they are intricately bound up with the social processes and practices of those around them. Ignoring these broader social contexts will simply result in the production of an impoverished and significantly incomplete understanding of what these young boys are learning and how they are developing.

Second, stripping these boys of their social context will also lead to the generation of crude and simplistic accounts of their masculine identities and behaviour. This is especially true in relation to the young boys in the working class North Parade where they have adopted a distinctly physical and aggressive form of masculinity. Studied in isolation it is easy to reach the conclusion that there is something innately violent and pathological about some of these boys. And yet, placed in the broader context of the community in which they live and the way it has been ravaged by economic decline and sectarian violence then such forms of behaviour no longer appear abnormal but are actually a normal and rational response to an abnormal situation. Third, one of the main aims of this book is not just to understand better what is going on for young boys in terms of their attitudes towards and experiences of schooling but also to consider the implications of this for how we can work most effectively with them. Again, if we do not understand the broader context within which the boys are located then we are simply not in a position to make meaningful and appropriate recommendations in relation to practice. In the two case studies to follow it will become abundantly clear that the young boys' masculine identities and their attitudes towards education are essentially a reflection of, and intricately tied into, the communities within which they live. For any practical recommendations to be successful they therefore need to address not only the symptoms of the problem (in terms of the boys' actual behaviour) but also its causes (i.e. the broader culture and contexts within which they live).

With these points in mind, this study is therefore different to some other pieces of research concerned with the early years because of the emphasis and time it gives to understanding the wider social contexts within which the young boys are located. The focus for the remainder of this chapter, then, is to provide an essentially descriptive outline of the differences between South Park and North Parade and thus to highlight the role of social class in defining the broader parameters of the social worlds, educational opportunities and life-chances of the young children in the two areas generally. It is in the following chapters that this overarching analysis is then deepened first by a more detailed exploration of the perspectives of parents and the schools and then of how gender fundamentally intervenes in all of this – in the form of masculinity – in the lives of the two groups of young boys.

There are actually areas like North Parade and South Park to be found across Northern Ireland. Often, such communities can exist in close proximity to one another, sometimes within walking distance. And yet in many respects they are worlds apart. This will be illustrated below by making comparisons at three levels: general socio-economic differences; differences in their experiences of the political conflict; and then differences, more specifically, in terms of overall educational attainment and provision. It needs to be stated that what is offered below is very much a description rather than an explanation of the differences that exist. Such a description will certainly suffice in relation to providing the necessary context for then understanding and explaining, in the following chapters, the differences in educational performance and provision found in the two respective areas. However, given the broader figurational approach outlined and advocated in the previous chapter, it is not sufficient simply to describe the main characteristics of North Parade and South Park without any discussion of how they have evolved and developed. This is especially important in the context of Northern Ireland where the nature of the divisions that exist and the extent of the violence and conflict that has taken place in the region demand some explanation.

I am mindful in making this point, however, that providing an historical analysis of the economic and political processes that have led to the development of areas like North Parade and South Park may be too much for some readers who simply want to focus, more specifically, on the boys themselves. With this in mind, and because of the limits of space, I have provided such an historical analysis elsewhere (Connolly, 2004). As a sociologist I strongly believe that this account is important and will help readers to understand more deeply the nature of the two communities and to avoid the tendency to regard them as somehow natural and inevitable. While it is provided separately, therefore, it is a useful additional element to the analysis and is freely available.[6] I would urge you to read it as a complement to this chapter.

Socio-economic differences

Economically, South Park is ranked[7] within the top 10 per cent of the most affluent wards in Northern Ireland and is a leafy suburban community characteristic of many prosperous middle class areas to be found across the UK and Ireland. By contrast, North Parade is ranked within the bottom 20 per cent of the most deprived wards in the region and, in some respects, is indicative of many isolated, working class areas that have been decimated by economic recession. By way of comparison, a number of key social and economic characteristics for the two areas are provided in Table 4.1. As can be seen, the consequences of economic decline are certainly evident in North Parade. There are high unemployment rates and, for those in

Table 4.1 A comparison of key social and economic indicators for South Park and North Parade, 2001*

Indicator	South Park	North Parade
Economic Indicators		
% who are economically active	64	51
% in managerial and professional occupations	35	12
% in semi-routine and routine occupations	26	49
% who are unemployed	5	14
% children receiving free school meals in local primary school	5	68
Health Indicators		
% of working age with limiting long-term illness	16	26
% whose overall health was 'not good'	12	19
Educational Indicators		
% with degrees	21	4
% with no qualifications	38	61
Social Indicators		
% of households headed by lone parents with dependent children	8	14
% of housholds with no car or van	23	54
% of households that are owner-occupied	70	48
Conflict Indicator		
No. of deaths in the area since 1969	1	25

Source: 2001 Census except for: a. the number of deaths that was calculated from data provided by Sutton, undated; b. free school meals data that was gained from the Department of Education.

Note: * These figures have been calculated from the respective wards that comprise the catchment areas for the two schools – North Parade and South Park Primary Schools respectively.

employment, nearly half are in low-paid, unskilled and relatively insecure manual work. The effects of poverty in the area are also evident with just over a quarter of the adult population having a limiting long-term illness and around a fifth stating that their health was 'not good'. The majority of households have no access to a car and just over two-thirds of the children attending North Parade Primary School are in receipt of free school meals. The physical area itself reflects these broader characteristics. North Parade is an isolated community cut off from its surrounding area with only one main entrance into the estate. It has a distinctly desolate feel to it with very few shops and amenities and significant patches of wasteland and litter. Much of the housing is run-down with a number of dwellings boarded up.

In contrast, South Park displays all of the trappings of a relatively affluent and prosperous community. As can be seen from Table 4.1, two-thirds of the adult population are economically active and one in three of these is employed in a managerial or professional occupation. Unemployment is relatively low and there are very few children attending South Park Primary School who are in receipt of free school meals. A large majority of households have access to a car and, more generally, the overall standards of health of those in South Park are much better in comparison with those living in North Parade. The physical area itself is a quintessential leafy middle class suburb. The housing is in good condition and is a mix of semi-detached and detached properties, most with relatively large gardens. The area is quiet and many of the streets are lined with trees. There are also many local amenities with a number of specialist shops and boutiques within walking distance. Overall, the local area is well kept and generally free of litter and graffiti.

Differences in experiences of the conflict

Such social and economic differences are only part of the picture however in relation to the two communities. Another key distinguishing feature is the very different levels of sectarian violence and conflict that both areas have faced over the years. Northern Ireland as a whole has witnessed an intense period of violence over the last thirty years. Since the outbreak of the conflict (or what have often been termed 'the troubles') in 1969 there have been over 3,600 people killed and well over 40,000 injured (Morrissey and Smyth, 2002).

The violence itself has arisen from the deep divisions between two principal ethno-religious groups living in Northern Ireland – those that see themselves as Protestants and constitute the majority (53 per cent of the total population) and those that see themselves as Catholic and are the minority (44 per cent).[8] The conflict itself has involved a number of organisations including, primarily, the British army and the armed police force as well as paramilitary groups representing both sides – republican groups associated with the Catholic population (mainly the IRA but also the INLA and more recently splinter groups such as the Real IRA and Continuity IRA) and loyalist groups associated with the Protestant population (including the UVF, UDA, UFF and LVF).[9]

The early 1970s was a particularly violent period and some sense of the scale of this can be clearly seen in Figure 4.1 that shows the number of actual deaths per year caused by the conflict from 1969 through to 2001. As can be seen, 479 people were killed in 1972 alone and there were between 250 and 300 deaths per annum for the following few years. Overall, much of the violence during this period was rather indiscriminate and included city and town centre bombs detonating with little or no warning and a significant number of what were known at the time as 'doorstep killings' due to the fact that victims were often shot dead at point-blank range when simply answering their front door (Fay et al., 1999). It was also relatively common in certain areas for individuals to be viciously attacked or shot while walking home because of their perceived religious identity. There were also a number of notorious cases of individuals being bundled into cars, driven away and then sometimes being tortured

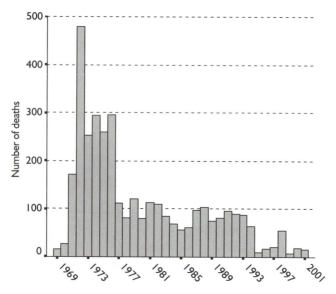

Figure 4.1   Number of conflict-related deaths in Northern Ireland 1969–2001
Source: Data taken from Sutton (undated).

before then being shot dead. More generally, while the early 1970s represented a particularly intense and violent period, it can be seen from Figure 4.1 that significant levels of violence continued up to the first paramilitary ceasefires of 1994. Between 1977 and 1993 there was an average of 89 people killed per year as a direct result of the conflict.

Given the intensity of the violence many people in Northern Ireland therefore tended to live in fear during this period. Not surprisingly, high levels of residential segregation emerged as people either moved to areas they felt more safe and secure in or were actually burnt out of their homes and forced to move by those living nearby from the other ethno-religious community. It has been estimated, for example, that just within the first few years of the violence (1969–72) between 8,000 and 15,000 families were forced to leave their homes and live elsewhere (Smyth, 1998: 15). Moreover, and as Boal (1999) has identified in his broader analysis of urban trends in the region, there was a 'ratchet effect' whereby intense periods of violence tended to significantly increase levels of segregation that would then never return to their previous levels during later times of relative peace (see also Murtagh, 2002, 2003).

Overall, in terms of current levels of segregation an analysis of the 2001 Census data reveals that a quarter of all wards (25 per cent) in Northern Ireland have a population that is at least 90 per cent Catholic or Protestant. In fact well over half of all wards in Northern Ireland (58 per cent) have a population that is at least 75 per cent Catholic or Protestant. While patterns of segregation can be found in middle class (Smyth, 1998) and rural areas (Murtagh, 2003), the highest levels of segregation are to be found in the urban, working class areas of Belfast and Derry/Londonderry where the violence has also been most intense (Fay et al., 1999; Morrissey and Smyth, 2002; Smyth and Hamilton, 2003). This is illustrated in Figure 4.2 that shows the ethno-religious composition of the 51 wards in Belfast in 2001 as an example. As can be seen, the relatively long tails at either end of the distribution illustrate the high levels of segregation that exist in certain areas. In fact the majority of wards in Belfast (57 per cent) consist of populations that are more than 90 per cent Catholic or Protestant.

The notion of interdependent relationships, which represents one of the principal features of a figurational analysis as outlined in the previous chapter, is a particularly useful one here for understanding the evolving nature of the relationships between Protestants and

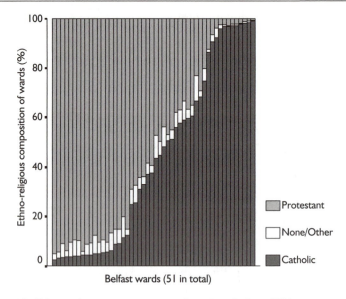

Figure 4.2   Ethno-religious compositions of wards in Belfast, 2001
Source: Data derived from 2001 Census.

Catholics during this period. In this particular sense, interdependence is not to be understood functionally, as a positive and mutually-beneficial relationship. Rather, the two ethno-religious groups were interdependent in as much as the lives of those within each group tended (to varying degrees) to be determined by, and thus ultimately to be dependent upon, the actions of those within the other group (Elias, 1978). In those areas that tended to experience high levels of violence, especially those where Protestant and Catholic communities lived buttressed up against one another, members of one community tended to live in the shadow of the other. Routine choices in terms of where to shop, which routes to take and even what to wear all tended to be determined against the backdrop of the threat created by the other community. Many of these behaviours and choices became internalised and taken-for-granted as part of a community's collective habitus. Moreover, the very real threat that exists has ensured that Protestants and Catholics have, more generally, learnt a whole range of ways of 'telling' each other apart (Burton, 1978). An array of complex signifiers have therefore developed to distinguish members of one community from another. Some are fairly obvious and include where a person lives, what school they attended, what their name is and what football team they support. However, they can also include much more subtle indicators such as the route a person is taking out of the town centre, the wearing of certain jewellery, how their name is spelt or even how they pronounce the letter 'h'. All of these forms of knowledge and ways of being have become 'second nature' for some people in Northern Ireland, especially those living in areas that have experienced high levels of violence.

This is certainly the context that North Parade and its residents have found themselves in. North Parade is an overwhelmingly Protestant community and, as shown in Table 4.1, there have been 25 killings in the local area related directly to the present phase of the conflict. This is actually not as high as some other areas but it has certainly added significantly to the sense of a community under threat. While the scale of the violence within Northern Ireland has certainly reduced since 1994 with the onset of the current 'peace process' and the paramilitary ceasefires, North Parade still lives with relatively high levels of sectarian tensions and threat. This sense of threat has been translated primarily into a very strong sense of territory within the community. North Parade is known locally as a distinctly loyalist estate with local loyalist paramilitary groups operating relatively freely in the area. The estate itself is clearly marked out by the prominent flying of British Union flags from lampposts and the painting of kerbstones and railings on roads leading into the estate red, white and blue. There is also a fair amount of political graffiti both offering support to the local paramilitary groups and also making derogatory and threatening statements against Catholics.

In contrast, South Park appears to have avoided much of the conflict altogether. As indicated in Table 4.1, it has experienced very little violence over the last 30 years with just one conflict-related death occurring in the area during this entire period. There is no graffiti and no signs of sectarian divisions or paramilitary activity at all. As stated earlier, in walking along the tree-lined roads of South Park it is almost impossible to distinguish the area from many other affluent middle class areas to be found across the UK and the Republic of Ireland. Moreover, and in contrast with the residents of North Parade, the onset of the peace process has brought with it significant benefits for those living in South Park. While sectarian tensions may still be high in localised areas like North Parade, more generally the peace process has brought with it a noticeable 'demilitarisation' and 'normalisation' of life in the region. With the notable exception of the Omagh bomb in 1998, the days of indiscriminate bombings have largely gone and the chances of coming across an army patrol or police road block or even having one's bags searched in shopping centres (all routine occurrences before the paramilitary ceasefires) are now all but gone. Those living in South Park, therefore, are now increasingly able to venture out of their own neighbourhood and travel around Northern Ireland without having their lives impacted upon by the conflict at all.

Differences in educational achievement and provision

Given these very different socio-economic and political conditions that the residents of North Parade and South Park find themselves in, it is not surprising to find equally stark differences in relation to the educational opportunities open to both groups. The data in Table 4.1 already provide some indication of this with nearly two-thirds of all adults in North Parade having no qualifications at all whereas, in contrast, just over one in five adults in South Park actually have a degree. To a large extent, these differences can be understood in terms of the effects of poverty and disadvantage on educational achievement, effects that have been well documented by researchers for a number of decades now (see Newson and Newson, 1965; Douglas, 1967; Mortimore and Blackstone, 1982). The extent of this relationship is clearly evident in Figure 4.3 that has simply taken the 51 wards in Belfast as an example and plotted each of them in relation to a measure of its overall level of multiple deprivation and then the percentage of adults within that ward who have no formal education qualifications. As can be seen, a strong relationship exists with increases in levels of multiple deprivation being closely associated with increases in the proportions of adults with no qualifications. In fact the strength of the relationship ($r = 0.868$, $p < 0.0005$) suggests that three-quarters (75.3 per cent) of the variation between wards in terms of the percentage of adults with no educational qualifications can be accounted for by levels of multiple deprivation.

However, and as already stated, levels of deprivation are only part of the picture. In areas like North Parade, they also suffer from relatively high levels of sectarian conflict and violence. It is therefore likely that the combined effects of poverty and the insecurity and

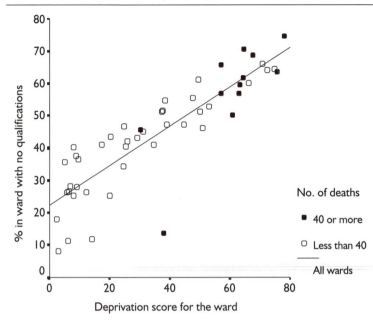

Figure 4.3 Relationship between levels of deprivation, proportions of residents with no formal qualifications and number of conflict-related deaths in Belfast wards

Source: Data relating to qualifications taken from 2001 Census. Deprivation score relates to the Noble measure of multiple deprivation and taken from NISRA, 2001. No. of conflict-related deaths taken from Sutton, undated.

trauma brought on by routine levels of violence can only tend to reduce further the levels of educational achievement in such areas. This is certainly illustrated in Figure 4.3 where those wards that have suffered from the highest number of conflict-related deaths (i.e. 40 or more killings since 1969) have been highlighted. As can be seen, with very few exceptions, these wards are all bunched together at the top end of the regression line. What this shows is the way in which the highest levels of educational disadvantage seem to be associated with those areas that suffer from both the highest levels of multiple deprivation and sectarian violence.

This is precisely the picture found in North Parade where the evidence suggests that the young children there are already significantly trailing behind their counterparts in South Park even before they start school in P1 (ages 4–5), the reception class (see also Strand, 1999a). (The children in question are now in P2. However, these

Table 4.2 Results of baseline assessments of the children in the two respective P2 classes* at North Parade and South Park Primary Schools (%)

Area of development	Stage achieved	School	
		North Parade	South Park
Personal, social and emotional development	PT**	32	–
	1st	64	20
	2nd	4	80
	3rd	–	–
	Total	**100**	**100**
Language development	PT**	8	–
	1st	84	12
	2nd	8	84
	3rd	–	4
	Total	**100**	**100**
Mathematical development	PT**	8	–
	1st	84	4
	2nd	8	76
	3rd	–	20
	Total	**100**	**100**

Notes: * *n* = 25 for both classes.
       ** progressing towards 1st stage.

baseline assessments were carried out on them during the previous year when they were in P1, and had only just started school.) This is illustrated in Table 4.2 that compares the baseline assessments of the children in the two P2 classes (ages 5–6) from North Parade and South Park Primary Schools.[10] These assessments were undertaken the previous year by the then P1 teacher in October when they had been in the reception class for about two months. It provides an evaluation of their levels of development in three basic areas: personal, social and emotional development; language development (including talking and listening and early reading and writing skills); and their mathematical development (including their skills at talking about maths, understanding of patterns and relationships and grasp of early number concepts). Each child's development in relation to these three areas is categorised into one of four stages. The second stage is that which is generally expected of children when they begin school, the first stage indicates that the child has not yet fully developed the skills expected while the third level indicates that the child has progressed beyond what is normally expected. Additionally, those children that have not yet progressed to the first stage are categorised as 'progressing towards the first stage'.

As can be seen from Table 4.2, there are significant differences between the teachers' assessments of the relative progress made by both sets of children by the time they start school. For the children at South Park, the vast majority (between 80 and 96 per cent) were assessed as having at least reached the expected stage of development (i.e. second stage) in relation to the three core areas by the time they started school. In stark contrast only a small minority of children at North Parade (ranging from 4 to 8 per cent) were assessed as having reached the expected stage. Moreover, some (8 per cent) were assessed as having not even progressed to the first stage in language and mathematical development and a third (32 per cent) as having not progressed to the first stage in personal, social and emotional development. It is this perceived lack of social development among the children at North Parade that has important implications for how the school has defined its educational role, as will be seen in Chapter 7.

As other research has also found (Strand, 1999b), such initial differences tend to then be repeated, and often increase, during the first years of schooling. This was certainly evident from two short tests that the same children (now in P2) were asked to complete during the fieldwork for the present study. Both classes undertook the two tests during the same week in February 2002. The first test

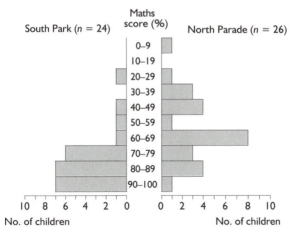

Figure 4.4 Distribution of maths scores for the respective P2 classes at South Park and North Parade Primary Schools

involved each child being asked to complete a standardised maths assessment.[11] The results from this test are shown in Figure 4.4. As can be seen, the children at South Park tended to perform significantly better with an average (median) score of 81 per cent compared to 64 per cent for the children at North Parade. It is interesting to note the greater variation in the scores for the North Parade children compared to those at South Park. While some achieved very high scores a fair proportion also achieved very low scores. In contrast, with just a few exceptions, the children at South Park tended to perform at a consistently high level.

The largest differences in performance between the two groups of children, however, were found in relation to their reading skills. The second short test each child was asked to complete was to read from a list comprising 100 common words. Each child was then given a score reflecting the number of words out of 100 that they were able to recognise. The results from this test are shown in Figure 4.5. As can be seen, there is a noticeable difference in the overall performance of the two groups of children. The average (median) number of words that children in South Park were able to recognise was 85 compared to just 19 for those in North Parade. Moreover, this time there is much less variation in the scores of the children in North Parade with the vast majority clustered at the lower end. By way of contrast the scores of the children at South Park are actually

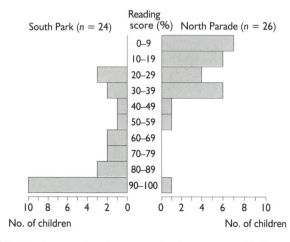

Figure 4.5 Distribution of reading scores for the respective P2 classes at South Park and North Parade Primary Schools

more varied. However, while there is a rather long tail of children at South Park scoring fairly low on the reading test, over half of the children in the class were able to recognise at least 80 words out of 100.

As a final source of information on the general educational differences between the two groups of children it is useful to compare two recent inspection reports undertaken for the two schools respectively. Because of the need to maintain anonymity, it is unfortunately not possible to provide verbatim extracts from the reports here. However, on reading both reports it is clear that they both provide further evidence not only of the very different dispositions towards education found between the two groups of children but also the equally different approaches to education undertaken by the two schools partly as a consequence of this. The inspection report on South Park Primary School, for example, emphasises the good behaviour, excellent relationships and positive working atmosphere found in classrooms. The young children are also noted for their abilities to concentrate and to present their work tidily and the teachers' work is praised for being thoughtful, well-planned and challenging.

In contrast, the inspection report on North Parade Primary School notes the difficult problems faced due to its location in a violent and economically-deprived area and praises the school for the emphasis it has given to its pastoral care and the emotional support of the children. However, the report also notes the discipline problems experienced by the school and the tendency for a significant number of children to be rowdy and difficult to control. Many children were viewed as being easily distracted and the tendency for a significant proportion to have restricted language development was also noted. Moreover, a fair amount of the teachers' work in class was felt to be low-level, rather repetitive and not sufficiently challenging for the young children.

Overall, three points are worth making regarding the interpretation of the evidence presented above in relation to the general educational differences found between the young children in the two areas. First, it is important not to read such differences as implying simply that there is something 'lacking' in working class family homes. The key point is, as Brooker (2002) has recently stressed, that it is not so much that working class (and minority ethnic) families lack basic cultural and educational practices but rather that the practices they have are simply different from middle class families (Tizard and Hughes, 1984; Wells, 1986). As will be shown in the following chapters, the problem arises in that it is those practices and skills encouraged within middle class homes that are the ones valued by schools and which have been used to define what counts as a 'good education' (Bernstein, 1971, 1975; Bourdieu and Passeron, 1977; Heath, 1983). Given that these are the skills that children are required to learn to achieve formal qualifications then the fact that working class children are less likely to have them is a problem. In the short-term (and certainly until there is a fundamental change to the educational system) there is a practical imperative for us all to focus on how we can help working class children successfully acquire these key skills. It is important, however, that adopting such a focus is not read as implying a 'deficit' model of working class family life that was originally made popular in the UK with the publication of the Plowden Report (1967).

Second, and with this first caveat firmly in mind, it is clear from the evidence provided above that the two groups of children do differ markedly in relation to their preparation for formal schooling, the progress they are able to make during the first years of school in terms of educational attainment and their broader dispositions towards the type of education provided by the schools. As can be seen, the children in South Park would seem to have internalised many of the social and emotional skills necessary for schoolwork and also the necessary self-discipline and motivation to learn. In contrast, the children in North Parade would appear to be much less well 'prepared' for the demands of formal schooling especially in terms of its routine practices and discipline. Given that many of these differences are evident in the baseline assessment – i.e. when the children have only just started school – then this does highlight the need to examine the experiences and perspectives of the parents and how the children's lives at home either correspond to or conflict with the demands of the school.

Third, while it is clearly wrong to simply blame the schools for the differences that exist between the two groups of children, the inspection reports do suggest that they have some role to play; certainly in reinforcing any differences that may be evident when the children first enter the reception class. In this sense the two schools do seem to have adopted very different roles for themselves in terms of the education they provide for their children. At South Park Primary School it is clear that there is an explicit emphasis on the children's formal academic development – particularly in the core curriculum subjects. Lessons tend to be planned 'conscientiously' and the curriculum delivered in a 'systematic and thorough' way. As will be discussed further in Chapter 6, the evidence from classroom observations certainly supports this overall picture. In contrast, North Parade Primary School would appear to have defined its educational role quite differently. A key emphasis – particularly in the early years – would seem to be given to social, personal and emotional development. Indeed this emphasis on a pastoral approach would seem to be partly at the expense of a focus on formal academic development. For both schools, therefore, what we have is a complex process whereby the approach taken by each school not only reflects the different needs and characteristics of the particular communities they serve but also tends to reinforce and exaggerate these. This, in turn, points to the need to examine the perspectives and experiences of the schools as well, and the relationships they have developed with the parents, and to identify the processes that have led them to define the particular roles they have for themselves.

Conclusions

Overall, this chapter has provided an introduction to the two case studies by comparing and contrasting the two areas of South Park and North Parade and thus setting out the very different social contexts within which the two groups of boys are located. As has been seen, the two groups of young boys are 'worlds apart' in terms of their experiences, opportunities and future life-chances. As will now be seen in the following four chapters, it is these differing social worlds that the boys come to internalise through the construction of their differing masculine identities and thus, as a result, their very different dispositions towards education. The following two chapters will focus on the middle class boys in South Park while Chapters 7 and 8 will then focus on the working class boys in North Parade. In both cases the analysis will begin with a more detailed study of the immediate social contexts within which the boys are located day-to-day – in this sense the home and the school – before then examining, more specifically, their own experiences and perspectives.

Chapter 5

Home–school relations South Park

Introduction

This and the following chapter examine the social worlds of the young middle class boys at South Park Primary School. In locating these two chapters in relation to the theoretical model outlined in Chapter 3 (and summarised in Figure 3.3), then the following chapter focuses on the boys' habitus while this chapter focuses on the broader figurational context within which this habitus is formed. The actual perspectives of the boys, the nature of the masculine identities they tend to form and the impact these have on their dispositions towards education and schooling will thus be explored in Chapter 6 whereas this chapter provides the immediate context for all of this by considering the nature of the influences of home and school. As will be seen, the overall approaches taken by parents and the school to education and the particular values they place on it have a significant effect on the way the young boys construct their sense of identity and the place of education within this.

One way of understanding this immediate context is to apply the figurational approach outlined in Chapter 3 to consider the nature of the interdependent relationships between parents and the school. As will be seen below, this will help to highlight the nature of the roles and expectations that parents and the school have of each other and the balances of power that underpin these. Moreover, in also doing the same in Chapter 7 for North Parade, this will also provide a mechanism for more clearly highlighting the key differences found in relation to the two areas.

The premise underlying this chapter (and Chapter 7) is that interdependency tends to be a general, characteristic feature of relationships between parents and schools. At its most basic level, parents clearly depend upon schools to *educate* their children.

However, schools also depend upon the parents to be *compliant* and thus to accept and support the way that they, as schools, educate their children. The key issue, and the one that differentiates South Park and North Parade, is how these two terms – to educate and to be compliant – are defined and understood in practice. The focus for this chapter is how parents and the school define these terms in South Park.

Academic success and the educational role at South Park Primary School

South Park Primary School is a very popular school with an excellent reputation locally. As Mrs Bell, the School Principal, explained:

> We are oversubscribed in first preferences and also we have second and third preferences from other schools so it all adds up. So the job of then sorting out who comes in, applying the criteria etcetera is a fairly major job. ... The school does have a good reputation. Very often when I look at the application forms there's a space at the bottom of the application forms for people to put their reasons ... [and some] people say that it's the reputation of the school. I would have anything up to 10 or 12 occasions when I show small groups of parents round the school. I think that helps and I think when people see the school and they see the children's work, they see how well settled the children are and they see how happy they are, I think that all of that helps.

The reputation of the school, which Mrs Bell alludes to in the comments above, is based largely around academic success and it is this that drives its educational role. Thus the key factor that would appear to impress potential parents visiting the school is the (quality of) the children's work and how settled they are (or, in other words, how organised and disciplined and therefore activity-focused the classes are). Academic success was also a key motivating factor for some of the parents as will be seen below. It was certainly a taken-for-granted factor underpinning their choice of school. Even when some parents were aware of and laid emphasis on the need for young children to 'play' and be exposed to a wide range of activities, there remained a fundamental acceptance of the need for a clear academic focus as well. This is evident in the following comments from one of the mothers who was explaining why they had chosen South Park Primary School for their son. While listing a number of social factors, the need for the school to have clear academic expectations was also mentioned in an almost taken-for-granted way:

> Marriott Place would be our local primary school [but] we didn't like it and so I went and visited South Park and spoke to Mrs Bell and I felt quite happy with it then to give it a go. I liked the building. I liked the fact that it had lots of play equipment. I thought that was more appropriate for [young children] than, you know, Marriott Place [that acts] more like a Victorian primary school, you know, walk down the corridor and children have to line up in a particular way with their bags in one hand and all this, you know, it was very regimented and I liked the way South Park was more flexible. *It seemed strict, of course. They had clear expectations which was good*, but these big play areas ... with different themes at different times of the year I felt was good. I liked the fact that they had animals, they had guinea pigs.
>
> [emphasis added]

Given the broader emphasis on school performance and parental choice, the school was therefore under pressure to maintain its high academic standards. Moreover, it was a pressure also exerted to a considerable degree by some of the parents themselves who are dependent upon the school to formally educate their children and thus who take an active role in ensuring this with their children's class teachers. This is clearly evident in the experiences of Mrs Summerbee, the P2 class teacher at South Park:

> The parents are very forward. They're in and out of the school all the time. And that's a good thing. They know they can talk, they're not scared of the teacher, you know. They're very one-to-one with the teacher. ... They feel it's their right to come in and talk to you. Which it is of course. Sometimes though it's respecting your space, you know, and they could be in all the time. They're never nasty though. I've had one or two instances but generally speaking they're very well behaved, they're very nice and supportive. ... Yeah, you're doing the job with them but they're professionals as well, they do other things that are similar, you know, it's 'we're all one in this together' sort of thing.

There are two key points to note from the comments above. First they give a sense of the highly motivated nature of some of the parents, the emphasis they give to education and the way in which they can successfully make use of their professional skills and training to deal with teachers (Vincent, 1996; Reay, 1998). Second, while their active interest is clearly experienced as a pressure by the teacher, her final comments suggest that it is not entirely unwelcomed. Indeed for the school to perform well academically and thus maintain its reputation it needs the support – and thus the *compliance* – of parents. More specifically, alongside the parents depending upon the school to educate their children, the school depends upon the parents to support their efforts in two main ways. First, they need parents to prepare the children for the demands of formal schooling in terms of self-control, social skills and also the ability to listen and concentrate. This is certainly what the school feels the parents tend to do well and this is reflected in the baseline assessments outlined in Table 4.2 of the previous chapter. As Mrs Summerbee, the class teacher, explained when comparing the children in her current class with a class she taught some time ago in another school located in a deprived working class area:

> The children are able to concentrate more and their language is better, their ability to cooperate is better and all that kind of thing. They are more able to concentrate really and therefore you could [expect] more interest, more support [from them].

These are sentiments also expressed by the School Principal, Mrs Bell:

> The children here are great, they are enthusiastic. Most of the time they are very happy. They are very open. Relate well to the staff and in the main they relate well to each other and their behaviour is, I think, fairly good. Most of the time we are very pleased with the behaviour, you get the odd wee blip, but they are very open and enthusiastic and they are keen to learn. Very keen to learn.

Second, and alongside this general need for parents to prepare their children for the demands of formal academic schooling, the school also depends upon the parents in terms of them providing ongoing support in relation to the academic work they are doing with the children in class. This is evident mainly through parents showing interest in their children's work (by attending parent evenings and taking seriously any comments or requests made by the teacher) and also, more routinely, in helping children with their homework. Again, the school would appear to be very happy with the support that the parents offer in this regard. This is evident in Mrs Bell's comments regarding parental attendance at school events and in relation to parent evenings:

> We would have a very high response to our formal interviews. We would have virtually 100 per cent attendance at school interviews. ... Virtually all the parents came in [to the open afternoon]. I would say, yes, they all did. And if the parent couldn't come granny came instead if it was going to be very difficult. Again for the book fair next week we find that parents come. We encourage the children to come, it's immediately after school, it's open to parents to browse before they collect their children. And we encourage parents and children to come together to buy a book. You know, giving the message that books are still so important and it's an important thing to do together. And we would get a big response to that.
>
> The parents' evening in June, in the beginning of June for the P1 parents, we would get a *very* high response for that. And the parents who can't come *all* contact the school and explain why. And usually they have *extremely* good reasons for not making it. So I think they're very interested in their children's education.
>
> [original emphases]

Given the high expectations of some of the parents, however, there remains a certain level of pressure that the school has to manage. As Mrs Bell explains, they attempt to do this by carefully controlling the information they give to parents about their children's progress so as to manage their expectations:

> We try to be very honest [with parents and] I think that contributes to a realistic picture. However, it takes some people quite a long time to come to accept the realistic picture if it is not what they would wish it to be. And I think that, yes, there are some parents who have unrealistic expectations for their children and at times can put pressure on. ... We try to [encourage a more realistic view] in our reporting to parents. We have looked

at the language we use. We have considered how we write about children to try to get comments that are similar across the year band when we are describing similar things. … We have looked at what we say about a child for instance who is progressing well at reading and what we say about a child who is not making the progress that we would wish and so we are feeding realistically to parents. We're not pretending. We're not saying 'he'll grow out of it' when we have the distinct feeling he won't.

Parents do, they will compare which reading book [their children] are on. Now with using a variety of reading books it makes it more difficult [*laughs*] to compare … than if you're just going through book 1, book 2, book 3, book 4. But parents do, they do compare.

Overall, it should be apparent from the discussion so far that the relationship between parents and the school in South Park is one characterised by interdependency. The middle class parents clearly depend upon the school to educate their children to a high academic standard. However, in turn, the school depends upon the support and compliance of the parents in order to achieve this academic success. This interdependency encourages us, in turn, not to view power as somehow absolute (i.e. that power is unilaterally held by one side over the other) but rather to think in terms of balances of power or what Elias (1978) has also referred to as power ratios. This is certainly alluded to in the final comments above from Mrs Bell where there is a real sense of careful and strategic negotiation taking place on the part of the school as it attempts to manage the pressures that the parents exert on it. However, such practices are equally evident among the parents as they attempt to carefully manage and influence the school. It is worth spending a little time looking in more detail at the perspectives and experiences of these middle class parents given the central influence they have on shaping their children's attitudes towards education. As Brooker (2002: 16) has shown: 'children's dispositions towards learning bear the imprint of their parents' experiences and expectations'.

Parental compliance and the middle class habitus

We have already seen in Table 4.1 of the previous chapter that a significant proportion of parents living in South Park are employed in managerial and professional occupations. Given this, these middle class parents will tend to have internalised a particular way of thinking and behaving in the social world, a certain set of habits or taken-for-granted practices, that reflect their day-to-day working lives (Ball, 2003). This middle class habitus, as it can be called, tends to be characterised by a level of self-confidence in approaching other professionals (in this case teachers) and an expectation and belief in the ability to work in partnership with them. This has certainly already been evident through the experiences of the class teacher Mrs Summerbee. It is also evident in the comments of one mother who was asked whether she felt the teachers were approachable:

> Yeah, very much so. ... When I have been with Mrs Summerbee *it's been much more us working together to make sure we get the right thing for Matthew [her son]* and also I've always felt she's been very interested in him and so I've never gone with a complaint and I've never had a complaint.
>
> [emphasis added]

This middle class habitus found among some parents also reflects a sense of autonomy that is a characteristic feature of those working in management and professional roles and thus, by definition, involves the internalisation of a level of personal organisation and self-discipline. One of the ways this can translate into practices within the home is through the notion of 'routine'. As one parent explained:

> Children need routine – it's the one thing I have learnt. You only have to be on holiday for a good while and then they become, erm, cheeky and just the whole thing goes if their routine [goes]. ... Routine and children is definitely the thing, no doubt about it. Even at their age. If they have too many late nights and just, you know, haphazard meals and things like that, they just love routine, it just seems to work, in our house anyway.

This sense of routine, therefore, reflects a certain middle class disposition for organisation and control. It is also a significant vehicle through which some middle class children come to internalise the habits of learning and educational study. As another mother explained in describing her 'routine' with her son when he arrives home from school:

Well he knows that I like to get homework done as soon as he comes home. Usually when he comes in he has a drink, some toast and a biscuit, watches Disney Channel for 10 or 15 minutes and then we start. It's just reading, spelling and his number work. I would always make him write the spellings down in a book, you know. And he does the reading with me – we do it page by page. Because he has the book for two or three days, you know, so I do one set and he does the other half and we change about the next day. It's never any problem. He's quite happy to do it because he loves to get out and he knows he can't get out until the homework's done. He's good about doing the homework. I wouldn't say he enjoys it but he knows if he wants to get out he has to do it!

Schoolwork is therefore simply a part of some middle class children's routines at home; a taken-for-granted and increasingly unquestioned aspect of their lives. As another mother and father explained when talking about their own two children:

Mother: Both of them come in and sit down and do their homework at the same time, depending upon how much they have. ... He does it all, he doesn't complain really.
Father: I think he knows himself what he's got to do, to just get on with it.

However, not only is the practice of schoolwork internalised within some of the middle class children's habitus, but its value and importance is also clearly learnt through the keen interest and active involvement of some parents in their children's work. In this sense, and as Allatt (1993) has argued, the clear association between educational qualifications and managerial/professional occupations means that notions of middle class happiness are often predicated upon educational success (see also Ball, 2003; Power *et al.*, 2003). The centrality of educational success to some forms of middle class habitus is certainly evident in the anxiety that some parents feel in the lead up to their children starting school and the need to ensure they are adequately 'prepared'. The comments from one mother regarding the preparatory work she engaged in with her own son illustrate this:

I would have done extra bits and pieces with him before he went to school in terms of writing and showing him words and letters so he was familiar with them. Now, they tell you not to do that but then I found with Daniel that I was the only one that hadn't [*laughs*], you know, and you think well what is the point in them saying: 'oh don't be showing them letters' or 'don't worry if they can't hold a pencil' and you go to school, your child goes to school, and they're the only idiot in there that doesn't know how to do it! [*laughs*] And I think that's unfair, that's bad advice and all teachers do it – all their children read and write before they go to school. They're very sly! [*laughs*] So I think that you need to look after your own child and you know what's best for them. And no matter what they say, even if they're going to school at four and it's very unfair, it's horrific I think, ... but in saying that they had to go and so they needed to be prepared and I did spend time with Daniel certainly in the summer time before it teaching him letters and reading and writing and just spending wee bits of time doing concentration work on books to get him used to that. I think it really did help because I think he had enough to learn when he went to school about the routine and adjusting to the change and everyone else.

What we also get a glimpse of here is the careful but highly strategic practices that some middle class parents engage in when managing their relationships with the school. In this sense, while they are 'all professionals together', some parents feel obliged to respect the professional expertise of teachers in relation to the education of their children. As Sharp and Green (1975) highlighted in their classic study of infant classrooms, this leads some parents to expend much effort and skill in successfully creating the impression of not interfering while actively and routinely doing so. One of the main examples of this is in relation to homework. For some parents there is a strong feeling that their children are not being 'stretched' enough by the school, as the following mother explains when talking about her daughter who is in Mrs Summerbee's P2 class at the school:

They [*the school*] don't tend [to] push them terribly hard. Now you can say that, well, why would you want to push them at that stage they're only wee, [young children]? [But] I worry about the fact that I don't want her to get bored. ... I mean, she's very, very happy there and it's a wonderful school for getting them into the school routine. ... [However,] I feel as the year's progressing she needs a challenge, you know, everything's very easy to her and I feel that from that point of view she's maybe not getting as much out of it.

In not wanting to appear too 'pushy' or 'interfering', one way around this for some of the parents is for them to extend or adapt the homework that has been set for their children. This is evident in the following comments from one mother who simply extends her son's reading homework by asking him additional questions about the book after reading it:

It's never terribly taxing. I think at this stage they should be getting a wee bit more, you know, I don't think one written bit of homework a week is enough. ... If it's a book, we'd just do the reading and then I'd ask him questions to see if he remembers what he's read and whatever and that's it usually, you know.

A similar practice is also engaged in by another mother, this time in relation to adapting her daughter's maths homework:

They're doing [the number] nine, you know, what makes nine. But she knows what makes nine so it's not good in that sense where she's getting [homework] like two plus seven is what? She knows she's working on nine so she knows what the answers are going to be. So I have to sort of try and put in it what makes eight, you know, because she's not concentrating at all because she knows it's going to be nine. ... She's not even trying to count it. So I sort of have to then go, well, do different sums where she knows – she's going 'that's not what I have to do!' – so she has to sit and count it, you know.

This emphasis on homework and the value of educational success – that is slowly becoming internalised into the taken-for-granted practices of the young children – is also evident in the following example where the father is complaining that his slightly older son at the same school was unfairly penalised in one test where he 'only' achieved a mark of 92 per cent:

Mother: All his assessments came back and he got 98 per cent, 87 per cent, you know, so ...
Father: There was one of those assessment tests where I thought, whenever I got to the bottom of it, I thought 'hang on a

minute!' [*laughs*]. I actually wrote at the bottom of it that I thought the marking scheme was too severe – it was on measurements. One of the questions, he got 92 per cent, and it was really brilliant work, excellent work. I was looking through it saying that was good, that was good, that was good. So where did he go wrong? There's this line/

Mother: /Yes, that's what it was, it was one line/

Father: /where he had to [measure it and] write down how many centimetres, how many millimetres and then [what this] equals in millimetres. And he got the measurements one millimetre wrong. So they took off a mark because he's written down 8 cm and 9 mm – it should have been 8 cm 8 mm. Right, so they took one mark off for that and I thought fair enough so he's lost one mark for that. He got it wrong. The next one then is, he also lost a mark because he translated 8 cm 9 mm to 89 mm so they took another mark off because it should have been 88 mm! But as far as I was concerned he got his process incorrect by getting the measurements wrong but the next step in the process he got right because he correctly translated the measurements into millimetres. And so they knocked another mark off. And as there were only 25 marks to get then he got 23 out of 25 which was then 92 per cent. So I thought hang on this is not fair [*laughs*]! I was really happy that he got 92 per cent but I thought he should have got 96! ... There was another test that there was something else that I thought they were a wee bit severe on but then I think they probably do deliberately over-severely mark if you are getting really high scores/

Mother: /That's not fair either really though, that's not fair.

Father: It's fair as long as they are being equally severe to all the ones who are equally high marks so as to sort of try and squish the marks down a bit to compress them so you don't get incredibly high marks and incredibly low marks.

This emphasis on schoolwork and the value placed on educational success is therefore simply a routine part of life for some middle class children. Moreover, it is not just confined to homework but can also be embedded in many other aspects of routine family life, as the following comments illustrate when one mother talks about what activities they tend to do as a family:

For us, well we're, we have a season ticket to the zoo we just renew every year and a season ticket to the aquarium. Ours are all animal fanatics. We go to the cinema, we do all kinds of mad things. We go on brilliant holidays. We go on weekends to London and see Robot Wars, you know, they get quite a lot of opportunities, you know, compared to other children. ... We love going to France, that would be our main thing. We love going camping and we always try to have a mixture of relaxing, sort of camping, and easygoing type times and also go sightseeing so, in the summer there, we took them to the D-Day beaches and the boys just loved it. Even Michael who isn't as interested in army and stuff like that. ... There's a fantastic circular cinema up there which shows you what the area was like during the war time. It actually had quite a lot to offer even the young children. ... There's lots of sightseeing points along there that they all really loved and loads of old relics and museums and stuff, so they loved all of that. And they've been all through Paris and the Eiffel Tower, oh [and] they're all into the cafés in London. You know, they're quite cosmopolitan, for their age! But they love all that and I love the fact that they can go places and, you know, it is educational in the broadest sense, you know, that they can go and see what the National History Museum is like.

Conclusions

Overall, it is clear from this chapter that the emphasis within South Park is on academic attainment and success and it is this that tends to structure the nature of the interdependent relationships found between parents and the school. As has been seen, educational success is a significant part of the middle class habitus for some parents and tends to underpin the hopes and aspirations they have for their children. Moreover, these middle class parents tend to have the educational background, the skills and the resources to be able to effectively support their children in achieving this educational success (Walkerdine and Lucey, 1989). Education tends, therefore, to be embedded in the routines of middle class family life and, consequently, becomes internalised by some of the children themselves as a taken-for-granted aspect of their own lives. These parents depend upon the school to successfully educate their children. However, and as has been seen, the school also depends upon the parents to be compliant and to support their efforts in educating the children. Thus, for the school to be successful it relies upon these routine family practices to adequately prepare the children for the demands of academic schoolwork and also to support them in the completion of their homework. In this sense, therefore, the dependencies tend to be mutually beneficial and the nature of the relationships between parents and the school tend to be largely harmonious. The balances of power are such that there tends to be a lack of underlying conflict and, instead, we find a series of carefully orchestrated strategies on both sides aimed at managing the expectations and impressions that each has of the other. This, then, is the immediate context within which the middle class boys in South Park are located and it is to them that we now turn.

Chapter 6

'Fish in water'

The schooling habitus of
young middle class boys

Introduction

This chapter focuses specifically on the experiences of and attitudes towards schooling held by the young middle class boys at South Park Primary School. The previous chapter has already demonstrated that a close correspondence exists between the routines and demands of home and those of school for some of these young boys. This chapter develops this theme in more detail. By focusing on the behaviour and perspectives of the young boys themselves, the chapter will show how they tend to move around their school worlds as 'fish in water', to borrow a phrase from Bourdieu (Power *et al.*, 2003: 81).

More specifically, and following the theoretical framework outlined in Chapter 3 (Figure 3.3), it will be shown how the broader social contexts of home and school as outlined in the previous chapter – with their emphasis on routines and control – have become internalised by these young middle class boys as a set of taken-for-granted habits and dispositions – in other words as their habitus. Within this context, the chapter will also draw out the young boys' overall dispositions towards schooling arising from this 'middle class habitus'. Having done this, the chapter will then examine the young boys' peer cultures in more detail. More specifically, it will outline the dominant form of masculinity that these boys tend to subscribe to and reproduce and how this, in turn, tends to mediate these overall (middle class) dispositions towards schooling. The chapter will end by examining the implications of all this for understanding the nature of young middle class boys' lower levels of educational attainment compared to girls in the early years.

The middle class habitus and schooling

In setting out the broader figurational context within which these young boys are located, the previous chapter focused on the interdependent nature of the relationships between the home and the school. It drew attention to the finely balanced nature of the power ratios that exist between parents and teachers and how their relationships tend to be rather harmonious and free of significant conflict. Underlying all of this is the shared emphasis upon the importance of academic attainment and the correspondence between the social practices of the home and those of the school in terms of the focus on routine and the close control and organisation of children's day-to-day activities. Of course the young boys are not just passively determined by these broader processes. Rather, it is possible to identify two further sets of interdependent relationships – between the boys and their parents and between the boys and the school respectively. While there is a high level of dependency of the boys on both their parents and the school (in terms of the need for physical care, self-esteem and emotional support and so forth), both the parents and the school also depend upon the compliance of the boys in terms of their ability to achieve educational success. As will be seen, such compliance is not guaranteed and at times needs to be actively sought.

However, given the young age of the boys concerned then the power ratios that underpin these two sets of relationships are high. In other words, there will clearly be a significant imbalance of power in favour of both parents and the school over the young boys. This can be seen in terms of the ability of parents and teachers to define and control the boys' immediate physical and social environments during these early years and thus effectively to set the parameters within which they then think and behave. It is with this in mind that rather than focusing on the nature and more subtle elements of the interdependent relationships that exist between the young boys and their parents and the school, this section will simply be concerned with outlining the consequences of such relationships; more specifically with outlining the tendency for some boys to internalise the social practices that characterise these relationships within their habitus. It is in the next section, which focuses more explicitly on their peer group relations, that the agency of these young boys will become more evident.

There are two particular elements that comprise the middle class habitus for some young boys as it relates to schooling that will be drawn out here. The first reflects the broader habits and largely unconscious patterns of behaviour that they have come to internalise through the social practices of the home that now tend to ease their adaptation into the routines and demands of formal schooling. The second relates, more specifically, to the interest and value in education that some of the boys have also acquired as a taken-for-granted aspect of their lives. It is worth looking briefly at each of these in turn.

Acceptance of routines and internalisation of discipline and control

In relation to the former, it was shown in the previous chapter how the professional backgrounds of the parents have disposed some to closely control the day-to-day activities of their children and carefully organise their lives, evident most clearly through the emphasis on routines within the home. However, this focus on control is not just evident in terms of the attempted control over the children's time and behaviour but also their physical appearance. In relation to school, it was noticeable for example that some parents placed signi-ficant levels of importance on presenting their children 'properly' and thus, presumably, displaying their commitment to formal education. This meant not just sending their children to school wearing the school sweatshirt but also with the correct accompanying polo shirt, grey or black trousers and black shoes. This attention to detail was also noticeable in terms of the tendency for some of the children to have the full kit for PE lessons, again down to the matching polo shirts, shorts and plimsolls. While one or two girls wore pinafores rather than trousers, the general tendency therefore was for both boys and girls to be dressed uniformly and for there to be relatively little to distinguish them, physically, in terms of gender. Some of the implications of this will be examined later.

This general emphasis on routines and close control was clearly evident in relation to the responses of the boys to the day-to-day practices of the school. Some boys had clearly already come to accept and internalise the key routines and organisational practices of the school and would tend to respond unconsciously to them. During playtimes, for example, once the bell had rung these boys would tend to instinctively gravitate towards the school door and create a line by way of habit without having to be routinely encouraged and cajoled. Similarly, prior to school assemblies each class would be led into the school hall in line and some of the children would take their place and sit down with little fuss or significant noise. On making their way back to class the teacher was also generally able to lead the way confident that the class would follow her. For the most part there was little effort required to quieten the children (whether boys or girls) as they walked along the corridors or to keep an eye on the 'stragglers' at the back of the line. These dispositions towards the passive acceptance of routines and the close control of their activities were therefore in many ways simply an extension of the practices of the home. They therefore represented part of the cultural capital that the children had inherited from their parents and were now able to realise to their benefit within the context of the school (Bourdieu and Passeron, 1977).

However, the most significant way in which this cultural capital tended to be realised by the children was through their capacity to engage in formal academic lessons. The following example is taken from my fieldnotes and describes a morning session where, with the exception of a 20 minute break for playtime, the children were engaged in whole-class English and maths lessons from 9.05 am through to 11.30 am. It is worth describing the morning session in some detail to give a proper flavour for the type of work engaged in by the children and their responses to it. Moreover, examples such as this were not uncommon and reflected a routine part of the children's schooling lives:

9.05am. All the children have arrived and are sitting at their desks. Mrs Summerbee [the class teacher] is standing by the whiteboard and asks for the children's attention in a calm, quiet voice. Most children immediately stop talking and sit round to face Mrs Summerbee. Some instinctively fold their arms. One or two children continue to whisper and Mrs Summerbee needs to repeat her call for their attention, still in a calm, quiet voice.

Mrs Summerbee explains that they are going to look at 'news' this morning and the children are going to write about their own news in their diaries. She asks the children where they had been at the weekend. A number of hands shoot up in the air and many of the children appear eager to gain her attention. Boys seem to be as eager as the girls. One boy shouts out an answer and Mrs Summerbee looks at him calmly and says in a quiet voice that she will not listen to children who shout out. She then turns to another boy who is sitting quietly with his hand in the air and asks him where he had been. From the answers Mrs Summerbee writes a numbered list on the board of names with a red pen (i.e. '1. Monsters Inc., 2. Green Park, 3. Swimming Pool, 4. Rollerskating').

Mrs Summerbee repeats the process to construct three further lists in different colours on the board relating to: people who the children visited at the weekend (i.e. '1. Friends, 2. Granny, 3. Grandpa, 4. Sister'); what actions they undertook (i.e. '1. Went, 2. Come, 3. Over, 4. Visited'); and what they felt about their activities (i.e. '1. Brilliant, 2. Exciting, 3. Fun'). During the whole of this process, that lasted about 20 minutes, the interest of both boys and the girls did not seem to diminish and most of the children remained focused and engaged in what Mrs Summerbee was doing.

Mrs Summerbee reads through each list of words in turn before asking the children to read through the list out loud with her. Nearly all of the children eagerly read out each word, in unison and quite rhythmically, as Mrs Summerbee points at each successive word in the list. At the end of the list she calls out 'Again!' and the children repeat the process. She then does the same for all four lists.

9.30am. The children are asked to retrieve their diaries and their own personal dictionaries. Mrs Summerbee explains that she wants them to write something about what they had done at the weekend on one page and then to draw a picture of it on the facing page. They are told to put up their hand if they do not know how to write a certain word.

Most of the children immediately set to work without requiring any further instructions. Mrs Summerbee and myself walk around the room responding to children who raise their hand. If the word they require is on the board then they are directed to it by being told it is 'red, number 2' (i.e. the second-numbered word in the red list). If the word they want is not on the board either Mrs Summerbee or myself write it into their personal dictionaries for them to copy out.

For the next 40 minutes most of the class remain focused on the work at hand. The children remain sitting at their desks and, generally, simply follow the practice of raising their hands and sitting quietly for a teacher to come to them when they have a query. Some talk among the children is tolerated and this contributes to a low level noise within the classroom that tends not to interfere with the children's ability to work. Most of the children are writing sentences that are clear and generally legible.

10.10am. Children are asked to pack their books and pencils away and line up at the door for playtime. Again, most of the children simply and immediately responded to this request. Some remain seated at their tables frantically trying to finish their pictures. Noise levels rise a little as more children talk among themselves and attempt to gain each other's attention.

10.15am. Children file out of the room, put on their coats and go outside into the playground.

10.30am. Children back in class. Without instructions most children sit down at their desk with a snack they had brought into school with them. Two children are busy walking between tables giving out milk to some of the others. Mrs Summerbee pays little attention to the class as she prepares for the next lesson, only looking up once or twice at tables where the children are being 'excessively' noisy. Her glances across to them are enough to reduce the noise to an acceptable level.

10.40am. Children are asked to pack away their snacks and drinks. Mrs Summerbee stands at the front of the class holding a maths stick (wooden stick with numbered intervals from 1 to 20 painted on it). With the whole class she asks them to count forwards and backwards. As with the reading, most of the class respond eagerly, in unison and rhythmically, counting the numbers as she points to them.

Mrs Summerbee then announces that they are going to do the 'Story of Seven'. Each child is given seven small counters. Initially, as a whole class, the children are asked to split the counters into two groups (e.g. a group of three and a group of four) and are asked to say how many are in each group and then, when added together, how many there are altogether. Mrs Summerbee then writes the corresponding sum on the board and asks the children to read it out (e.g. '3 + 4 = 7'). This is done a number of times for a range of different sums resulting in the answer seven.

11.05am. The children are asked to get their maths books out and write at the top of a new page: 'All About 7'. Mrs Summerbee then asks them, individually, to make up as many different sums as they can, using the counters and then writing the sums down in their books. As before, most of the children engage eagerly in the task and show a keen interest in each other's work with some competing with each other over how many sums they can write down. The children are told that when they have filled in a page of sums and had it checked by the teacher they can get some 'maths toys' from the drawers and play with them quietly. By 11.25am some of the children begin packing away their books and walk over to the drawers that contain a range of maths toys (mainly toys such as small plastic animals that could be used for counting, organising and grouping together). All of the children seem to know instinctively which drawers to get the toys from and what toys they can take to their table to play with.

11.40am. Children are asked to pack away and, when finished, to sit on the carpet ready for a story before lunchtime. Again, most children begin immediately to stand up and pack away. The classroom has an air of busyness about it as most children appear to be focused on the task of tidying up. A small number of the children (slightly more boys than girls) appear to get distracted and require a little encouragement by the teacher.

This morning session has been described in some detail as it illustrates some of the key features of the middle class schooling habitus that have been internalised by some of the boys and girls. It should be stressed that this is not typical of the whole school day. While such formal work was a routine aspect of most morning sessions, the afternoons were often more practically focused either in terms of PE or music and movement lessons or in terms of structured play. However, the fact that the children do have the capacity to effectively engage in such academic activities for such significant periods of time on a routine basis, especially in comparison with the working class children in North Parade (to be discussed in Chapter 8), is worth noting. More specifically, three points are particularly worth drawing out at this stage. First, it is clear that some of the children have internalised the passive acceptance of being closely controlled and organised as described earlier and therefore that much of their behaviour in school has become unconscious and routinised. It is this that is captured by the description of these young boys as moving around school like 'fish in water'. They tend, in other words, to be familiar and at ease with the demands of school life. When Mrs Summerbee addresses the whole class, for example, some of the children tend to stop what they are doing and, by force of habit, even fold their arms as a demonstration of active compliance. Similarly, some of the children unquestioningly and instinctively retrieve books, undertake tasks, tidy up and line up when asked to do so. They also simply 'know' what materials they can play with at any one time and where to find them. As Mrs Summerbee explained after the morning session when asked about the children playing with the maths toys:

> They know where all the maths stuff is, they know where all the English stuff is. It's sort of colour-coded to a degree depending upon what I want to do. Play things over there. And at certain times they know they can only get those things which should reinforce a wee bit, sometimes, the sort of things we have done.

Second, this element of their middle class habitus is not simply something that has been internalised at home but is also something that the school continually has to reinforce and maintain. This is evident from the subtle but nevertheless effective interventions that Mrs Summerbee makes to maintain order, whether that be through the use of a calm and controlled voice, the occasional use of disapproving glances or the general adherence to class rules such as not listening to children who shout answers out. Third, the evidence would seem to suggest that this emphasis placed on formal education, even at this relatively young age, is not entirely inappropriate for some of these children. They certainly seem to have the interest in academic work and the skills and the capacity to concentrate for prolonged periods of time. The key point here is that once we accept that there is no universal developmental pathway and that young children's learning and development is culturally-determined, then it will be the case that it may be appropriate to adopt a greater emphasis on formal academic learning at a relatively early age for some children, especially those for whom educational success actually constitutes an integral part of their cultural backgrounds. This, as seen in the previous chapter, is certainly the case for some of these middle class families and their children.

Interest in and recognition of the value of education

Alongside this internalisation of the passive acceptance of routines and being closely controlled, the second main element of the boys' middle class habitus is the more explicit interest in education and a taken-for-granted recognition of the value of schooling. The general interest that some of the boys had in education has already been documented above in relation to the descriptions of the behaviour of some of the boys and girls in Mrs Summerbee's class. From classroom observations it was certainly evident, for example, that some of the boys were eager to participate in class discussions, listened intently at story times and were keen to complete their work quickly and effectively. Indeed during one of the group interviews I held with the children, one of the boys clearly became frustrated with having to engage in discussions with me and, pointing to the classwork they had brought with them, asked: 'Can we finish this page now?' This also happened in the following discussion I had with Michael and James where they also demonstrated the general value that they placed on education and going to school:

Interviewer: What do you think would happen if you didn't go to school?
Michael: Erm, well, we'd be bored stiff, wouldn't we [*to James*]?
James: Yeah.
Interviewer: Why else do you think it's important to go to school?

Michael:	It's important to be teached and you learn and you can play so that's important. ... We learn writing and we learn to do capitals and we learn to do bubble writing.
James:	[*Impatiently*] Are we going to do our work soon?
Interviewer:	Yeah, we're going to start it now. But my last question is why do you think it's important to learn to write?
Michael:	Well, erm, it's important to know how to write so if you want to write, if it's somebody's birthday, you have to write the card an' all to your mum.

This taken-for-granted acceptance of the value and importance of education was also expressed by Stephen and Robert in another interview:

Interviewer:	Do you think it's important to go to school?
Stephen:	Yeah, it's really important.
Interviewer:	Why?
Stephen:	Because if you didn't go to school you wouldn't learn anything.
Robert:	And because you wouldn't even know what maths is!
Stephen:	Yeah and you wouldn't even learn to read or anything/
Robert:	/And you couldn't even say the alphabet.
Stephen:	No, or you couldn't say numbers.
Interviewer:	Is that important? Why does it matter?
Stephen:	Because it's very, very good to go to school because you learn a whole lot of things.
Robert:	When you grew up you wouldn't be smart or anything.
Interviewer:	What would happen then? If you didn't go to school at all what do you think would happen?
Robert:	Well, you would get very not smart and then you wouldn't know anything.

Such comments about schooling and the importance of education may not seem that remarkable in themselves. However, it is when they are set against the comments of the young working class boys from North Parade (to be discussed in Chapter 8) that their true significance will become apparent. For now it is sufficient to note the value that some of the young middle class boys place on education and the taken-for-granted role that they see school playing in their lives. It is also something that permeates through into the dominant expressions of masculinity found among these boys, as will now be seen.

Masculinity and the middle class habitus

This emphasis on routine, close control and educational success represents only part of the young boys' middle class habitus. Running alongside all of these dispositions are those relating more explicitly to their gender identities, in this case their sense of being male and masculine. The boys' attempts to make sense of who they are and to construct an identity for themselves can therefore be seen as attempts to manage and negotiate the variety of dispositions and habits they have acquired over time as a result of their social class and gender positionings. The sense of identity that results thus represents a fusion of these positions – it is gender viewed through the lens of social class or, equally, social class viewed through the lens of gender. As will be seen, what emerges is a particular form of identity, a middle class masculinity, which reflects the combined dispositions of social class and of gender.

This section will explore how the boys' sense of being masculine is constructed within the dispositions of their middle class positioning. It will first examine the 'boundary work', as Thorne (1993) has termed it, that the boys are actively engaged in through their attempts to construct a distinctive identity for themselves. The section will then focus, more specifically, on the dominant form of middle class masculinity found among these boys and then the ways this informs some of the boys' attitudes towards schooling.

Drawing the boundaries – lines of gender and social class

All social identities are inherently relational in the sense that they are defined with reference to others. This is certainly the case with regard to gender where definitions of what it means to be a boy are often constructed in a negative sense in terms of not being a girl (Thorne, 1993; Jordan, 1995; Francis, 2000). However, this is equally true in relation to social class where, as will be seen, being middle class can often be defined by way of contrast with what are perceived to be working class characteristics and behaviour. What all of this suggests is that the relationships between boys and girls or between middle class and working class children are also ones that are essentially interdependent. To explain this further it is worth looking at the boundary work engaged in by some of the young middle class boys at South Park and the lines they have drawn in terms of gender and social class in turn.

With regard to gender, the nature of the interdependent relationships that exist between boys and girls can be understood at two levels. First, in terms of the drawing of boundaries, given that masculinity and femininity are classically defined in oppositional terms then a boy's masculine identity depends upon the existence of girls who are feminine (Francis, 1998; Frosh *et al.*, 2002). Boys can therefore only claim to be strong and good at sport if there is a reference group (girls) that they can contrast themselves against and who are, by definition, seen as weak and not good at sport. Such differences need to be effectively managed, however, for the more that boys and girls transgress these boundaries the more that these dominant definitions of masculinity and femininity are undermined. Boys therefore cannot be 'allowed' to skip and play girls' games while girls cannot be allowed to demonstrate strength and sporting prowess (Hough, 1985; Thorne, 1993). Second, boys and girls depend upon one another to actively recognise and confirm each other's roles. A boy's sense of attractiveness is therefore dependent upon girls showing him interest. Thus, while boys may 'complain' about girls paying them attention and chasing them round the playground these are necessary practices for these boys who depend upon them to effectively demonstrate their masculinity. The same, clearly, is true of girls and their attractiveness in relation to boys and it is this that may account for the popularity of games of kiss-chase and discourses on boyfriends and girlfriends in many primary school playgrounds (Epstein, 1997; Connolly, 1998a; Skelton, 2001; Renold, 2002, 2003).

For some of the boys at South Park, however, their boundary work at this age tended to be confined largely to the former level of simply distinguishing themselves from girls. This is evident in the discussion with Adam, Michael and James below where, as can be seen, they were incredulous of me even asking whether they would prefer to be boys or girls:

Interviewer: If you had a choice would you want to be girls or boys?
Adam: Boys!
Michael: BOYS!
James: BOYS!

Interviewer: What's good about being boys?
...
James: Because boys get to do much better stuff than girls.
Interviewer: Like what?
James: Well, [*pause*] they get to go on rollercoasters and girls are scared of it.
...
Adam: Boys can do more funny things than girls.
Interviewer: Like what?
Adam: Being a clown. Being a magician.
James: And boys are better doing sports.
Interviewer: If you were a girl couldn't you do everything a boy could do?
James: No.
Adam: NOOOO!
Michael: No way!
Interviewer: Why?
Michael: Cos, cos they don't know how to do it!
James: Cos they, my sister screams when I hurt her!

What is noticeable from the above is the fact that being a boy appears to be defined more in terms of simply not being a girl than in relation to a specific set of characteristics. In fact, as can be seen, the boys had to think for a while about what made them boys. Being a boy, then, had become very much a taken-for-granted and largely unquestioned aspect of their lives. However, it is interesting to note some of the characteristics that the boys did come up with, when pushed, to distinguish themselves from girls. As will be discussed later, these characteristics tend to be less concerned with strength and physical skills and tend more to reflect the broad range of experiences that some of these middle class boys have been exposed to through their family life with its emphasis on the acquisition of knowledge and specialist skills. Very similar themes are also evident in the following discussion with Keith and Nathan:

Interviewer: It's funny because you say you play with Robert and Nathan says he plays with those other two boys, do you not play with girls?
Keith: NOOO!
Nathan: URRRGGHHHH!
Interviewer: You don't?

Nathan: Girls are yucky!
Interviewer: Are they? Why?
Nathan: Because, I just think so.
Interviewer: Does that mean you wouldn't want to be a girl if you could?
Nathan: Uhh, urrgggh!
Keith: [*laughs*]
Interviewer: So you want to be a boy then?
Nathan: Yep, that would be much better.
Interviewer: Why? What's good about being a boy?
Nathan: Just because you get to do cool stuff.
Interviewer: Like what?
Nathan: I don't know! Lots of cool stuff.
Interviewer: What about you Keith? What do you think's good about being a boy?
Keith: Ermm, you can run faster.
Nathan: Oh yeah, you can run faster.
Interviewer: Than girls?
Nathan: Yeahh!!
Keith: Girls can hardly run.
...
Interviewer: If you were a girl could you do everything a boy can do?
Keith: No!
Nathan: Nooh!
Keith: My sister can't even play my Gameboy! She can't get past Level 1! I can get past Level 9!
Nathan: I've got a game where it goes up to Level 62 and I've got up to number 61!
Interviewer: But isn't there some boys that can't get past Level 1?
Keith: Well, some. Babies can't.
Nathan: Babies can't even play Gameboy! [*laughs*]
Interviewer: Well could it be just that your sister's bad at it rather than that she's a girl?
Nathan: No! My mum can't even get past Level 9. She can get to Level 9 but she can't complete it!

This general necessity to carefully manage and police the boundaries between boys and girls was also clearly evident in the playground. Interestingly, footballs were not allowed in the playground at South Park Primary School but various toys were made available to the children including a significant number of skipping ropes. Given the popularity of skipping among girls and the possible accidents that could occur, a particular section of the playground was set aside for this activity. While the area was open to boys and girls in principle, it was seen very much as a girls' area. This was confirmed to me one day, for example, when I was standing on the edge of the skipping area watching what was going on. A girl came up to me and I commented how 'there are not many boys around here, are there?' She agreed replying 'no'. When I asked her why not she answered: 'because it's a section for girls'.

Being clearly identified as a girls' section, however, meant that it attracted the attention of some of the boys who would possibly feel threatened by its existence. Moreover, some of the boys used it as a way of publicly demonstrating their distance from it and thus confirming their own masculine identities. Some boys, therefore, set themselves the task of attempting to break into the area to disrupt the girls' games. As one of the lunchtime supervisors commented to me: 'You've got to keep an eye on them here skipping. The boys won't let them [skip] if you give them half a chance.' On several occasions, small groups of two or three boys would be seen hiding round the corner of the building occasionally peeping round to view the skipping area. Following much activity that included intense whispering and pointing they would run into the skipping area, in a line, and crouch down as if engaged in a military operation. Sometimes they would be content just to run through, around and out again and other times they would push a girl or purposely grab hold of her skipping rope.

As mentioned earlier, however, in the policing of these gender boundaries particular attention needs to be paid to ensuring that they are not transgressed (Thorne, 1993; Francis, 1998; Lynch and Lodge, 2002). This was evident on one occasion, for example, where a boy who clearly enjoyed skipping had decided to skip on his own in the skipping area. His behaviour quickly caught the attention of two other boys who stood for a while on the edge of the skipping area looking at the boy in question and whispering to one another. After a while they ran into the area and stood immediately behind the boy. The boy continued to skip and one of the other two put his leg out and kicked him up the bum. The boy stopped skipping, turned around and shouted: 'Stop it!' He then tried to continue to skip and the same boy kicked him again up the bum. After again being told to 'Stop it!', the boy turned to his friend and they both laughed. The other boy then grabbed his skipping rope and pulled at it. The boy just stood there holding onto his rope. After a while the two boys ran off.

Overall, therefore, a significant amount of effort is required for some of the boys in terms of drawing and policing the boundaries around their sense of masculine identity. However, from the boys' discussion reported earlier, it would seem that it is a particular form of masculinity that is being valued and protected, however vague and incomplete it may be. The boundaries drawn are therefore not just ones between boys and girls but also, for some of these boys, between them and other groups of boys. This is clearly evident in the following discussion with Benjamin, Oliver and Simon where they attempt to distance themselves from 'bad boys':

Interviewer: Why do you think school's important?
Benjamin: Because you learn lots.
Oliver: You learn lots of things.
...
Simon: And if you don't go to school you get put in the bad school.
Interviewer: Oh! And what's the bad school?
Simon: It's where you go every night and you have to sleep in the bad school an' all.
Benjamin: And the lady, if you speak when she tells you not to speak then she whacks you with a chain. She gets this big chain and whacks you on the bottom [*laughs*].
Interviewer: Do you know anyone that goes to the bad school?
Oliver: No. It's not called the bad school it's the bad boys' home. You stay there until you learn to behave!
...
Interviewer: Do you know any bad boys?
Simon: If you shoot somebody or if you stick a knife in somebody that's where you go – bad boys' home for you! If you're a bad boy!
Benjamin: The bad boys beat you up!
Interviewer: Are there any bad boys in this school?
Benjamin: No way!
Simon: They wouldn't allow bad boys here anyway! ... [They're] boys with knives and guns.

For some of the young middle class boys at South Park therefore, the dominant form of masculinity is not just constructed in opposition to girls but also in opposition to other (working class) boys. As some of the comments have already hinted at, it is a masculinity that is less physically embodied and expressed, whether through fighting and violence or through engagement in romantic relations and games of kiss-chase with girls. Indeed the physical expression of masculinity has been partly curtailed for some of these boys by the attention to detail their parents give to school uniform with the consequence that boys and girls tend to be dressed in very similar ways. Nor were these boys or girls likely to be sent to school wearing jewellery or, in relation to the girls, decorative bands or clips in their hair. There was a sense in which some of these children were therefore being sent to school to learn and that these markers of gender differences were regarded by parents as inappropriate in this context. For some of the boys and the girls, therefore, a significant amount of control was exercised over their physical appearance.

The overall effect of all of this for some of the boys has been to encourage them to develop a sense of masculinity that is less based upon physical strength and appearance and more in line with their broader middle class dispositions, with their passive acceptance of being closely controlled and emphasis on knowledge and mental skills. In this sense, it is therefore a difference between an *externally-expressed masculinity* with an emphasis on physical performance and displays of strength and aggression and the *internally-expressed masculinity* of some of the young middle class boys at South Park that is expressed more through self-control and the display of specialist knowledge and skills. This will now be explained in a little more detail.

Middle class masculinities and young boys

The emphasis throughout these case studies has been on understanding how the attitudes and behaviour of individuals tend to reflect the social contexts within which they are located. Individuals are not just free to pick and choose their own identities but will inevitably be moulded and shaped by the increasing tide of social processes and practices that surround them. This is certainly true for some of the middle class boys at South Park where they are bound to internalise, in the Vygotskian sense, the particular routines and values found in their homes and the school. As has been seen, there is a close correspondence between the home and the school with both placing an emphasis on routine, close control and the importance of academic success. These, then, are the general dispositions within which the young boys attempt to construct their own sense of identity and what it means to be a boy. They are dispositions that, as argued, tend to emphasise the successful mastery of knowledge and mental skills over physical prowess. This is not to say that some of the middle class boys do not value being physically strong and competent, as illustrated in the comments of Keith and Nathan reported earlier regarding how they can run faster than girls. However, such physical prowess and displays of strength simply do not take on the significance that they do for some of the working class boys in North Parade as will be seen in Chapter 8. This is evident, for example, in the way that some of the boys uncritically accept the behaviour of other boys in their class who cry, as illustrated in the following discussion with Benjamin and Simon:

Interviewer: Does everyone like school or do you not like school?
Benjamin: Well first when I started I was crying but now I'm OK, I like school, I really do like school now.
Simon: Yeah, you used to cry a lot, didn't you?

For some of these middle class boys, then, successful displays of masculinity involve the ability to demonstrate specialist knowledge, technical expertise and particular mental skills. A key medium through which this is done is the home computer as shown in the following discussion between Oliver, Benjamin and Simon. As can be seen, it not only illustrates the academic 'training' that the young boys routinely receive at home through the computer but also how specialist knowledge about particular games (in this case 'Sammy Snake') is highly valued and competed over by the boys:

Interviewer: What about computers? Do you like playing computers?
Oliver: Yeah!
Simon: Yeah!
Oliver: I love it!
Benjamin: I learn on my computer which numbers, like 80 plus 66 plus 88!
...
Oliver: I play games likes racing, race the car and rockets.
...
Simon: I play Woody and Sammy Snake. I play all the games that he [*Oliver*] plays.

Interviewer: What's Sammy Snake?
Simon: Erm, there's a snake in your house and/
Oliver: /No, but that's not the same as mine! My Sammy Snake, there's this man who tries to shoot Sammy Snake and he gets the gun out and tries to shoot that man but the man runs away – that's what's in my Sammy Snake.

The sense in which the home computer represents a key resource for these boys is also evident in the following discussion with Keith, Nathan and Harry. As can be seen, alongside the demonstration of intricate details and facts regarding one particular computer game, it is also evident that these boys regularly access the internet through their computers as well:

Interviewer: And do any of you have a computer at home?
Nathan: Yeah.
Keith: Yes.
Harry: My dad's got a computer and my sister's got one and it has a printer with it.
Interviewer: And what do you do on the computer?
Harry: Play games.
Interviewer: What sort of games do you play on it?
Harry: An aeroplane game.
Keith: I play Star Wars and I can get up to Level 4 but I can't complete it because the gear stick's a little hard to move. If you press the top it shoots big bullets. If you press the button underneath it's small bullets. But you can run out from the big bullets but you can't run out the small bullets. And it shows you how many big bullets down here. And it shows, if there's red people shooting it's a goody and if it's in green it's bad. And you have to complete it by shooting the ships and you have to shoot every one of them and I've completed it! But Level 2's a little tricky because there's these big, big, big black things that you can crash into and you have to have lots of big bullets, lots and lots of big bullets to blow it up but I've never blown it up.

...
Interviewer: Do you only just play games on the computer? Do you do anything else on the computer?
Keith: I go onto the internet for games/

Nathan:	/So do I!/
Harry:	/And me!/
Keith:	/And I go on the website for Ice Hockey to see who's winning. My daddy and my mum does [goes onto the internet] everyday after school. My dad does it at night and in the morning.
Harry:	[I go to] Disney.
Nathan:	I go into Disney too.

Very similar themes concerning the significance of computer games and displays of knowledge are also evident in the following discussion between Nathan and Harry where the boys had begun talking about the computers in the classroom and a particular maths game they liked playing. The correspondence between home and school life is clearly apparent when comparing the following with the comments reported in the previous two discussions:

Interviewer:	And what do you like about the computers?
Nathan:	You can do maths and there's also word games and you have to do sums to get past things. You have to get the diamond and the eye and when you get the eye you can press on the eye and then you get the demon. But if you land on the demon you have to do lots of sums/
Harry:	/Six sums./
Nathan:	/But if you get them right it banishes away.
Harry:	And if you're on Level 10 there's 10 demons and 10 diamonds. … The first level's very easy, there's just one, two, three, four gates to open.

At the time of the fieldwork one of the most popular topics for discussion was Harry Potter and the first of the feature films that had just been released in the cinema. As can be seen in the following discussion between Michael, Adam and James, there was a premium attached to knowledge of the Harry Potter stories and of the fantasy gadgets and events that took place within them:

Michael:	I went to see Harry Potter!
Adam:	We're going to see it!
James:	And I'm going to the pictures maybe tomorrow to see the Lord of the Rings!

Adam:	I don't like the Lord of the Rings very much.
Interviewer:	[*to Michael*] Did you like [Harry Potter]?
Michael:	Yeah! At the end, at the end Harry was on a chess set and his friend got killed and Harry became a rich boy!
James:	Remember, remember Harry Potter sticks his wand up the Ogre's nose!
Michael:	Yeah! [*laughs*]
James:	And remember when he pulls it out all the snot and everything!
Michael:	It was disgusting!

...

Michael:	It was Christmas day and Harry Potter got this new cloak and if you put it over you you'd turn invisible don't you?
James:	Yeah, yeah. And he went down to the library and got the Book of Spells and he put a spell on the Ogre, when the Ogre came.
Michael:	And he found this book and opened that and this big monster head came out!

...

Interviewer:	Has anybody got any Harry Potter stuff at home?
James:	Yeah! Me! Me! Erm, Harry Potter pen, Harry Potter gameboy and/
Michael:	/I, I, I'm getting the Harry Potter thing you make stuff in.
James:	Oh! I'm getting that and I'm getting the Harry Potter Book of Spells.

...

Interviewer:	And what about the books? Have you got any Harry Potter books?
Oliver:	Yes, yes, my brother has.
James:	Yes, my sister has.
Interviewer:	Have you tried reading them?
Oliver:	Yes!
James:	Yes!
Oliver:	Quite easy for me!
James:	Yes, quite easy!
Interviewer:	And do you like reading them?
James:	Yeah, I've got 1,600 pages to read.
Oliver:	I've got 10 hundred and 89 to read.
James:	It only goes up to 659.

Such interests and dispositions with their emphasis on the successful display of specialist knowledge and mental skills were also reflected in the career aspirations of these young boys. Through all of the group interviews, the boys were asked whether they had thought about what they would like to do when they grow up. While it is important not to read too much into the list of careers and jobs provided by the boys as shown below, it does give some indication of the nature of their social worlds and their habitus with their emphasis on professionalism and also fantasy action and adventure. As before, however, the true significance of this list will only be apparent when comparing it to the respective list compiled in relation to the working class boys of North Parade (see Chapter 8):

- 'Professional skateboarder'
- 'Doctor'
- 'Jet pilot'
- 'Footballer'
- 'Racing car man'
- 'Scientist'
- 'TV presenter'
- 'Artist'
- 'A person who finds dinosaur bones and fossils'
- 'Sea-diver'
- 'Policeman'.

Middle class masculinities and schooling

It should already be apparent from the examples above that a close correspondence exists between the broader elements of the young boys' middle class habitus and their favourable dispositions towards education and schooling. The type of competition evident among the boys and the ability to display individual success are all translated effortlessly into the schooling arena (Mac an Ghaill, 1996b). As Simon commented during one interview: 'I like reading cos I like the teacher saying I'm the fastest boy doing it'. The emphasis on academic competition was also evident during one classroom session where Keith, Nathan and Thomas were stting at one table working through maths sheets that Mrs Summerbee had prepared. As can be seen, a number of different sheets were used reflecting various levels of difficulty and the boys were acutely aware of this:

Keith:	I'm doing the hard ones cos I've got a '3' on mine!
Nathan:	This one's really hard cos it's got four things.
Thomas:	No it's not – I done it!
Nathan:	No – you've only got a '2' on yours!
Thomas:	[*Looking at his worksheet*] That's easy!

The way in which academic success forms part of the middle class masculine identity is also evident in the following conversation with Michael and James. As can be seen, the reason they like schoolwork is because it's 'easy':

Interviewer:	Do you like school?
Michael:	Yes.
James:	Yeah.
Interviewer:	What do you like about school the best?
Michael:	Well I like playing, playing games and dressing up.
Interviewer:	What about sums, do you like sums?
Michael:	Yeah.
James:	Yes because they're really easy!
Interviewer:	What about writing, do you like writing?
James:	Yeah, I love writing stories. We like to write pirate stories don't we Michael?
Michael:	Yeah.

While there is a strong level of compatibility between the form of middle class masculinity described here and educational achievement, it is not completely without its tensions, however. This is most evident in terms of the boys' attitudes towards reading where their desire for factual knowledge and fantasy action is not always met through the books they are required to read. This can be seen in the following discussion with Oliver and Jason where they begin by talking positively about their schoolwork and are keen to demonstrate their mathematical knowledge. However, as they move onto reading it is evident that they do not like all forms of reading and make a clear distinction between factual and fictional stories:

Interviewer:	What about at school, now, what you're doing now? Do you like writing?
Oliver:	Yeah, I like doing work.
Jason:	I like doing sums.
Oliver:	I like making things as well.

Jason: I know what 100 plus 100 is!
Interviewer: What is it?
Jason: 200!
Interviewer: Wow!
...
Interviewer: What stories do you like the best?
Oliver: Well [*pause*].
Jason: I like ones about, like, not the ones over there about ... but the ones over there about dinosaurs and stuff.
Oliver: About dinosaurs, bugs, sharks and volcanoes.
Interviewer: What are the books over there that you don't like then?
Oliver: Well, those/
Jason: /Well actually they aren't true.
Oliver: No, we like those ones that are true. But sometimes when we were in P1 we liked the story ones.
Jason: Yeah but now we don't!
...
Oliver: My favourite ones are dinosaurs because they're so cool because they lived a long time ago.
Jason: They actually lived before Jesus was born.
Oliver: I know!

Similar sentiments are also expressed by Keith, Nathan and Harry in the following discussion where, this time, the emphasis is more on the lack of fantasy action in stories and how that makes reading them boring:

Interviewer: Why do you like maths better than reading?
Keith: Because you get the time to play.
Interviewer: Do you not play games when you're doing reading?
Keith: No!
Harry: Nooo!
Keith: That's why it's so rubbish!
Interviewer: Why? Is it not interesting?
Harry: No!
Keith: You say words and words and words, even if you don't know them you have to say them.
Interviewer: Don't you find some of the stories interesting? ... What about if it was a story about Star Wars?
Harry: [*excitedly*] Yeah!
Keith: Yeah! Yeah!

Nathan: I'd be interested to that!
Interviewer: And would you like reading then?
Keith: Yeeaaahh!!
Interviewer: So what stories don't you like to read? ... Do you like this one you're reading [in class] now?
Keith: No, because it's too long!

Given the final comments above and the boys' apparent enthusiasm for reading science fiction stories like Star Wars, it would certainly be tempting to conclude that the problem (as far as it is a problem) of these boys' disinterest in reading could be addressed successfully by simply giving them more factual and fantasy action books to read. This, however, would be a short-sighted approach for reasons discussed in Chapter 2 (see section on 'Feminine schools'). It is worth repeating the point here that such approaches to 'masculinising' the curriculum may have some limited short-term successes in terms of increasing boys' motivation to read a certain type of book. However, it does not actually help to increase boys' appreciation of the wider range of literary styles and forms. On the contrary, such interventions are only likely to collude with the boys' existing dispositions and result in legitimating and reinforcing their narrowly-defined interests.

More generally, and in the interviews with their parents, there was certainly evidence that some parents did tend to collude with their sons and effectively condone their relative disinterest in particular aspects of their schoolwork. As the comments of one mother indicate, some parents do find it difficult to motivate their sons:

And I don't know, I mean, I hope I'm not painting a picture of Simon being stupid because he's not, at all, it's just applying himself. He finds it very difficult.

Given the problems that some parents face in encouraging their sons to do their schoolwork, especially their literacy work, it is not surprising that some gain solace through recourse to biological arguments that attempt to naturalise these problems and thus effectively remove the need to try too hard with their sons. As another mother explains:

I just think wee girls have more concentration than wee boys. Wee boys just seem to jump about and just don't seem to want to sit and do, you know. ... Wee girls just have more patience and everything, definitely. And as I say, Robert would be, just, he's not hyper or nothing by any means, he's just a typical wee boy, just in-out, in-out, in-out, you know. But he has it but just doesn't [apply himself]. But I would say Joanna [*his sister*] will go far but will have to really work at it but he'll not. I know that. He'll not have to push himself at all but she'll have to work really hard to achieve.

Given the centrality of academic success to the middle class habitus of some parents, as described in the previous chapter, then the fact that some of their children may not be achieving as much as they should does present a problem. As evident in the mother's comments above, one way around this is to emphasise the natural academic skill of her son and how this will 'win through' in the longer-term. However, one of the dangers of doing this is the need to substantiate these claims through negative comparisons with girls. Girls' abilities would appear once again to be denigrated as their achievement is simply explained away by diligence and hard work rather than natural flair (Walkerdine and Lucey, 1989). Another danger inherent in such a perspective is the complacency it encourages precisely because it is assumed that the boys' natural ability will eventually save them. As the following mother explained when talking about her son's reluctance to read:

I think it's fairly normal. I'm not too worried about James because I think, talking to other mums at the school, and talking to friends who have got teenagers, I think boys tend to be not as interested so I'm not as concerned as, you know, to give him extra tuition. He's doing quite well ... I think things kick in later on. I don't know at this age ... and as I say he's got the ability, he's a very bright little boy. ... He has got the ability to do it and that's what would frustrate me. And he, because he's so good at reading but he just doesn't want to practise it.

Of course the worrying fact is that the statistics show that things do not tend to 'kick in' later on but rather, as outlined in Chapter 1, the gaps that already exist at Key Stage 1 in relation to attainment levels in English simply grow bigger through Key Stages 2 and 3 and onto GCSEs.

Conclusions

This chapter has outlined some of the key elements of the schooling habitus of some of the young middle class boys at South Park Primary School. It needs to be reiterated that this is not offered as a comprehensive nor a representative account of all 5–6-year-old boys at the school. Rather it has been an attempt to identify those particular social processes and practices that might contribute towards an explanation of the general patterns of educational achievement found among middle class boys as highlighted in Chapter 1.

Perhaps the most obvious point to make concerning the data discussed above is that there is little sense in which these young boys can be described as 'underachievers'. Some of these boys are, as we have seen, highly-motivated and disciplined. They move around the school environment, as suggested earlier, as 'fish in water'. They have thus come to accept and internalise the routines of the school and consequently respond well to the demands placed upon them. These particular boys tend to value education and have constructed a masculine identity that corresponds well with, and actively promotes, educational achievement and academic success. As has been argued, the dominant form of masculinity found among the boys, to varying degrees, can be seen as the internalisation of the passive acceptance of being closely controlled and a sense of routine and also the value of education found in the home and the school. As such, it is not so much based upon an external expression of masculinity through strength and physical prowess but its internal expression through the mastery of particular mental skills and the demonstration of specialist knowledge and technical expertise.

While these young middle class boys are not 'underachievers' as such, there is a small achievement gap between boys such as these and their middle class female counterparts that does need to be explained, particularly in relation to literacy. The fact that the gap is relatively small can be accounted for by the general emphasis on educational success that tends to be found within middle class homes. In this sense the pressure is on boys and girls to achieve and thus there is comparatively little room for gender to take a determining role in the educational performance of middle class boys and girls. From the evidence provided in this chapter, one of the reasons for the small achievement gap that does persist is the rather restricted form of masculinity that the boys have tended to internalise with its disposition towards a limited range of factual and fantasy-action literary forms. Moreover, the tendency for parents (and possibly teachers) to collude in this has meant that such limited interests tend to go unchallenged. Some of the implications of these findings will be explored and discussed further in Chapter 9.

Chapter 7

Home–school relations in North Parade

Introduction

This and the following chapter focus on the experiences and perspectives of the working class boys in North Parade in a similar way to that which has been used in relation to the middle class boys in South Park in the previous two chapters. This chapter begins this process by examining the nature of the immediate contexts of the home and the school within which the boys at North Parade are located. Chapter 8 will then set out how these contexts tend to influence and shape their masculine identities and thus their particular dispositions towards education and formal schooling. In focusing on the home and the school, this chapter will follow the approach taken in Chapter 5 in relation to South Park by exploring the nature of the interdependent relationships between parents and the school in North Parade. As will be seen, these relationships differ markedly from those found in South Park and reflect a very different definition of the educational role of North Parade Primary School. The nature of this role will be outlined first before then examining some of the problems the school faces in attempting to secure the compliance and support of parents in relation to this role.

It is important to note at the outset that this is not a particularly representative nor accurate account of the approach taken by the school or of the relationships it has developed with the parents. As explained carefully in Chapter 4, this has never been the intention. Rather, the point of this chapter is simply to understand the differences in educational performance and provision in North Parade compared to South Park by identifying some of the processes that tend to contribute to these. While all of the processes reported below are 'real' in the sense that they reflect the real perceptions and experiences of the teachers and the parents involved, they do not paint a comprehensive picture. This is certainly sufficient for the purposes of this book. However, even though the school and its staff have been anonymised, I do feel that it is important to stress that the account offered below, in just focusing on those processes that tend to exacerbate differences, is an unduly negative one. Not all of the teachers had negative perceptions of the parents and some worked extremely conscientiously and made notable efforts to engage with and support parents. Moreover, the behaviour and attitudes of the School Principal (Mrs Marsh) and the P2 class teacher (Mrs Lee) were also far more complex than implied below and included a number of genuine attempts to begin to address some of the problems faced by parents in the local area. Some of these included basic numeracy and literacy classes for parents established by Mrs Marsh and also a number of carefully-planned and innovative approaches to teaching adopted by Mrs Lee in the P2 class. For the sake of clarity and the need to focus specifically on understanding and explaining the key differences that exist between the two schools, these have not been included in the account below. However, some of these will be discussed in the final chapter that considers the implications of these case studies and what needs to be done to work more effectively with young boys. For now it is important simply to remember the type of approach that has been adopted in the analysis below and thus to avoid the temptation to interpret what follows as a representative or comprehensive account.

Pastoral care and the educational role at North Parade Primary School

In understanding how relations between parents and the school in North Parade tend to differ to those in South Park we need to remind ourselves of the core characteristic features of the interdependency that tend to underpin relationships between parents and schools. It will be recalled that parents depend upon schools to *educate* their children while schools depend upon parents to be *compliant* – to accept and support the efforts that they make to educate their children. At South Park the nature of these interdependent relationships was relatively harmonious and finely balanced as both parents and the school worked around a definition of education in largely academic terms. Now the problem faced by North Parade Primary School is that it cannot rely upon its parents to 'prepare' the children for formal academic schooling in the same way that South Park

Primary School could in relation to its parents. As outlined in Chapter 4, North Parade is a very different place to South Park. As Mrs Marsh, the School Principal, explains:

> Well we're working in what is officially described as a multiply-deprived area with a lot of socio-economic problems. There are 68 per cent of children on free school meals which is quite a good social indicator of the problems that we would have as far as their, the financial problems we would have with the children. And of course what happens in [relation to the political violence] impinges very much here. Well parents I know are involved in, or have very strong opinions on, what goes on and those opinions are soaked up by the children and so their, I suppose their attitudes might be different from the ones we would share. ...
>
> And I do feel a bit like King Canute, you know. Other agencies need to be on board, it's not just an education issue. They need economic activity in this area so that the parents feel they have a job and a bit of self-respect. There's a lot of petty crime in the area. There would be a culture of bullying in the area and the police don't come in very much. All of those sorts of things need to be sorted out. It's not just an education issue by any means.

Given this, it is the perception of the school that some of the parents simply do not have the capacity to be able to effectively support their children's educational development. It will be remembered from Table 4.1 in Chapter 4 that nearly two-thirds of all adults in the area have no formal qualifications at all. Moreover, the general lack of resources available to them – evident in the higher rates of long-term unemployment, their poorer living conditions and lower levels of health – mean that there are very few opportunities open to them to encourage and facilitate their children's learning. Thus, while the parents do tend to care passionately about their children's education, the reality is that some of them do not have the necessary knowledge, skills and/or resources to be able to offer their children the support they need to succeed in formal education. This is certainly a perspective that is dominant among some of the staff at the school. As Mrs Lee the P2 class teacher explained:

> The parents are keen. They'll attend meetings. Most of them – there were about five or six that didn't come to parents'

interviews – most of them are keen that their child will learn. They're very keen on the books and homeworks, you know. If you don't send the homework home you get a few of them coming in saying 'There's been no homework! Why has there been no homework?' And I do find they're keen.

[However] a lot of them don't really know what to do. Even though they're keen they don't really have the background to know what to do. For example, I was talking to one parent about a little boy, saying, you know, he seemed to have an enjoyment of books. He likes reading books, does he read books at home? And dad turned round and said: 'Well, yeah, he'll go upstairs and play on the Playstation all night!' And that's not really [*laughs*] what, you know, a Playstation is not any educational value at all really! But that's what they would do at home really, tend to play at home on the Playstation or videos, tend to watch a lot of videos. They don't really play any games like take turn games or board games. Even just general snap and that kind of thing they don't tend to play games like that.

This is also the perspective held by Mrs Marsh, the School Principal:

The vast majority of parents work with us in so far as they understand the education process. In that most parents would say to us that they want their children to do well at school and I believe that to be true. ... They want their children to do well. You know, 'well' in commas! But they, they have no point of reference about success really because they haven't had, most of them haven't had any success themselves; particularly in academic life. Now that's not to say they haven't had success in just surviving because it's not easy here, you know, and perhaps they're much better at that than I would be. In fact they probably are, I couldn't live in the sort of uncertainty that a lot of them live in. But really they don't know, they're not aware of what it takes to do academically well. ... They really don't know what's involved so that can cause us problems. Not problems, but it just means that what they mean by support is ... they give the support they're able to give but there's a true ignorance about some of the support that could be given.

As can be seen, a strong perception exists among some within the school that it is not possible to depend upon the parents to support them in the academic education of their children. More fundamentally, and reflecting the baseline assessments of the children reported in Chapter 4 (Table 4.2), there is also a feeling that the general living conditions and lifestyles of many of the parents are such that the children are not even adequately prepared for the routine demands of formal schooling. In stark contrast to the strong sense of organisation and control that some middle class parents instil in their children at South Park, there is a perception among some staff at the school that the lives of many of the working class parents at North Parade are that much more unstructured and hectic. As Mrs Marsh explains when asked to compare her children with those in a previous middle class school where she once taught:

> The parents [at the other school] would have their lives better organised. ... There'd be a group of parents here who would live a very hand-to-mouth existence. They stagger from one crisis to the next to the next. I can think of one or two who really, they cope with enormous difficulties, some of their own making. And you think that 'I would have avoided that situation'. But I don't know, they're sort of sucked into it. They don't have the mental energy to take stock of their lives and say, you know, 'I'm in a mess, how can I get out of this? What strategies can I use?'

It is clear in these comments, and those reported earlier, that such views are imbued with value judgements and a rather negative view of the parents and their lifestyles. However, they do reflect an underlying reality whereby the effects of poverty and social exclusion, together with the ongoing impact of the violence, do tend to cause some parents to experience relatively high levels of stress and anxiety and to feel 'out of control' (Brooker, 2002). For these parents, they simply do not have the resources nor opportunities to exercise the same level of control over their lives as found in relation to the middle class parents in South Park. It will be remembered from Chapter 4 (Table 4.1) that adults in North Parade are almost three times more likely to be unemployed than those in South Park. There are also around twice as many single parents in North Parade and a substantially higher proportion who either have a limiting long-term illness and/or whose health is 'not good'. The majority of households in North Parade (54 per cent) also have no access to a car compared to under a quarter (23 per cent) of those in South Park. Given these conditions and the demands that bringing up young children places on parents, then it is not surprising to find that some not only tend to feel 'out of control' of their own lives but also tend to lack the resources and thus the opportunity to exert the same level of organisation and control over their children's day-to-day activities as some of the professional middle class parents in South Park. Moreover and just as with the middle class parents, these working class parents are also likely to internalise these broader experiences into a set of predispositions or taken-for-granted ways of thinking and acting but with very different effects. Not surprisingly, this working class habitus tends to lack the emphasis on organisation and control found among the middle class parents in South Park. These are simply not characteristics that some of the parents in North Parade tend to experience and/or have the opportunity to develop. Rather, for some parents their habitus is characterised by an emphasis on the 'here and now', on surviving and thus on meeting the material needs of their children and themselves. Within this, success is more likely to be defined materially with a strong desire among some parents to provide the best for their children in relation to such things as clothes and toys (Connolly, 1998a). This will be seen in the following chapter, for example, in the tendency for some of the children in the P2 class at North Parade to be dressed in expensive, designer clothes and to wear jewellery.

For some staff at the school, however, such parental displays of love and care for their children can be perceived as misguided and inappropriate. As the School Principal, Mrs Marsh, explained when talking about the parents:

> The vast majority, I would say, 99.999 per cent of the parents here love their children. But that love can manifest itself in different ways. For example, here the love would be demonstrated in expensive toys. Quite often, quite inappropriate toys. For example, a quad bike will be bought or a television and a video as well, you know, and they put themselves in debt. Whereas in [a more middle class area] that love would be thinking about a secure home background, [about] the here and now and how that will affect the children in the future and their education prospects and all those sorts of things.

Moreover, some of the parents' behaviour is not just seen as misguided but also as conflicting with the needs of the school. As Mrs Marsh went on to explain later in the same interview:

There are times, for example, when it's the children's birthday so they'll celebrate the birthday by being absent from school. Or they'll, you know, they'll want to go somewhere so they'll keep them off because they won't send them in for the morning because they'll feel uncomfortable about collecting them in the morning, at lunchtime, so they'll just keep them off the whole day.

The sense of unease that some parents feel in relation to the school, as alluded to in the comments above, is something that will be returned to shortly when examining the perspectives of the parents in a little more detail. The key point for the moment to draw out from the above is the perceived incompatibility between the behaviour and lifestyles of some of the families and the academic demands of formal schooling. As has also been found elsewhere (see Connolly, 1998a; Skelton, 2001), there is an imperative on some children living in economically-deprived areas to grow up more quickly. This is especially the case in areas like North Parade that are also characterised by high levels of violence. Children need to learn, from an early age, to become streetwise and to protect themselves. The practical implications of this for the development of the boys' masculine identities in North Parade will become clear in the next chapter. It is a reality that not only leads some parents to dress their children in designer clothes and jewellery, as mentioned above, but also to them tending to entrust their children with greater responsibilities more generally. The tensions that this can cause between parents and the school is evident in the following example provided by Mrs Marsh:

> There would be a sort of carelessness here that probably wouldn't be found in [a more middle class school]. If they're sick and you ring [the parent] and say so-and-so's sick, er, [they may reply] 'just send them on up home'. Now we have a policy that once a child is at school that unless it's the official hometime a child must be collected by an adult known to them because obviously there are dangers with them wandering out of school in the day. Whereas in [a more middle class school] if you phoned and said that the child was sick the vast majority of the parents would say, you know, they'll either have some arrangement for collecting the children or they'd arrive themselves for them. That would be an illustration of what I'd call carelessness.

Similarly, the tendency for some parents to give their children greater responsibility and freedom in relation to playing outside is also interpreted negatively by some in the school as inappropriate and in conflict with the needs of the school. As the P2 class teacher, Mrs Lee explained:

> It's a very difficult school. The area's very tough. A lot of children kind of run wild after school and at night time as well, especially coming into the summer term. Erm, and also by September as well a lot of them just run wild for two months over the holidays so we find it takes a long time for them to settle down, you know, and get them into the routines. ... Last year it took them until about Hallowe'en before they really calmed down. It's just getting them into the routine of work and, erm, school. ... This year I think they were wilder [*laughs*], it seems, wilder at the beginning of September! By Hallowe'en they did settle down. It is quite a large class and you just have to be on them the whole time. You can't relax really for a minute with them really, there is quite a lot of pressure that way, I think.

These final comments encapsulate the fundamental mismatch between the home and the school at North Parade. The reality of life in North Parade is very different to that found in South Park. As argued above, the approach of the middle class parents with their strong emphasis on organisation and control tends not to be as apparent in North Parade where the experience of parents is more likely to reflect a sense of being out of control and the need to live day-to-day. Young children being raised in such an environment are required to 'grow up more quickly' and all of this, together, can result in working class children in North Parade being less likely to have the cultural capital that their middle class counterparts in South Park have (Bourdieu and Passeron, 1977). This is most evident in the final comments above where Mrs Lee describes the difficulties in encouraging the children to settle down into the routine of the school – a routine that, as seen in Chapter 5, has already been internalised and is part of the taken-for-granted lives of some of the middle class children in South Park.

Ultimately, therefore, the school cannot define its educational role in strictly academic terms as it simply cannot depend upon the parents to be compliant in and thus effectively support and facilitate this. In such circumstances what the school has been required to do is to re-define its notion of education away from strictly academic concerns towards a much greater emphasis on pastoral matters

(Gallagher *et al.*, 1998; Connolly, 1998a; Acker, 1999; Skelton, 2001). In the early years this re-definition of roles is most clearly illustrated in the greater emphasis North Parade Primary School gives to social and personal development compared to South Park. As Mrs Lee explains:

> [Our aim] is to develop the children's ability to socialise and to, not to introduce them to formal education until they're ready. Not to force them into picking up a pencil and writing until they get the basics and the principles behind things. ... What we're moving towards, especially in P1, is a lot of games to develop turn-taking and sharing. A lot of physical development to develop their gross and fine motor control before they even pick up a pencil. ... And also in the afternoons then there's three days of PE – two days with equipment and one with the dance. I think it really helps, especially up here where they don't play games really at home and they're not used to sharing and taking turns and talking and they don't, you know, their oral language is very important and trying to get them to express themselves better.

At one level these are very laudable principles and goals for the early years. The problem arises, however, when they are pursued against the background of negative perceptions of the parents and low expectations of the children. It is interesting to note the contradiction in Mrs Lee's account where, for example, she is able to criticise the tendency for children in North Parade to lack the opportunities to play and develop social and physical (gross and fine motor) skills while, at the same time, claiming that they are left to play outside and 'run wild' (and thus, presumably, have plenty of opportunity to develop these skills). Overall, the problem that arises when this emphasis on the pastoral role sits alongside such negative perceptions has been clearly highlighted by the inspection report discussed in Chapter 4 in the neglect of academic progress through a focus on activities that were seen to be relatively low-level, repetitive and unchallenging.

Securing parental compliance in North Parade

Within all of this, the main problem for the school is that it remains dependent upon the parents to be compliant with their approach to educating the children. At one level this is achieved simply by the greater imbalance of power that exists between parents and the school in North Parade. As research has shown for some time now, some working class parents not only lack knowledge of the education system but also lack the confidence to approach the school. They can often feel ill at ease with teachers and out of their depth when discussing educational matters. All this can be exacerbated for those who have had poor experiences at school themselves and who thus may well feel particularly inadequate when in the company of a teacher (Jackson and Marsden, 1962; Halsey, 1972; Midwinter, 1977; Mortimore and Blackstone, 1982; Moles, 1993; Brooker, 2002). In North Parade, such experiences can provide an effective barrier between some parents and the school. This is partly evident in the lack of knowledge the parents have of what is going on in school. As one mother said when asked if she knew what the teacher was doing in the class:

> They just tell you it's more informal, more play. ... I find they don't tell you everything they do, you know, they tend not to say anything. I don't know.

Another mother commented:

> The teacher doesn't know us. ... She didn't really bother, she doesn't really speak to us.

The following mother was clearly concerned about what she felt was her son's lack of progress but was not aware of the approach the school was taking and had not felt able to discuss her concerns with Mrs Lee. The concerns she expresses towards the end regarding her son's poor handwriting and the 'scrawls' he was making actually relates to Mrs Lee's use of creative writing techniques – an approach that the mother was unaware of:

> I wasn't very sure at first about [Mrs Lee's approach] because it seemed like even in the middle of P2 he wasn't doing an awful lot. When Davey came into the school, he started in the nursery, he could write 'Davey' and he knew his letters but I felt like he wasn't, for a while I thought he wasn't getting any further, they weren't actually teaching him much, he was playing more than anything ... He would have wrote stories but it was more just

letting him freely sit and write. It would've been a lot of scrawls and his writing and all was terrible. He wasn't really having much help about how his writing should be.

In this sense, therefore, compliance on the part of parents is achieved partly indirectly through a lack of knowledge and understanding. However, it can also be achieved through a sense of anxiety that some parents have of approaching the school and the fear that raising any concerns or making a complaint may have negative consequences. As the following comments indicate, some parents do have concerns about their children's education, in this case about the lack of homework that they are being given:

Diane: Callum's homework, when he gets it he does it like that [clicks fingers], it's too easy.

Joanne: Jason's is OK. He's in red [group]. I'm not sure what order it goes in.

Diane: I think it goes like that – red, green, yellow and blue.

Gillian: Adrian's in yellow same as Callum. They get two words/

Joanne: /And I think that's ridiculous.

Gillian: The red group, they get four words.

Joanne: He would have four spellings, reading and then either English or maths. If he went through it quickly and did it no problems I would write that Jason did this completely on his own, you know, that way.

It is clear from the comments above and the discussion more generally that these parents had little understanding of how the class was organised. Moreover, when asked whether they had raised any of these concerns about homework with the teacher, they all said that they would tend not to. As they went on to explain, underlying this was a fear of what might happen if they did 'complain':

Joanne: I think it's just more or less if your face fits. This is my opinion.

Diane: If there's no problems everything's like OK/

Joanne: /Everything's fine.

Diane: But once you have a problem that's you out/

Joanne: /That's you/

Diane: /You'll pay for it.

Interviewer:	And how will you pay for it?
Joanne:	Ignored.
Diane:	You'd not be asked to help out with things by certain staff now, not [all] ... And then you're caught between, do I say anything? You don't want your children, sort of, paying for it. ...
Gillian:	I just say nothing.

For these particular mothers, their concerns about approaching the school would appear to be a reflection in part of a previous encounter that some of them had had with one of the teachers. As Diane explained in relation to the time she went to see the teacher about a problem she was having:

Diane:	I was just told most of the parents here don't care anyway.
Joanne:	It's a deprived area.
Diane:	It's a deprived area and most of them don't care/
Joanne:	/Don't care.
...	
Diane:	I find if you disagree or speak up against the [school] that's it/
Joanne:	/You've had it!
Diane:	Because you live on this estate your children really aren't going to do very well. [You're told] 'We're just here to do a job, we'll teach them the basics. And don't have any expectations, they're not going to'/
Interviewer:	/You're actually told that?
Diane:	Not in so many words but you know you live on an estate, you know what estates are like/
Joanne:	/Well the exact words to me when I went to see the [teacher] I was told the parents don't care, I said 'well I care, I'm here' and she said 'well most of them don't. It's a cultural thing it's a North Parade thing' and that just makes you feel about that size.

Underlying some of these reactions from the school was a level of defensiveness. This is evident in the following comments by another mother who describes what the school's reaction was when her mother asked the teacher about her son's homework on her behalf:

Obviously you want to know sort of what kind of work and all they're doing and they were starting their maths and I didn't understand about their maths. So my mum says 'I'll mention to the teacher about it'. So the teacher was really annoyed that mum had said to her and said, you know, 'why are you questioning why we're doing our maths?'. But mummy wasn't, she just wanted more information. So the next morning the Principal was actually waiting for my mum coming in. The teacher had been round and said to Mrs Marsh about my mum questioning about the maths and said to her 'look, that teacher's highly qualified, she's a very good teacher, she was annoyed that you had asked her about the maths'. But she just almost like puts a barrier up as soon as you approach her as if, you're like, you know, and it's not the case.

This level of defensiveness, and the negative reactions that some of these parents experienced from the school more generally, can be understood partly in relation to the school's attempt to maintain its re-definition of its educational role as essential pastoral rather than formal academic, especially in the early years. As has been seen, while some of the parents do not have the necessary knowledge and skills to be able to effectively support their children's academic learning, they still care passionately about ensuring that their children gain a 'good education'. These parents are less willing to agree with or support the school's re-definition of its educational role. Moreover, some of them have had sufficient confidence to approach the school with their concerns. This, however, places the school in what it will perceive to be an impossible situation. From their perspective, any attempt to place a significant emphasis on a more formal academic education will be doomed to failure as the majority of children are not sufficiently prepared for it and a similar proportion of parents are unable to support their children in this. It is therefore likely to lead to unrealistic expectations and also the inevitable poor academic performance will reflect badly upon the school. In this sense it is much safer to maintain the focus on an essentially pastoral educational role in which the school can demonstrate success.

This would seem to be the viewpoint of Mrs Marsh, the School Principal, in the comments below. Here she is talking about the increased interest that she feels the parents are beginning to show in their children's education, especially in relation to the transfer test (also known as the 'eleven plus'). Northern Ireland still operates a selective post-primary education system where children in the final year of primary school are able to take a series of tests to determine which type of school they then transfer into. While all children are eligible to sit these tests, about a third of children do not and these are more likely to be children living in poorer, working class areas. At North Parade Primary School only a small handful of children are entered for the test each year. As Mrs Marsh explains:

> We are beginning to see a change in the parents' attitudes. Now it is slow but one of the indicators would be that they are taking more interest in the transfer test. Now it may not be what we really want them to take an interest in [*laughs*] but at least you know we're getting a group this year for example of P6 parents, a group of 16 or 17 came in a couple of weeks ago to listen to me talking about the transfer test and what's involved.

The underlying concern here for the school then is that the more children they enter for the transfer test, the more will fail and thus the more this will reflect negatively on the school. Re-defining the role of the school as essentially pastoral rather than academic helps to avoid this problem. The attempts by the school to 'cool down' some of the parents' academic expectations is certainly something that is picked up by some of the parents. As the following parents explained during one discussion:

Gillian:	I found with the transfer we were called to a meeting about last February and I found it was quite off-putting. There was no encouragement to sit it, sure there wasn't.
Diane:	I was actually told by the teacher that Callum wasn't capable. Not in so many words but, just, don't bother doing it, he's going to go to the [local secondary school] anyway.
Gillian:	Well from the start I found that at the meeting it wasn't 'push it, go for it, try it' it was 'it's a lot of work, here's the papers' and/
Diane:	/They were more or less putting you off it.

This is also the perception gained by the following mother whose aspirations for her son have clearly been dampened by the response of the school:

Suzanne: I would love them to have a career. ... I always regret not, I left school and never stayed on or went to college and I always regret that. I wish I had done that.

Interviewer: Do you ever think about going back to learning now?

Suzanne: Och, when I left school all I wanted to do was work and earn money [*laughs*]. I've always worked so I have never been out of work. But I'd always wanted to be like a nurse, I loved like looking after people sort of thing. So I hope they'd go for a career.

Interviewer: Does North Parade operate the eleven plus?

Suzanne: Well, there's a handful of kids that do it. Some of the parents I have talked to, Mrs Marsh doesn't encourage the eleven plus at all, actually it's the other way around. She'd prefer they didn't do it.

Interviewer: Why?

Suzanne: I just think, I don't know, I get the impression that it's more work for the teachers that they don't want. ... I think all kids should have the opportunity if they want to do it but that school doesn't encourage it.

Interviewer: But if your children are still there and the eleven plus is still in operation how are you going to do it?

Suzanne: I would like them to do it obviously but I mean if they're not going to be encouraged it is very difficult, definitely. ... That school there definitely doesn't encourage it.

Conclusions

What can be seen in this chapter is the very different nature of the interdependent relationships found between parents and the school in North Parade in comparison with those described in Chapter 5 at South Park. For South Park the relationships were largely harmonious as both parents and the school worked with similar conceptions of the school's role as one concerned largely with academic attainment. Moreover, the nature of family life in South Park meant that the young children tended to internalise through their habitus a taken-for-granted disposition towards formal learning and a passive acceptance of routine and control – precisely those skills required of children by the school. There is, as many researchers have pointed out, an almost seamless transition from home to school for these children (Bernstein, 1971, 1975; Bourdieu and Passeron, 1977).

Not only are parents therefore happy with the formal academic focus of the school but the school is also able to depend upon the compliance of the parents in supporting them in their role by adequately preparing their children for the demands of school life and consequently supporting them with their schoolwork.

For North Parade, however, the story is a very different one. The school is not able to adopt a similar academic emphasis in relation to its educational role as it cannot depend upon the compliance and support of the parents as South Park Primary School could. According to some staff at North Parade, the parents tend not to have the educational knowledge and skills to be able to appropriately support their children's learning at home. Moreover, the struggles that they face simply to survive and the day-to-day demands placed upon them are such that they do not have the resources to adequately prepare their children for the demands and routines of school life. As has been seen, the response of the school to this has been to re-define its educational role around a greater emphasis on pastoral care rather than academic attainment, especially in the early years. This, in turn, has provided an opportunity for the school to demonstrate its success via other means. The problem for the school, however, is that it remains dependent upon the compliance of the parents and thus their willingness to accept and support this re-definition.

In relation to some of the parents this compliance has been gained simply by virtue of the greater power imbalances that exist between parents and the school compared to those in South Park. The fact that some parents have little understanding or awareness of what goes on in school and also may lack sufficient confidence to approach the school with any concerns they may have has meant that their compliance is gained by default. However, and as has been seen, other parents have had the confidence and have been sufficiently concerned to approach the school. It is here where the school has had to struggle to maintain the compliance of these parents and would seem to have done so partly through the adoption of a rather defensive stance and also partly through a strategy of attempting to dampen down parental expectations. In some cases such practices have tended to quash the challenge presented by these parents and thus to (forcibly) secure their compliance. This, then, is the context within which the young working class boys are beginning to explore and construct their own masculine identities and, through these, their dispositions towards education and formal schooling. It is to these that the next chapter turns.

Chapter 8

'Fish out of water'

The schooling habitus of young working class boys

Introduction

This chapter focuses on the experiences of and attitudes towards schooling held by the young working class boys at North Parade Primary School. It has already been shown, in Chapter 6, that their middle class counterparts tend to move about school like 'fish in water'. More specifically, a close correspondence exists between the routines and control found at home and those required of pupils at school. There is thus an almost seamless transition for some middle class young children as they begin school life (Bernstein, 1971, 1975; Bourdieu and Passeron, 1977). As will now be shown, the experiences of the young working class boys are very different. The lack of correspondence between life at home and school, as highlighted in the previous chapter, has meant that some of these young boys' experiences of schooling are like 'fish out of water'.

To aid comparison with the middle class boys in South Park, this chapter will follow the same broad structure as Chapter 6. It will therefore begin by continuing with the analysis provided in the previous chapter by outlining how the particular social processes and practices found at home and school have become internalised by these young boys in terms of a specific working class habitus and how this, in turn, has come to inform their attitudes towards schooling. The chapter will then go on to examine the young boys' peer group relations and the dominant form of working class masculinity that tends to underpin these. In doing this, it will also assess how this form of masculinity tends to exacerbate the boys' overall dispositions towards schooling as outlined earlier. As in Chapter 6, the chapter will conclude with a consideration of the implications of all this for understanding the nature of working class boys' underachievement in the early years.

The working class habitus and schooling

The broader figurational context outlined in the previous chapter focused on the nature of the interdependent relationships between parents and the school. As we have seen, these relationships tend to be very different to the ones found in South Park where the school has been able to define its role in terms of formal academic achievement with the full compliance and practical support of the parents. The relationships between parents and the school in South Park tend therefore to be relatively harmonious and built upon a shared commitment to academic attainment and a correspondence between the routines and practices of the home and the school. By contrast, this correspondence between the home and school is lacking in North Parade. While some of the parents care passionately about their children's education, they simply do not have the knowledge, expertise nor resources to effectively support an emphasis on academic attainment by the school. With this in mind, and working with a culturally-deficit model of the local community, the school has therefore re-defined its educational role away from a focus on academic attainment and more towards one based around pastoral care. As outlined in the previous chapter, the compliance of parents with regard to this re-defined role has been gained by the school through the relatively high imbalances of power that tend to characterise their relationships. Thus some parents are simply unaware of what the school is doing and others lack the confidence to approach teachers about this. Moreover, while some parents have attempted to challenge the school this has tended to be quashed through the defensive reactions of some teachers or the more general attempts to dampen down the parents' educational aspirations.

This, then, is the immediate social context that the young children living in North Parade come to internalise and which then influences and shapes their own general dispositions towards education. In looking at what has actually been internalised by the young boys, and thus what we can call their working class habitus, it is worth following the structure of Chapter 6 and focusing on two levels, in turn. The first relates to the broader habits and largely unconscious patterns of behaviour that some have come to internalise through the social practices of the home. However, and as will be seen, what is lacking in this instance is the correspondence between these practices and those of the school as found with the young middle class boys. The second level relates, more specifically, to the general dispositions that these young boys have towards education because of their *working class* position.

Growing up quickly and learning to survive

As outlined in the previous chapter, some of the parents in North Parade are not able to exercise control over their own lives and homes to the same extent as the professional, middle class parents in South Park. It will be remembered that residents in North Parade are far more likely to be unemployed and experience poor health than those in South Park. There is also a much higher proportion of single parent families in North Park and of families that do not have access to a car. Given these conditions it is not surprising to find that some parents simply do not have the resources or energy to supervise and control their young children to the same extent as those in South Park can. Rather, the emphasis for these parents is simply living day-to-day and using all of one's efforts and skills simply to survive. At one level, therefore, there is a tendency for the young children living in North Parade to have their day-to-day activities less closely controlled and organised in comparison with their middle class counterparts in South Park. Some of these young working class children are therefore quite used to a significant degree of freedom and assuming a fair amount of responsibility in relation to their daily lives.

At another level, the social and economic conditions of life in North Parade have also led to some parents having to develop an emphasis on the practical and the material. While middle class parents may be able to demonstrate success through the academic achievements of their children, some working class parents are forced to demonstrate such success simply by feeding and clothing theirs. As touched upon in the last chapter, it is therefore not surprising to find that some parents will take great pride in being able to give their children 'the best' – often going to great lengths and making huge personal sacrifices in order to provide them with the latest toys and games and to dress them in designer clothes. This was certainly evident in relation to some of the young children in North Parade where they were much more individually and distinctively dressed at school than their counterparts in South Park Primary School (Connolly, 1998a). While most of the children at North Parade still wore the school sweatshirt there tended to be little attention paid to conforming with other aspects of the school uniform. Rather, some boys would wear expensive jeans and trainers while some girls would wear brightly coloured leggings and satin-style and/or sequined jeans. Moreover, some girls came to school wearing gold rings and jewellery, including necklaces and earrings; some had their nails painted and others had rather colourful bands and ties for their hair. Similarly, some boys would also come to school wearing necklaces and a number had their ears pierced; some would also tend to have their hair cut short and styled.

This general emphasis on the practical and the material in the lives of these young children also tended to be forcefully consolidated by the fact that they lived in an area experiencing relatively high levels of violence and sectarian tensions. The background to this was touched upon in Chapter 4 and is explained in more detail elsewhere (see Connolly, 2004). Residents of North Parade therefore tend to live with a real and ongoing sense of threat and an undercurrent of apprehension and fear. The ever-present nature of the violence in the area is something certainly picked up by the young boys as the following comments from Martin illustrate:

Martin: There's bad men up at that shop there! There's all UVF an' all there.

Interviewer: What's the UVF?

Martin: Bad people! They've got guns and they shoot at people for nothin'.

Interviewer: Do they?

Martin: They want to shoot people for fun. They kill people and then go running away. They shoot people. That's all the writing up there [*referring to the UVF graffiti on the shop walls*].

As explained in Chapter 4, given this level of violence and the feelings of insecurity and threat that accompany it, it is not surprising to find that a strong sense of community and territory has developed within North Parade, evident in the marking out of the estate's boundaries through the painting of kerbstones and the flying of flags. In terms of cultural practices, one significant way in which this sense of territory and community is actively expressed is through local bands and parades. Orange Parades have become one way in which some Protestant communities tend to develop and express their own sense of identity. A number of parades take place, particularly in the summer, and will attract significant audiences as people line the streets to cheer the parades and the accompanying bands on. A carnival atmosphere is often created and it is not uncommon to find stalls selling food and drink as well as flags and other loyalist merchandise.

The bands that accompany the Orange Parades often tend to be formed in and represent particular areas and comprise mainly young men playing drums and flutes. Band members will also tend to wear distinctive uniforms, often military and/or paramilitary in style and, not surprisingly, being a band member carries a significant level of status with it. Many of the bands also tend to associate themselves with particular loyalist paramilitary groups and paramilitary emblems can be seen at times painted on the sides of the large drums and sewn into some of the band members' uniforms. While representing a positive expression of some Protestant communities' identities, these displays of paramilitarism and the fact that some parades do tend to march by or through Catholic areas have therefore made the whole issue of Orange Parades an extremely contentious one over recent years. The widespread outbreaks of civil disorder that have followed some marches – particularly those in Drumcree during the mid-to-late 1990s – and which have attracted international media attention are testament to this.

Given the high political symbolism that has tended to accompany bands and parades and, moreover, the attraction they will have to young children because of the noise, colourful uniforms and general sense of occasion, it is not surprising to find that some of the boys expressed a great deal of interest in the local bands, as the following discussion with Jamie and Lee indicates:

Interviewer: What do the bands do? I've not seen the bands before.
Jamie: [*excitedly*] The bands?
Interviewer: Yeah.
Jamie: They play drums like this [*jumps up and pretends to play big drum while marching round the room*]. Boom! Boom! Boom!
Interviewer: Do you both like the bands?
Jamie: Yeah!
Lee: Yeah!
Interviewer: What do you like about them?
Jamie: The big drums – the big bangs!
Interviewer: Would you both like to be in the bands?
Lee: Yeah!

Jamie:	Yeah because it's noisy! Boom! Boom! Boom!
Interviewer:	Do you know anybody who's in the bands at the moment?
Jamie:	Aye! My grandpa, my daddy and my mummy!

As can be seen from Jamie's final comments, bands tend to be rooted in local communities and it is thus not uncommon for family members to be involved. This is also evident in the following discussion with Martin and Billy. This time, as can be seen, Martin makes reference to the fact that his father is a member of the North Parade Defenders Flute Band – a band closely associated with the loyalist paramilitary group the UVF:

Interviewer:	Somebody was talking about bands before. I've not seen a band – what are they?
Martin:	I've seen a band!
Interviewer:	Have you?
Martin:	They play drums like that one there and they play whistles, they play flutes. And the leader goes like that there sometimes [*stands up and shows how the leader twirls and throws the baton*].
Interviewer:	And why do they do that then?
Martin:	It's a parade. They do it to make everyone happy, to watch it.
Interviewer:	And do they do it round here?
Billy:	Yeah. My daddy used to be in a band.
Martin:	My daddy is in the North Parade Defenders. He's still there.
Interviewer:	And would you both like to be in a band?
Martin:	Yes.
Billy:	Cos you get to play everything.

The identification with the bands and the desire to be a member are also evident in the discussion with Lee, Davey and Martin below. As can be seen, there is significant status and competition surrounding claims about who is a band member. The conversation began with me asking Davey about a hat I saw him wearing earlier that day in the playground. It had a UVF emblem on it:

Interviewer:	Davey, you had a hat on today, a nice blue hat.
Lee:	[*sniggers*].

Interviewer:	What did it say on the front, I didn't see?
Davey:	Ulster Volunteer Flute Band.
Interviewer:	What's a flute band?
Davey:	A band!
Interviewer:	Are you in the band?
Davey:	[*nods*].
Lee:	He's in no band!
Davey:	I am so!
Interviewer:	What do bands do?
Lee:	Play drums!
Martin:	I know they go boom! Boom! Boom!
Lee:	They have baseball bats!
Davey:	I'm already in the band.

The association between support for the bands and identification with the local paramilitary organisation, the UVF, is evident in the above discussion. Indeed the ongoing sectarian violence and tensions in the area and the prominence of the paramilitary-style local bands with their association with the UVF form an important backdrop against which the young boys come to develop a sense of identity, as the following comments from Martin and Lee graphically illustrate:

Interviewer:	What do you want to do when you grow up?
Martin:	Join the UVF!
Lee:	[*laughs*].
Martin:	UVF! [*chants*] U-V-U-V-F! U-V-U-V-F!
Interviewer:	What's the UVF?
Martin:	They fight! They shoot guns!
Interviewer:	Do they?
Lee:	They have big guns!

The implications of the above comments for the development of the young boys' masculine identities is all too apparent and will be explored in more detail in the next section. For now it is important to draw out the underlying nature of the working class habitus that has been internalised by some of these young boys and girls. It is a habitus that is much less concerned with the mastery of specialist knowledge and technical skills and also about the passive acceptance of discipline and control as tends to be the case with the young middle class children. Rather it is composed of a set of habits and dispositions that are much more physically- and materially-oriented and based upon a greater sense of control over one's own day-to-day life. For some of these working class boys and girls, therefore, the emphasis is upon how they look and what clothes and jewellery they wear. It is upon being streetwise and, for the boys, displays of physical competence. Given the real dangers associated with living in an area like North Parade it is therefore a habitus that is, above all, driven by the instinct for survival and thus the need to grow up quickly (Skelton, 2001).

Thus, in terms of the general habits and behavioural dispositions that these young boys are coming to internalise, there is little correspondence between these and the demands of formal schooling with their emphasis on routines and the close control of their behaviour. It is this that underlies the comments of the class teacher, Mrs Lee, in the previous chapter. Classroom observations of the children tended to confirm her opinion that it was an extremely difficult task to get them to 'settle down' and into the routines of school life. Given their tendency to be afforded greater freedom and control over their own lives, there was thus much less of a tendency for the young children to respond instinctively to the commands of the teacher and some needed to be asked repeatedly to do a simple task like sit down, stop talking or line up at the door. When the children had created a line at the door or in the playground it was common to see some children pushing and shoving one another. It was also necessary for the teacher to keep a close eye on the children at the back of the line when walking them through the school and she would, at times, need to directly intervene to cajole them along.

Most significantly, there were clear limits on how Mrs Lee could organise her days with the class and what she could reasonably expect of the children in terms of schoolwork. As already mentioned, the school had adopted a strong pastoral emphasis in terms of its educational role. This meant a much more fragmented day than that found at South Park with a greater emphasis on informal play and practical activities. No particular activity or session would usually last for more than half an hour. To give some indication of this, a 'typical day' is outlined below. While some of the actual activities changed from day to day it does give a flavour of the way in which the day is organised and the balance between play, other practical activities and formal academic sessions:

- 8.50–9.45   Structured play.
- 9.50–10.05   Listen to story on carpet.

- 10.05–10.20   Numeracy activities sitting at desks.
- 10.20–10.35   Milk and snacks and then toilet.
- 10.35–11.00   Breaktime in playground.
- 11.00–11.30   Visit to library within school.
- 11.30–11.50   Creative writing sitting at desks.
- 11.50–12.00   Tidy up and toilets.
- 12.00–1.00   Lunchtime (lunch and then play in playground).
- 1.00–1.30   PE in assembly hall.
- 1.30–1.50   Singing.
- 1.50–2.00   Sitting on carpet, preparation for hometime.

As can be seen, there tend to be just two short sessions (15 and 20 minutes respectively) where the children actually sit at their desks and engage in formal academic work. This is clearly not to suggest that they are not also engaged in other meaningful numeracy and literacy learning activities throughout the day. Rather, it is simply pointed out as a comparison with the respective class in South Park where, with the exception of breaktime, they are routinely able to engage in this type of work for the whole of the morning.

Moreover, it was sometimes a difficult task for Mrs Lee to maintain the compliance of the children even for these relatively short periods where they were expected to remain seated. Some of the children were observed to find it difficult to follow instructions given and, without one-to-one direction from Mrs Lee or the class-room assistant, would often become distracted. One way Mrs Lee dealt with this was to provide three or four differing (but themed and inter-related) activities on the respective tables (whether numeracy- or literacy-based) and organise it so that the children moved from one activity to another after five or ten minutes.

Attitudes towards education

Alongside the internalisation of a set of dispositions that are much more physically- and materially-oriented, the young boys' working class habitus also included a more specific set of taken-for-granted perceptions of schooling and of the value of education. For some of the young boys, they were already internalising a sense of the insignificance of school, as can be seen in the following comments from Cameron and Davey:

Interviewer: Do you think it's important to go to school?

Cameron: Nooo!
Davey: Nah!
Interviewer: Why? Does it not matter if you go to school or not?
Davey: No.
Cameron: I hate it.

For others, when asked what they thought would happen if they did not ever go to school, their answers suggest that they do not seem to value schooling. As we saw in Chapter 6, when the middle class boys in South Park were asked this question they tended to list a number of things that they would miss out on if they could not attend school. These tended to be academic and included being able to read and write, to do sums and be 'smart'. In stark contrast, some of the working class boys in North Parade did not mention anything that they would lack by not going to school. Rather, and possibly reflecting the general sense of a community that routinely experiences significant levels of external control, their only concern was with being punished if they did not attend. As Billy commented:

Interviewer: What do you think would happen if you didn't ever go to school?
Billy: Er, I know!
Interviewer: What?
Billy: A teacher would take you away and send you to jail!
Lee: [*laughs*].

This is also a sentiment expressed towards the end of the following discussion with Dominic, Martin and Lee where they talk about how their parents would be sent to jail if they did not go to school. While they also conclude by saying they do not think it matters if they go to school or not, they do begin the discussion with some positive points about school. Interestingly, however, none of these are academic but rather relate to practical activities:

Interviewer: Do you think school's important?
Lee: Yes.
Dominic: Yeah.
Interviewer: Why? Why's it important?
Lee: Because.
Dominic: Cos you get to go to PE.
Martin: PE and playing.

Interviewer:	What would happen if you didn't go to school?
Lee:	Er, go to jail!
Dominic:	Your mum and dad would go to jail.
Interviewer:	Would they? But do you think it would matter if you went to school or not?
Lee:	Erm, nope.
Martin:	Sometimes I don't want to [go to school].
Interviewer:	Why don't you want to?
Martin:	Cos, my sister gets to stay off but I never get to stay off.

The following discussion with Jamie, Campbell and Lee also shows how the elements of schooling that some of the young working class boys like tend to be much more practically-based rather than academic:

Interviewer:	Do you like school?
Jamie:	Yeah.
Campbell:	Yes.
Interviewer:	What do you like about school?
Jamie:	I like doing PE.
Interviewer:	What about you, Campbell? What do you like about school?
Campbell:	The computer.
Interviewer:	What do you like doing on the computer?
Campbell:	Printing!
Lee:	I like art.
Interviewer:	Is there anything else about school that you like the best?
Jamie:	I like playing the honeycomb game.
Lee:	I like making things.
Campbell:	I like the blocks on the carpet. You can make a house and a car. You can make anything.

Masculinity and the working class habitus

The focus of the discussion so far has been on some of the ways in which social class has tended to influence and shape the young boys' perspectives and behaviour in North Parade. As we have seen, some of these boys tend to live in families that are struggling to survive. They have little support and few resources available to them to cope with the demands of bringing up young children. Some parents therefore simply do not have the time or ability to be able to exert the high levels of control and organisation that some of the middle class parents in South Park tended to do over their children. The young children are therefore less likely to develop and internalise a passive acceptance of routines and being closely controlled and organised. Rather, the emphasis is more fundamentally on practical and material concerns; on the here-and-now and on surviving. As outlined above, within this context these young boys are expected to grow up fast. The way they are dressed and the greater expectations on them in terms of being able to look after themselves are all elements of this. Moreover, this pressure is increased by the fact that they are growing up in a dangerous and fairly violent neighbourhood. They therefore have to learn to be streetwise from an early age – to know how to act and behave and how to look after themselves (Connolly, 1998a; Skelton, 2001). As shown above and as will be explored in more detail below, these are all factors that are already beginning to influence and shape the lives and identities of these 5- and 6-year-old boys.

Moreover, these broader practically- and materially-based dispositions tend to have the effect of impeding the young boys' ability to succeed in school. As shown above, not only do they tend to lack the necessary habits and dispositions to fit easily into the routines and demands of formal schooling but some boys also do not seem to value education and particularly the academic elements of schooling. In many ways there is little correspondence between their day-to-day lives at home and on the local estate and such formal academic work. While their parents may care passionately about the need for their children to be educated, they simply do not have the necessary knowledge and expertise to convey to their sons and daughters in order for them to gain a practical sense of the importance and necessity of formal academic education. Given this, it may be for this reason that some parents have, out of desperation, resorted to 'threatening' their children with the possibility of being 'taken away' and 'locked up' if they do not go to school – something that would certainly help to explain some of the children's comments reported above.

Either way, these are the broader working class dispositions that provide the parameters within which the young boys are left to construct their sense of masculinity. It is to this that the chapter now turns. To aid comparison, the following analysis of the dominant form of masculinity among these working class boys will take the same approach as that used for the young middle class boys in Chapter 6. The analysis will begin, therefore, with an examination of the 'boundary work' engaged in by some of the boys in marking out the distinctive space for their own identities (Thorne, 1993; Francis, 1998). It will then look, in more detail, at some of the main elements of the dominant form of masculinity subscribed to by some of the young boys before concluding with an exploration of how this has tended to mediate the broader working class dispositions to schooling outlined above.

Young working class boys' boundary work

It was argued in Chapter 6 that the nature of the interdependent relations between boys and girls can be understood on at least two levels. On one level, all social identities are relational in that they tend to be defined by way of reference to others. In terms of gender, being a boy and thus being masculine is as much about *not* being a girl and thus feminine as anything else. Given the way in which gender identities are oppositionally defined in this way then success-fully demonstrating one's masculinity requires young boys to actively disassociate themselves from girls (Francis, 1998). This is clearly evident in the responses of Davey and Martin below to my asking them whether they would like to be girls:

Interviewer: Would either of you two like to be a girl?
Davey: [*laughs hysterically*] Nooo! No! No!
Martin: Nooooo!
Interviewer: Why not? Why do you like being boys?
Davey: Cos.
Martin: Cos it's better.
Interviewer: Why is it better?
Davey: You get to play wrestling.
Martin: You get to go to BB [*Boys' Brigade*].
Davey: And you're allowed to fight! Remember when I punched you and you slammed on your knees and I hurt you? Remember once I bit you and you were bleeding! [*laughs*]
Martin: [*No response*].

The young boys' responses are illuminating because they illustrate the key features of masculinity that they tend to value and subscribe to. As can be seen they tend to reflect a specific emphasis on physicality and violence (Jordan, 1995) – an emphasis very different to the middle class boys' focus on the mastery of specialist knowledge and technical skills. Very similar sentiments are also evident in the discussion with Lee and Billy below:

Interviewer: Would you not like to be girls?
Lee: No!
Interviewer: Why?
Billy: Cos boys would be stronger.
Interviewer: What's good about being boys then?
Billy: They're stronger than girls.
Lee: They [*girls*] make you all dizzy an' all and can't remember what you're drawing!
Billy: You get to play football an' all and fight and wrestling.
Interviewer: Oh! And girls don't do that then?
Billy: No – they don't have muscles.

This need to disassociate themselves from girls is also evident in relation to flute bands. While some girls are members of flute bands, this is not something that some of these boys can countenance. For them, flute bands with their association with violence and paramilitary symbolism are a male preserve. As Martin and Billy argue:

Interviewer: And would you both like to be in a band?
Martin: Yes.
Billy: Cos you get to play everything.
Interviewer: And are there girls in bands as well?
Martin: No!
Billy: The girls can be a leader.
Interviewer: Oh. And do they play the drums and flutes and all that?
Martin: NO!
Interviewer: Why not?
Martin: Cos they're not that good.
Billy: They're no good.

The distinction introduced in Chapter 6 between externally- and internally-expressed masculinities is one that certainly seems to convey the differences between the dominant forms of masculinity subscribed to by some of the working class and middle class boys respectively. For the working class boys above, their sense of masculinity is very much expressed externally through physicality and strength (Mac an Ghaill, 1994; Connolly, 1998a; Skelton, 2001; Nayak, 2003). Having muscles and the ability to fight and wrestle are all elements of this form of masculinity. In contrast, and as shown in Chapter 6, some of the middle class boys actively disassociated themselves from this form of masculinity, promoting, instead, a more internally-expressed form based around the successful display of specialist knowledge and skills.

There is a second level by which boys and girls are interdependent, however, and this involves the need for boys and girls to actively recognise and confirm the gender roles and identities of one another. Thus a boy's sense of masculinity and attractiveness depends upon girls showing him interest. As argued earlier this, in turn, may partly explain the popularity of discourses on girlfriends and boyfriends and games of kiss-chase in primary playgrounds (Epstein, 1997; Connolly, 1998a; Renold, 2002, 2003). It was argued in Chapter 6 that such interdependencies were not particularly evident among the young middle class boys at South Park, possibly due to the types of internally-expressed masculinity developed at that particular age and also the tendency for some of the parents to pay particular attention to school uniforms and thus dress their sons and daughters in relatively asexual and indistinguishable ways. In contrast, and as already outlined, much clearer distinctions were evident between the boys and girls at North Parade Primary School in terms of their dress and general presentation. The symbolism of gender and the emphasis on masculinity and femininity tended to be much more evident among these children. It is this that may partly explain the greater significance of discourses on girlfriends and boyfriends there than in South Park, as the following discussion with Cameron and Dominic shows:

Cameron: I'd play with Lee and Jamie and Dominic.
Interviewer: They're all boys. Would you play with any girls?
Cameron: Nooo! [*laughs*]
Dominic: No! No!
Interviewer: Why?
Cameron: They'd kiss us!
Interviewer: Would they?
Dominic: Yes!
Cameron: Me and Jamie keep getting chased by girls!

These 'complaints' about girls chasing and kissing them are actually necessary elements of the boys' successful demonstration of their masculine identities. The dependency of some of the young boys on girls being attracted to them is also evident in the discussion below with Jamie and Martin:

Interviewer: So that's all boys that you play with. What girls do you play with in the playground?
Martin: [*laughs*] Nooooo!
Jamie: No way!
Interviewer: Why?
Martin: No girls!
Interviewer: Why?
Jamie: Cos girls chase me!
Interviewer: Girls chase you, Jamie? Why?
Jamie: Cos.
Martin: They love you! [*giggles*]
Interviewer: Do they?
Jamie: Nearly all of 'em! All of 'em nearly chase me!

Working class masculinities and young boys

Overall, this boundary work engaged in by the young boys has clearly marked out the parameters within which their masculine identities are formed. As has been seen, they are parameters that tend to emphasise external expressions of masculinity in terms of muscles and strength as well as physical skills such as fighting and wrestling. Through the discourses on girlfriends and boyfriends they also place an emphasis on being physically attractive and, increasingly at this age, on displays of (hetero)sexuality. It is worth looking in a little more detail at some of these themes to gain a better understanding of the particular ways in which they are played out, practically, in the young boys' day-to-day social worlds.

It is already clear from the comments reported above that being able to fight, and thus 'look after yourself', is a key element of the dominant form of masculinity already being subscribed to by some of these young boys. This is evident, for example, in some of the boys' interest in wrestling and the attention to detail they tend to pay to learning and rehearsing the many different moves. This can be seen in the following discussion with Cameron and Matty:

Interviewer: And what do you play in the playground? What games
do you play?
Cameron: Wrestling.
Interviewer: Wrestling?
Cameron: Aye, but sometimes you get shouted at for it/
Matty: /I know all the moves.
Interviewer: Do you? Tell me what moves you know.
Matty: 'Choke-slam'! 'The last ride'!
Interviewer: What's that one?
Matty: It's where you go [*demonstrates*] – flick 'em up and
then choke slam them.
Cameron: Er, 'people's elbow'!
Matty: 'The rock bottom'!

Significant levels of status were therefore gained by some boys
not only in terms of their knowledge of wrestling moves but, more
practically, in terms of their ability to actually display them and
thus to demonstrate their own strength. As can be seen in the
following argument between Davey and Martin, being the strongest
in the class was a highly sought-after position:

Interviewer: So who's the strongest in your class then?
Davey: ME!
Martin: Me.
Davey: ME!
Martin: Me.
Davey: No, big Tommy, remember? Big Tommy!
Interviewer: Big Tommy?
Martin: No way, I can twirl him around and drop him.
Davey: Well, I can do a death throw on him, splat him down!

For some of the boys, much of their free-time was spent carefully
practising, rehearsing and demonstrating their physical strength and
fighting skills. The most common place for this to occur was in the
playground where much of the boys' activities largely went unnoticed
by the teachers and lunchtime supervisors whose role tended to be
restricted mainly to intervening to break up 'proper' fights or to
responding to complaints or problems that individual children would
approach them with. Given that all of the staff were female, most of
the time that they did spend interacting with the children was taken
up joining in and organising games with the girls, particularly

skipping. A larger skipping rope would sometimes be used with an adult rotating one end, a girl the other, and other girls either queuing up to take turns to skip or crowding round to watch and/or join in the rhyme that was being sung. Such skipping games proved to be very popular and would often attract the involvement of more than two-thirds of the girls in the playground.

For some of the boys, therefore, they tended to be left to their own devices to rehearse and demonstrate their wrestling skills and also to re-enact many other forms of fighting and violent behaviour they had either witnessed directly or seen on television. Some of these re-enactments involved carefully choreographed displays of violence and aggression sometimes reflecting local paramilitary activities. On one occasion, for example, three boys were seen to be chasing a fourth. When they had caught him, two of the boys held each of his arms and pulled them, tightly, round his back so that his chest protruded forward. The third boy then stood in front of him and proceeded to pretend to punch him, violently, in the stomach. On each 'punch', the boy who was being held jerked his body forward and let out a deep groaning sound. The two boys behind him would then sharply pull his arms back, thus thrusting his stomach out again, and the boy in front of him would proceed to pretend to punch him again. On another occasion, four boys were seen to be playing a shooting game where they would pretend to have handguns and be shooting at each other. Again, however, the actions of the boys were heavily choreographed and stylised with the boys standing with their legs astride, their arms outstretched and with their hands clasped together pointing the 'gun'. Each shot they made was accompanied by a deep shooting sound and the gun sharply recoiling back and upwards.

To a lesser extent such re-enactments of violent events were also to be seen in the classroom, especially during structured play in the morning. Three boys, for example, were playing on the carpet during one session with the toy cars and garage. They were carefully recreating a bank robbery and had planned the route for the getaway and where to hide the cars. With great excitement and attention to detail, the boys manoeuvred their cars along the roads marked on the carpet and around and through the garage, imitating the screeching of tyres and the shooting of guns as they went along. On another occasion I was sitting on one of the children's chairs observing a group of children on the other side of the classroom. I felt something pressed into the back of my head and turned around.

Standing there was a boy with a gun he had made out of Lego. He was holding it in both hands, with his arms outstretched and standing there with his legs astride adopting a military-style shooting position.

Alongside such stylised and carefully choreographed displays of violence, overtly aggressive behaviour and fighting would also occur at times, mainly in the playground. On one occasion, for example, two boys were chasing a third boy, grabbing him by the jumper and swinging him around. The aggressive nature of the two boys' behaviour as they violently pulled at him and caused him to stumble over twice clearly indicated that this was not 'play'. The third boy became increasingly distressed as the other two boys pulled off his jumper and then teased him with it. He sat on the ground and began to cry. The other two boys then looked around nervously, saw that none of the lunchtime supervisors had noticed the incident, threw the jumper at the boy and ran off laughing. The third boy remained sitting on the floor, clutched the jumper to his chest and then slumped forward on top of it, rolling himself up into a ball. He maintained this position for about a minute before slowly pulling himself to his feet and walking away.

More generally, the predominance of such levels of violence, even if largely stylised and rehearsed, did tend to create the context within which a certain aggressive and intimidating manner was becoming internalised by some of the boys and would sometimes be expressed unconsciously, as a habit. This can be seen in the following discussion between Billy, Lee and Martin where their conversation soon included aggressive and misogynist themes:

Interviewer: What do you play in the playground?
Billy: Fight!
Martin: Steal money!
Interviewer: In the playground? No, what games do you play?
Billy: 'Power Rangers' and 'Space'.
Interviewer: Do you play with girls and boys?
Billy: [*laughs*]
Martin: We pull her trousers down! I know!
Interviewer: What?
Martin: We burn something! I know, pull her trousers down and burn her!
Lee: We pull her pants down and burn her!
All: [*hysterical laughter*]
Interviewer: You do what?

| Lee: | I know, get her later and burn her bum! |
| Billy: | I got one – burn her arse! |

More generally, there tended to be a level of intolerance of emotion and difference found among some of the young boys. One boy in the class, for example, had a rather nervous disposition and tended to speak quickly with a high-pitched voice. On one occasion in the playground he came up to me and began telling me about the game he had just finished playing. Davey came over and stood up close behind him mimicking his voice with disdain. On another occasion just before breaktime in the classroom the children were sitting at their desks with the drinks and snacks they had brought in. Cameron was having difficulty opening the bottle of drink he had brought in. Martin and Billy were sitting opposite him and began laughing at the fact that he could not open his bottle. Cameron soon became extremely frustrated and began to cry. The two boys continued to laugh at him, however. Moreover, Martin tried to attract the attention of Lee on another table to point out to him that Cameron was crying and to encourage him to join in their mocking behaviour.

Overall, therefore, the dominant form of masculinity aspired to by some of the boys at North Parade was one based around an externally-expressed masculinity with its emphasis on being strong (both physically and emotionally) and on being able to fight as well as able to attract girlfriends (Jordan, 1995; Connolly, 1998a). With this in mind, it is not surprising to find that the young boys' career aspirations were also much more limited and practically-oriented. As the following discussion with Adrian, Tommy and Kurt indicates, their aspirations tend to reflect the realities of life in North Parade and the tendency for those in employment to have manual jobs:

Interviewer:	When you grow up and you leave school what jobs would you get?
Adrian:	I would get the best job – building houses.
Tommy:	I'd get, I'd fix some cars!
Kurt:	No, I wouldn't get a job. I would clean carpets with my daddy's carpet machine – my daddy cleans carpets.
Interviewer:	And would you work with him?
Kurt:	[nods].

While it would be wrong to read too much into the young boys' aspirations at this young age, it does tend to indicate quite clearly the effects of the wider social contexts in which they live on their attitudes and dispositions. This is especially the case when comparing the aspirations of these boys with their middle class counterparts in South Park. It will be remembered from Chapter 6 that the middle class boys tended to have relatively high aspirations, reflecting the professional backgrounds of their parents and the wide range of experiences and resources they had access to. For the working class boys in North Parade, however, their aspirations were much more grounded and reflected their experiences of life on the estate and the limited opportunities that accompanied these. This is evident in the answers the boys gave during interviews when asked what they would like to do when they grow up, as listed below:

- 'Build houses'
- 'Fix cars'
- 'Footballer'
- 'Kill rats and get a gun'
- 'Join the UVF!'
- 'Work with my daddy'
- 'Make stuff with wood'
- 'Join the army'
- 'Fireman'
- 'Clean carpets'
- 'Just go to work'.

Moreover, it is also worth showing the answers given by Lee, Billy and Martin when they were first asked what they would like to do when they grow up. While they were clearly joking, it does give some insight into the contexts within which these boys live:

Interviewer: Have you got any ideas what you'd like to do when you grow up?

Lee: Aye – stay in the house! [*laughs*]

Interviewer: Stay in the house? What about you Billy?

Billy: I know – say bad words! [*laughs*]

Interviewer: Martin, what do you want to do when you grow up?

Martin: Steal trophies and money! And kill somebody and kill people!

Billy: I've got a real gun!

Martin: So do I!

Working class masculinities and schooling

While a close correspondence seems to exist between the dominant forms of masculinity found among some of the young middle class boys and the demands of formal education, it is already apparent from the above that this is not so for some of the young working class boys in North Parade. In the context of the school, these are young boys who are like 'fish out of water'. The dominant form of masculinity that is already emerging and that they tend to subscribe to, with its emphasis on strength and physical prowess, does not fit well with the routines of schooling with their dependency upon children passively accepting the close control and detailed organisation of their time and activities, evident in the need to be able to sit for significant periods of time and engage in fine and intricate activities such as reading and writing and other academic tasks. It is not that these young boys are in any sense incapable of doing so. Rather, and as we have seen, for some of these boys they are activities that they are simply not used to; activities that have just not been part of their day-to-day lives. While the passive acceptance of being closely controlled and the ability to deal with formal academic work have already been internalised into a set of taken-for-granted habits for some of the young middle class boys, these working class boys have to struggle to learn them. This is evident in the following discussion with Cameron and Jamie:

Interviewer: What about reading, do you like reading?
Jamie: No.
Cameron: No.
Interviewer: No? Why not?
Cameron: I don't.
Jamie: It's wick! It takes my memory away.

A very similar experience is also apparent in the discussion below with Adrian and Tommy. Interestingly, however, they do seem to like writing as can be seen:

Interviewer: In school what about sums, do you like doing sums?
Adrian: No.
Tommy: No.
Interviewer: Why?
Adrian: Because too boring.
Interviewer: What makes it boring?

Adrian:	Because you have to, like/
Tommy:	/You have to, you have to think about it and write the number – a hundred plus a thousand an' all.
Adrian:	I know.
Interviewer:	And do you find it hard or easy?
Adrian:	Hard.
Tommy:	Hard.
Interviewer:	What about writing, do you like writing?
Adrian:	Yes.
Tommy:	Yes.
Adrian:	I love it.
Interviewer:	What do you like about writing?
Adrian:	Cos you can write, you don't have to spell like, you don't need to spell, you can just draw a picture.

The type of writing these boys are referring to is a particular form of creative (or emergent) writing used fairly successfully by Mrs Lee with the class. It is an approach to writing where children are encouraged to 'write' whatever they like and thus to develop an understanding of the notion of stories and the activity of writing and also, crucially, the confidence and enjoyment of engaging in it. At this age, much of what the children 'write' is no more than incoherent scribbles. However, when asked to talk about what they have written, many of the children are able to interpret their writing and to recount very detailed and intricate stories. No attempt is made, at this stage, to correct their writing. Rather, the idea is that the children's writing will naturally begin to evolve into identifiable letters, then words and ultimately coherent sentences. As can be seen from the comments above, for these boys at least, it is an activity they enjoy, mainly because it is not embroiled in the same types of rules and regulations associated with formal writing and other activities like maths.

Not surprisingly, some of the boys also had little interest in reading. Interestingly (and in comparison with the middle class boys discussed in Chapter 6) none of these working class boys during any of the interviews mentioned Harry Potter. Of the books that they did demonstrate some interest in, they were mainly action and adventure books where the interest was mainly confined to the photographs and pictures inside. As Lee and Billy commented:

Interviewer: What type of books do you like?

Lee:	[*excitedly*] Cars, racing cars, quad bikes and motor-bikes!
Billy:	I like, erm, the Titanic book and the shark one.

Similar sentiments are also expressed by Cameron and Martin below. As can be seen, interest in such topics can be used as a means of gaining status and thus is sometimes eagerly sought after:

Interviewer:	What type of books do you like to read?
Cameron:	Erm, scary ones!
Martin:	So do I! Hallowee'n book is scary isn't it?
Cameron:	[*laughs in agreement*]
Martin:	Volcano books [as well].

Conclusions

This chapter has focused on the some of the key elements of the schooling habitus of some of the young working class boys in North Parade. At the risk of sounding a little repetitive, it does need to be reiterated that this is not meant to be a representative nor a comprehensive account of either young working class boys as a whole or even the small group of boys in Mrs Lee's class. Some young boys in this class liked going to school and enjoyed reading and writing and other formal schoolwork. However, what we do know from Chapter 1 is that, in general, working class boys of this age do achieve less well than their middle class counterparts, especially in English. The aim of this chapter therefore has been simply to identify some of the processes and practices found among this particular group of working class boys that may help to contribute towards an explanation for these differences. Thus, what has been presented above can be seen more as the 'worst case scenario' evident for the young boys in North Parade Primary School in terms of how a number of different tendencies can work together to significantly limit their academic achievement.

As can be seen, some of these working class boys are struggling with the demands of formal education even at this early age. They are, as described earlier, like 'fish out of water'. There is a fundamental mismatch between their experiences and lives at home and what is required of them at school. The children live in an area that suffers from relatively high levels of poverty and violence. They are located in a context, therefore, where they and their families have little support and few resources to cope with the demands of bringing up young children. The parents simply do not have the time nor the opportunities to exert the same degree of close control and high levels of organisation of their children's activities as some of the middle class parents in South Park do. Their priority, instead, is simply surviving. With an emphasis on living day-to-day, it is not surprising to find the development of a set of dispositions among parents and their young children that are more practically- and materially-oriented. This, together with the realities of living with routine levels of sectarian tensions and violence, can help to contextualise the tendency for some young boys to develop a masculinity that is based upon strength and physical prowess. The dominant form of masculinity already emerging for these young boys is therefore one that is externally-expressed and, ultimately, based around the need to be streetwise and to 'look after yourself' and thus survive. And it is here that the incompatibility between such forms of masculinity and the demands of formal schooling are apparent. As we have seen, some of the young boys are simply not used to the high levels of close control required in order to sit for long periods of time and concentrate on intricate academic work. Moreover, such forms of activity bear little relevance to the actual experiences of some of these boys and the manual work engaged in by adult males around them.

This incompatibility between the dominant forms of masculinity subscribed to by some of the young boys and the demands of formal schooling helps to explain the relatively low levels of achievement experienced by these boys. Additionally, the fact that the achievement gap between young working class boys and girls is larger than between young middle class boys and girls can be explained by the general lack of emphasis placed on formal academic achievement by some parents. It was argued in Chapter 6 that the high priority given to educational success and the pressure placed on children within some middle class homes has had the effect of limiting the ability of gender to take a determining role in the academic performance of these middle class boys and girls. In contrast and as shown in this and the previous chapter, there is much less emphasis on educational attainment in some working class families. Not only do some parents simply not have the knowledge and expertise to help and encourage their children in school but formal education has much less practical significance in the lives of those living in North Parade, especially given the high levels of unemployment and the dependency upon routine manual work. Within this context, therefore, gender is free to play a more central role in influencing working class boys' and girls' attitudes towards schooling. And it is here where the greater variation in responses (and thus gaps in achievement between boys and girls) can be found, given that formal education with its emphasis on being dependent and passive tends to conflict generally with dominant forms of masculinity but can correspond fairly well with dominant forms of femininity (Francis, 1998, 2000).

In making these arguments, two points need to be stressed in conclusion. First, and following on from the arguments made in Chapter 2, describing such forms of masculinity as 'laddish' is fundamentally to misrepresent the type of behaviour described here. It is not a particular lifestyle that boys can simply choose to adopt as the term can imply. Rather, this form of behaviour is more deeply-rooted and engrained than this; found within the very fabric of some of these boys' ways of being. It has therefore become an unthinking and taken-for-granted aspect of their lives – a set of unconscious habits rather than a conscious lifestyle choice. Second, the term 'underachievement' is also an inappropriate one to use to describe the predicament that these young working class boys find themselves in. As Troyna (1984) has argued in relation to the emergence of the concept of underachievement to describe the experiences of Black boys, it tends to lay the emphasis for change on the boys themselves rather than on the structures around them. And yet, as this and the previous chapter have attempted to show, these boys are not simply 'choosing' to underachieve. Given the sets of habits and dispositions they have come to internalise, some young working class boys are incapable of achieving on a par with their middle class counterparts at this moment in time. They therefore simply lack the necessary knowledge and practical skills to be able to successfully meet the demands of formal schooling.

This is not to suggest that nothing can be done to address the problem. There is no biological reason, for example, why these working class boys cannot perform as well as their middle class counterparts. However, it is to suggest that this cannot be achieved through superficial programmes aimed simply at encouraging and motivating young working class boys. More fundamental change is required that can successfully address their more underlying and deeply-engrained dispositions towards education. Moreover, such dispositions themselves will only change when the conditions that give rise to them are dealt with, in turn. This means, as Mrs Marsh the Principal of North Parade Primary School clearly pointed out in the previous chapter, that the low academic performance of working class boys is not just an educational issue. Rather, it will only ever be tackled through a multi-agency approach that can also address the problems of long-term unemployment, poor health and bad living conditions (and in the context of Northern Ireland, the continuing political conflict). The implications of all this will be explored a little further in the following, concluding chapter.

Part IV

Implications for practice

Chapter 9

Conclusions
Working with young boys

Introduction

This book has covered a lot of ground in relation to the schooling of young boys. It has examined, in detail, the actual statistical evidence and the key explanations offered in relation to the phenomenon of young boys' lower levels of achievement compared to girls. It has also looked again at how young children's learning and development can be theorised and the place of gender within this. In addition, the last five chapters have provided two detailed case studies of the schooling experiences of young middle class and working class boys. The aim of this chapter is to draw all of this together and to examine the implications of the theories and evidence presented for how best to work with young boys to improve their educational experiences and to raise their levels of achievement. The chapter will begin by providing a brief summary of the main points to arise from the preceding chapters before looking at the key conclusions to be drawn from these and then some of their implications for those working with young boys.

Summary of the book

The rhetoric and reality of boys' underachievement

The first section of the book (Chapters 1 and 2) provides a detailed assessment of the rhetoric and the reality of 'boys' underachievement'. One of the main findings from an analysis of national data is that all of the patterns found at GCSE level in terms of the differences between boys and girls are already evident in the early years. Moreover, the patterns found in the early years (and also through to GCSE) show that there is a considerable difference between the rhetoric of 'boys' underachievement' and the actual reality. The evidence at Key Stage 1 certainly does not support the taken-for-granted picture of boys universally failing in schools and also continuing to fall further and further behind girls. Rather, the reality is much more complex than this and can be summarised in relation to three key points. First, the overall gap between young boys and girls is not increasing but has actually been stable for some time now and, if anything, there is some evidence of the gap beginning to close over recent years.

Second, it is fundamentally misleading to continue to compare boys and girls as if they represent two homogeneous groupings. There are many groups of young boys performing well above the national averages at Key Stage 1 (and all the way through to GCSE examinations). Similarly, there are particular groups of young girls performing well below average. The key point to emerge is that while there is a small gap between young boys and girls in terms of their overall levels of performance, this tends to be dwarfed by the much more considerable effects of social class and ethnicity on pupils' achievement levels. It is therefore not appropriate to focus simply on 'young boys'. Rather, there is a need to be much more specific and to identify particular groups of young boys in terms of their ethnicity and social class background. There is a world of difference, for example, between the general schooling experiences and educational opportunities of young White middle class boys compared to, say, young Bangladeshi working class boys. Third, the actual gap between young boys and girls is not constant but varies between differing social class and ethnic groups. The basic picture to emerge is that the gap is smallest among those groups who are already performing well in education and is largest among those who traditionally perform least well in education.

With all of this evidence in mind, Chapter 2 then went on to examine what explanations have currently been put forward for the phenomenon of 'boys' underachievement'. While these explanations have tended to be focused on older children, it has been worth re-assessing these in some detail in order to gain a fuller picture of the key issues at stake that can then help to focus the current research on boys in the early years. As was seen, a variety of competing arguments has been offered ranging from those that focus on essential biological differences and those that blame schools (either in terms of being biased in favour of girls or simply providing poor or mediocre teaching) to arguments that tend to cite wider changes in society and their adverse effects on boys and men. The problem with many of these explanations is that they tend to be based on simple comparisons between all boys and all girls and, therefore, fail to account for the complex reality described in Chapter 1. In fact, as Gorard *et al.* (1999) have argued, the lack of attention that has been paid to the actual evidence of gender differences in achievement has led many researchers and educationalists to focus on trying to explain and develop strategies to combat problems that do not actually exist.

In carefully re-assessing some of these key arguments in the light of the actual evidence, Chapter 2 concluded that, notwithstanding the intervening effects of social class and ethnicity, the overall differences between boys and girls in terms of their levels of achievement can be explained most fundamentally by the dominant forms of masculinity that boys tend to subscribe to. At a very general level, such forms of masculinity do not sit easily with the routine demands of schooling in terms of the need to be diligent, passive and hardworking whereas dominant forms of femininity tend to conform more readily to these (Salisbury and Jackson, 1996; Younger and Warrington, 1996; Francis, 2000). Boys are therefore more likely to react negatively to working hard in school and to see it as 'uncool'. Clearly, however, there are many differences within this as differing groups of boys adopt differing forms of masculinity depending upon their social class and ethnic backgrounds. One of the findings from previous research on older boys tends to suggest, for example, that while some middle class boys still wish to avoid being seen to work hard in school, they do value academic success and can use it to bolster their particular form of masculinity with its emphasis on superiority and natural intelligence – a type of 'intellectual muscularity' as Redman and Mac an Ghaill (1997) have termed it (see also Bourdieu and Passeron, 1977; Aggleton, 1987: Mac an Ghaill, 1994). In contrast, for some working class boys and/or boys from particular minority ethnic groups, the feelings they already have of being alienated from school may lead them to develop more exaggerated forms of masculinity as a response that then tends to encourage them to reject school altogether (see, for example, Willis, 1977; Corrigan, 1979; Mac an Ghaill, 1994). Overall, the evidence for older boys is that while their constructions and displays of masculinity can explain their general tendency to lag behind girls, the differing size of the gaps found within specific social class and ethnic groups can be explained by the specific forms of masculinity constructed by those particular groups of boys.

However, what we know much less about is whether these arguments about the effects of differing forms of masculinity are applicable to young boys. Just because the same patterns of achievement are evident in the early years that are found later at GCSE, we cannot simply assume that the same explanations apply. It is with this in mind that the book has offered two in-depth case studies involving a focus on a group of (White) working class and middle class young boys. The aim of these case studies has been to get beneath the surface of the national evidence to begin to understand the dominant forms of masculinity found among these two groups of young boys, whether they differ and what effects they tend to have on their dispositions towards education.

Theorising masculinities in the early years

Having identified the focus for the case studies, the next task has been to develop a suitable theoretical framework able to help us understand how young boys come to develop particular forms of masculine identities and the ways these come to influence and shape their attitudes towards schooling. It has been argued that the need for such a theoretical framework is especially important given the way in which traditional developmental accounts of childhood – encapsulated through the work of Jean Piaget – have created a context where it has been very difficult to understand the effects of gender in young children's lives and almost impossible to advocate intervention strategies to deal with gender issues in the early years. As a consequence, until relatively recently, comparatively little time has been spent on focusing on gender issues in the early years (Yelland, 1998; MacNaughton, 2000; Skelton and Hall, 2001). With this in mind, the second section of the book (Chapter 3) has spent some time looking again at the work of Piaget and some of the key problems associated with it. As was argued, with its emphasis on the natural development of children through a number of clearly-defined and universal stages, there is little scope to incorporate an understanding of the differing ways in which gender impacts upon the learning and development of boys and girls. Moreover, with his emphasis on child-centred learning and the notion of 'readiness', Piaget has constructed a theoretical framework that actively disapproves of any attempts by adults to intervene in young children's learning processes (MacNaughton, 2000).

Given the continuing influence that such Piagetian theories of child development still have within early years practice, it has been necessary to look for alternative approaches to understanding young children's learning and development and especially ones that can help us understand how broader factors such as gender and the social class and ethnic backgrounds of the children impact upon their development. This has been the aim of the remainder of Chapter 3 that has attempted to build an alternative theoretical framework for understanding young children's development based upon the insights offered in the work of Vygotsky. As argued in the chapter, Vygotsky's theoretical approach provides an important starting point given his emphasis on the way in which children's development is essentially characterised by the *internalisation* of the social relations they are engaged in. Young children learn and develop, therefore, first by engaging in particular social activities and then, second, by internalising these as a set of cognitive schemes and dispositions. While this is a relatively simple point it does have major implications for how we understand and study young children's development. On the one hand it effectively undermines any notion of children passing through universal stages of development. As their learning tends to reflect the particular contexts within which they are located, then there will be as many different developmental pathways that children will follow as there are differing social contexts within which they are located. On the other hand, recognising this means that children's development can therefore only ever be understood by focusing on the wider social contexts and relationships within which they are located. It is for this reason that the two case studies have given so much time to describing the wider contexts of the local neighbourhoods, families and schools that the two groups of young boys are located in and how the relationships found within these contexts have then become internalised by the boys in relation to a particular set of dispositions and ways of thinking.

Alongside his emphasis on social context, the other major contribution that Vygotsky has made of relevance to this current book is his notion of the *Zone of Proximal Development* (ZPD). As explained in Chapter 3, this represents the space in which children are actively learning at any point in time. It is therefore the distance between what a child can already achieve under their own initiative and what they can potentially achieve with the help of an adult or more experienced other. Of course, the more that they are helped and thus able to achieve more complex tasks, the more they will eventually come to internalise these and thus be able to complete them on their own. The key point in this is the role that Vygotsky gives to adults in helping to support and encourage young children's learning. Rather than being banished to the sidelines, as Piagetian theory tends to advocate, Vygotsky's work encourages adults to take an active role in young children's development. As will be seen a little later in this chapter, this has important implications in terms of justifying and also providing the theoretical basis upon which particular intervention strategies can be developed for working with young boys around the issue of gender.

It was argued in Chapter 3, however, that there has been a problem with how Vygotsky's work has been applied to date in terms of the limited way in which the broader social context within which young children are located has been actually studied. With this in mind, the chapter concluded by suggesting an alternative way of applying Vygotsky's overall approach through the twin concepts of *figuration* and *habitus*. How these two concepts 'map onto' Vygotsky's theoretical framework was illustrated in Figure 3.3. It was argued that each child is located within a number of different sets of social relationships or what are referred to as figurations. For each figuration, the child is engaged in a number of complex interdependent relationships characterised by differing balances of power and undergoing processes of change. The child's routine experiences of these relationships will slowly come to be internalised into a set of predispositions to thinking and acting in certain ways. It is these predispositions that make up the child's habitus. The habitus is therefore not just composed of all the specific cognitive schemes that we traditionally focus on in terms of the early years (i.e. modes of reading, ways of adding and subtracting numbers etc.) but it also includes more general perceptions and values – reflecting those of the community in which she or he belongs – that tend to influence their overall dispositions or motivations to education and learning. It is here that the influence of gender and social class can be successfully incorporated into an understanding of a young child's development.

This broadly Vygotskian approach, enhanced with the twin concepts of habitus and figuration, therefore provides the theoretical framework with which to make sense of the two case studies that provide the focus for the third section of the book (Chapters 4–8).

Case studies of boys and schooling in the early years

As already mentioned earlier, the purpose of the case studies has been to focus in-depth on two groups of young boys (one middle class, the other working class) in order to understand precisely how they come to construct and express particular forms of masculinity and how this, in turn, impacts upon their dispositions towards education. In doing this the aim has been to identify some of the reasons both for the general tendency for young boys to lag behind girls in the early years and also for the significant differences in attainment that tend to exist between middle class and working class boys at this early age.

It has been stressed throughout that the two case studies are not offered as either representative or comprehensive accounts of working class and middle class young boys in general or even of these two groups of boys in particular. Rather, the method used has simply been to focus on those particular social processes and practices that tend to exacerbate the differences between these two groups of boys. Thus when looking at the middle class boys in South Park the emphasis has been upon what factors tend to lead them to achieve relatively highly in academic terms while, in the same way, the emphasis when looking at the working class boys in North Parade has been on drawing attention to those factors that tend to lead them to achieve much less well. What has therefore been constructed for both case studies is the 'best case scenario' in terms of South Park and the 'worst case scenario' in terms of North Parade. While they are all empirically-grounded in the sense that they are based upon real incidents and events, they are purposely constructed almost as caricatures of the experiences and perspectives of the two groups of boys.

This type of approach has been necessary in order to draw out more clearly some of the general processes that tend to differentiate middle class and working class boys. As was shown through the case studies and as will be summarised below, in setting these two case studies side by side some of the reasons why working class boys *in general* tend to achieve less well than middle class boys become apparent. However, there is a danger associated with this type of approach in terms of the potential it has for pathologising middle class and particularly working class communities. It is precisely for this reason that I have been at pains to stress that these are not representative accounts and that it is not possible to make definitive claims about *all* working class and middle class young boys from these two case studies. Indeed there are some working class boys in North Parade achieving very well and some middle class boys at South Park doing particularly badly. However, the point is that we know *in general* that young working class boys do less well than young middle class boys. It is therefore these general tendencies and processes that the case studies have tried to understand and draw out.

With these points firmly in mind, an attempt has been made to summarise the key findings from the two case studies in Table 9.1. As can be seen, the study of the young boys has been placed within the broader figurational contexts provided by the local neighbourhoods, the family and the school. The way in which some of the boys have tended to internalise the social processes and practices found in these figurations has then been outlined in terms of their developing habitus and, more specifically, the particular form of masculinity that some tend to subscribe to and then, in turn, the particular dispositions towards schooling that they are already developing at this age.

As can be seen from Table 9.1, the young middle class boys living in South Park, tend to be located in a context where they have significant access to a wide range of resources and learning opportunities. For some, their parents have the time and the ability to closely control and organise their activities. They also have the educational knowledge and expertise to instinctively know how to successfully prepare their children for the academic demands of school. Given all of this, the school is able to adopt a clear emphasis on formal academic achievement given the correspondence between the routines and practices of the home and those of the school.

For some of the young middle class boys, therefore, it has been argued that they tend to internalise these broader contexts in terms of subscribing to an internally-expressed form of masculinity with an emphasis on demonstrating specialist knowledge and technical skills. This, in turn, leads to these boys being highly disposed towards education and the ability to be academically successful for three main reasons. First, the close control and organisation of their time and activities at home has had the effect of disposing them towards a passive acceptance of the routines and demands of formal schooling. In other words, they are more likely to be already used to the type of control and increased discipline directed towards them by teachers in schools. Second, given the emphasis on educational success and the

Table 9.1 Summary and comparison of the findings from the two case studies

		South Park	North Parade
FIGURATIONS	BROADER SOCIAL CONTEXT	Relatively affluent, very little violence. High proportion of parents in secure middle class occupations. Access to wide range of resources.	Relatively high levels of deprivation and sectarian tensions and violence. High unemployment and dominance of routine manual occupations. Very limited access to resources.
	FAMILY LIFE	High levels of control and organisation of young children's time and activities. Parents have knowledge and expertise to support young children's education.	Parents less likely to have resources and the time and physical energy to closely control and organise their young children's time and activities. Parents also tend to lack knowledge and expertise to support their young children's education.
	SCHOOL	Emphasis on formal academic achievement.	Emphasis on pastoral care.
YOUNG BOYS' HABITUS	DOMINANT FORM OF MASCULINITY	Internally-expressed. Emphasis on demonstration of specialist knowledge and technical skills.	Externally-expressed. Emphasis on strength and physical prowess.
	DISPOSITIONS TOWARDS SCHOOLING	High levels of achievement. Strongly disposed towards demands of schooling in terms of: • Passive acceptance of being closely controlled and highly organised; • High value placed on education; • High correspondence between academic achievement and dominant form of masculinity with its emphasis on demonstrating knowledge and skills.	Low levels of achievement. Poorly disposed towards demands of schooling in terms of: • Less likely to be used to being closely controlled and highly organised; • Insignificance of education to the lives of those around them; • Mismatch between dominant form of masculinity with its emphasis on strength and physicality and the focus on formal, academic achievement.
	EXPLAINING THE GENDER GAP	Gap is small because of high pressure on middle class boys and girls to succeed in education. Little room, therefore, for gender to be a determining influence. Slightly lower levels of attainment by boys remain however, and these can be partly explained by the collusion of parents (and possibly teachers).	Gap is large because education lacks practical significance to those living in North Parade. Lack of pressure on working class children to succeed. Gender therefore has more room to play a determining role. Dominant form of masculinity tends to exacerbate further the boys' low levels of achievement compared to girls.

active support their parents are able to offer them at home, some of these boys have also come to regard schooling as a taken-for-granted aspect of their lives and thus place a high value on education. Third, their particular form of masculinity, with its emphasis on the acquisition of specialist knowledge and skills, clearly disposes them extremely favourably towards academic achievement at school.

It will be remembered from Chapter 1 that young middle class boys, generally, tend to be high achievers in schools. While they do tend to lag behind their female counterparts, the gap tends to be pretty small. With the points outlined above in mind it can be concluded that one of the factors that can explain the small size of the achievement gap is the general pressure that middle class families (and schools) place on education and academic success. Within this context there is little room for gender to take a determining role in influencing the educational performance of boys and girls – the pressure is on both to succeed. However, one reason for the small gap that does remain is likely to be the tendency for parents (and possibly teachers) to collude to a certain extent with the boys and to not effectively challenge their limited set of interests and general unwillingness to work consistently hard at school.

In contrast, the young working class boys in North Parade are living in an area suffering from relatively high levels of deprivation and also under the cloud of continuing sectarian tensions and violence. They therefore have very limited access to wider resources and learning opportunities. Moreover, some of their parents are simply struggling to survive. They are more likely to be unemployed, to be single parents, to be in poor health and not to have access to their own transport. Within this context some do not have the resources nor opportunity to closely control and organise the time and activities of their children to the same extent as some of the middle class parents in South Park do. Moreover, given that almost two-thirds of all adults in North Parade have no formal qualifications whatsoever then these parents are also more likely to lack the educational knowledge and expertise they need to effectively prepare their children and support them in relation to the academic demands of schooling. Struggling against the effects of poverty and relatively high levels of violence in the area, the school has therefore tended to emphasise its pastoral role over that of promoting formal academic achievement. Working partly within a culturally-deficit model of the local community the school has prioritised the children's social and emotional development.

Given these broader figurational contexts, some of the young working class boys have tended to subscribe to a more externally-expressed form of masculinity with an emphasis on strength and physical prowess. This, in turn, reflects the real dangers that these boys face living in the local area and thus the need to 'grow up quickly' and to be streetwise. All of this, in turn, has led to some of these young boys being poorly disposed towards schooling and the desire to be academically successful for three reasons. First, there is a mismatch between their experiences of home and school. More specifically they are simply not used to the close level of control and the highly organised nature of the classroom in the same way that their middle class counterparts tend to be. It is therefore a struggle for some of them to fit into the routines of school life. Second, education has little practical significance to many of the adults in their lives. As already mentioned, two-thirds have no qualifications at all and there is a significant proportion who are unemployed. Of those in work many tend to be employed in routine manual occupations. Looking around them, therefore, the young boys will find it difficult to see what relevance education has to their day-to-day lives. Third, there is a fundamental mismatch between the dominant form of masculinity that some tend to subscribe to and the demands of the school. In other words, the boys' emphasis on strength and physical prowess tends to conflict with the school's need for these boys to be diligent, passive and hardworking.

For young working class boys like these at North Parade, it was seen in Chapter 1 that the general trend is for them to not only exhibit low levels of achievement generally but also for the gap between them and their female counterparts to be much larger than that between young middle class boys and girls. The generally low levels of achievement can clearly be explained, in part, by the fact that they are poorly disposed to the demands of formal schooling for the reasons outlined above. In addition, the tendency for the gap between the achievement levels of working class young boys and girls to be larger can be partly explained by the fact that education does tend to have less practical significance in the lives of some working class families. While many will care passionately about their children's education, some parents simply do not have the knowledge nor the expertise to be able to encourage and support their children. Because of this, there is less effective pressure placed on the young children and thus gender can exert a more determining role in relation to influencing the attitudes of young boys and girls to schooling. It has already been pointed out that schools require pupils to be passive. This tends to be a characteristic closely associated with dominant forms of femininity and in opposition to those of masculinity. Given that the boys are already adopting an externally-expressed and rather emphasised form of masculinity then it is not surprising to find gender playing a more significant role in increasing the difference between the dispositions of young working class boys and girls towards schooling.

Key conclusions to emerge from the research

Before focusing on more specific, practical issues there are five key conclusions to be drawn arising from the findings outlined above. First, the book has provided ample evidence of the need to begin any strategy aimed at addressing the poorer educational performance of boys in the early years. We saw in Chapter 1, for example, in relation to available statistics at a national level, that all of the key patterns of differential performance found at GCSE are already evident in the early years. Moreover, the two in-depth case studies have also tended to confirm this pattern. For the young working class boys in particular, some of them are already finding it difficult to see the significance of education to their lives and others are beginning to lose the motivation to learn at the ages of five and six. Given that the seeds are already being sown at this early age then it does seem rather misplaced to target efforts and resources mainly at raising boys' achievement at secondary level, that tends to be the case at the moment. The key point to arise from this study is that focused and targeted work needs to begin in the early years.

Second, it is clear that gender has only a partial role to play in influencing the differential patterns of achievement between boys and girls. Again, we have seen from the statistical evidence presented in Chapter 1 that social class and ethnicity have much more of a profound impact upon the chances of pupils succeeding in education compared to gender. Moreover, the realities of this have been underlined through the case studies reported in Part III where social class has tended to play a leading role for these two groups of boys in determining the wider parameters within which they then come to construct their particular forms of masculinity. Through the two case studies we have seen the complex ways in which gender and social class tend to interact in the lives of these young boys; with the effect either exacerbating poor levels of achievement (in the case of the young working class boys) or actually partly increasing the motivation to learn and succeed (in relation to the young middle class boys). The key point from this then is that raising boys' achievement cannot simply be about gender, it needs to be as much (if not more) about strategies focusing on social class and ethnicity as well.

Third, the use of the concepts of habitus and figuration has helped to emphasise the deeply engrained nature of the young boys' masculine identities and thus their differing dispositions towards education. In line with the approach offered in the work of Vygotsky, what we have seen in the two case studies is how these two groups of boys have come to internalise the social relationships around them into an increasingly durable and taken-for-granted set of habits. Their sense of masculinity is therefore something that is already finding its way into the young boys' subconscious and routinely influencing and shaping the way that they think and behave. While it is not something innate nor biologically-fixed, the boys' masculinity is therefore something that is deeply-rooted *and experienced as if it is innate and fixed*. The important point to stress from this is that we need to avoid the tendency to treat masculinity as if it is almost a lifestyle choice – something that boys can simply choose either to wear or discard at will. The notion of 'laddish culture' sometimes implies this with its focus simply on particular forms of behaviour with little attempt to explain where they have come from. However, and as we have seen, the 'laddishness' of the young working class boys with its emphasis on fighting and girlfriends is not simply a lifestyle choice but a set of dispositions reflecting the material conditions within which the boys are located. The key challenge arising from this point then is that attempts to encourage young boys to question their existing identities and, hopefully, to adopt more positive and constructive forms of masculinity will only have limited success unless the conditions that give rise to their existing identities are also addressed.

Fourth, the fact that the boys' masculine identities and dispositions towards education are so deeply engrained does tend to question whether the term 'underachievement' is an appropriate one to describe their experiences. As Troyna (1984) has argued previously in relation to the issue of the underachievement of Black pupils, it tends to individualise the problem and place the focus on the pupil him or herself to change. It implies, in other words, that the pupil is able to achieve more but is simply not trying hard enough. And yet, in relation to the young working class boys in North Parade, for example, at this moment in time they are simply not able to significantly improve their levels of attainment on their own. As we have seen, they do not have the necessary habits and dispositions to be able to deal effectively with the demands of formal schooling. Rather than underachieving, many are quite possibly achieving the best that they can given the conditions they are in.

Finally, and perhaps most importantly, it needs to be stressed that while the focus of this book has been about the achievement of young boys this should not be read as implying that girls no longer face any problems in relation to education. On the contrary, and as has been clearly demonstrated, not all girls are performing well in school and there are actually certain groups – particularly working class girls and/or Black and Pakistani girls – that are achieving significantly lower than the national average and whose performance should be a serious matter for concern (Mirza, 1992; Plummer, 2000; Osler and Vincent, 2003; Shain, 2003). One of the dangers in writing 'yet another' book about boys and achievement is that it can simply reinforce this uncritical focus on boys with the effect of further marginalising the issues and problems that girls continue to face in education (Yates, 1997; Epstein *et al.*, 1998a; Raphael Reed, 1999). There is an urgent need, therefore, for further research on girls' experiences and perspectives of schooling and how these are mediated by factors such as social class and 'race' and ethnicity.

Recognising this, however, does not negate the fact that we also need to continue to focus on and problematise dominant forms of masculinity within schools. This is not simply because, as this book has shown, masculinity tends to have an adverse effect on the education and general well-being of boys and men but also because it powerfully impacts upon the lives and experiences of girls and women (Connell, 1995; Salisbury and Jackson, 1996; Gilbert and Gilbert, 1998; Skelton, 2001; Martino and Pallotta-Chiarolli, 2003). While the focus of this book has been with how dominant forms of masculinity tend to limit the educational achievement of certain groups of boys, the case studies have also touched upon some of the other negative and adverse effects of masculinity. In this sense, and as other studies have consistently shown, boys' failure to reach their full potential in relation to education is therefore just one symptom of a more fundamental male malaise that in school also expresses itself in terms of: the routine sexual harassment and domination of girls by boys (Mahony, 1985; Lees, 1993; Kenway and Fitzclarence, 1997; Connolly, 1998a; Duncan, 1999; Renold, 2002, 2003); the tendency for boys to be much more likely to be both perpetrators and victims of bullying and other forms of violence (Elton Report, 1989; Ahmad and Smith, 1994; Kelly, 1994; Smith *et al.*, 1999); and the control and domination that particular groups of boys exercise over other boys and girls and the patterns of subordination and exclusion that result (Stanworth, 1981; Spender, 1982; Mac an Ghaill, 1994; Salisbury and Jackson, 1996; Skelton, 2001). Thus problematising and developing strategies to address the negative expressions of masculinity within schools – that provides the focus for the remainder of this chapter – should be of as much benefit to girls as boys.

Implications for practice

So, what are the implications of all of this for practice? How can the findings summarised above and the key issues to arise from these be used to inform the way in which we work with young boys in schools and early years settings? Given the five points made above, the answer to this question rests at two levels in terms of the young boys that provided the focus for the two case studies: strategies focusing on social class inequalities and also those focusing more explicitly on gender. In turn, the strategies focusing on gender can be seen largely as those aimed at challenging the dominant forms of masculinity apparent among the young boys and can, themselves, be understood at two levels: challenging dominant forms of masculinity through school policies and practices and also through direct work with young boys themselves. These three elements (i.e. social class strategies and gender strategies at the level of the school and also directly with the boys themselves) have to be seen as an integrated package of measures that need to be undertaken in tandem in order to effectively begin to address the issue of boys' levels of achievement. It is worth looking at each of these in turn.

Addressing the effects of social class inequalities

As mentioned in Chapter 2, popular debates about 'boys' under-achievement' and, in particular, about the problems of 'laddish behaviour' tend to be directed at working class boys rather than boys in general. For these boys, it is actually poverty and disadvantage that remain the key factors that tend to determine their levels of educational achievement rather than gender *per se*. This was clearly shown through the case study of the young working class boys in North Parade where, as has already been argued, the effects of masculinity were limited mainly to exacerbating the more fundamental problems posed by social class. Any attempts aimed at raising the achievement levels of these working class boys (and girls) therefore need to focus primarily on addressing the problems of poverty and disadvantage in the area, as well as the continuing levels of violence and sectarian divisions. These are the conditions, as we have seen, that give rise to the dominant forms of masculinity that these young boys are already internalising. So long as there are high levels of unemployment, poor health and few resources available in the area then the effects that a single school can have in changing the behaviour and levels of achievement of these boys is going to be limited.

What all of this points towards is the need for targeted and effective intervention in areas of high social need such as North Parade. Of course this has been something recognised explicitly by the UK government through a variety of programmes it has established over recent years including *Education Action Zones* and then *Excellence in Cities* as well as *New Deal for Communities* and obviously *Sure Start*. The potential as well as the problems associated with some of these programmes have been more than adequately discussed elsewhere and need not be rehearsed here (see, for example, Plewis, 1998; Hatcher, 1999; Power and Gewirtz, 2001; Simpson and Cieslik, 2002). The point, simply, is that given the multiple nature of the problems and disadvantages faced by areas like North Parade then a coordinated and targeted strategy is required that is multi-layered in its approach, based upon significant levels of long-term investment and aimed at genuinely empowering local communities. While schools and other early years settings have an important role to play in any such strategy the overall responsibility for it clearly lies elsewhere. Given that this is a book written for teachers and early years practitioners specifically then it is not necessary (nor appropriate) to begin to examine here what the precise nature of such a strategy should be. However, both the enormity of the task and also its central importance as a prerequisite to any effective intervention aimed at raising young children's educational achievements in the locality should not be forgotten.

Alongside such broader, structural approaches to the issue of raising young working class children's educational achievement, there are things that schools can practically do in the meantime that can also make a difference. There are two key issues as highlighted in the case study of North Parade that will be mentioned here. The first relates to the teachers' general expectations of the young children. As was seen, the school tended to work with very limited expectations of the parents and the young children. While this partly reflected the fact that the local community was suffering from high levels of disadvantage, the teachers' low expectations also tended to exacerbate the problem at times. This was seen, for example, in the repetitive and unchallenging work that the teachers tended to give the children as pointed out in the inspection report. It was also evident in attempts by the school to 'dampen down' the parents' expectations, especially around the transfer test. While schools need to be realistic, there is also a danger that this can lead to all children and parents being negatively labelled. It is therefore important that schools and individual teachers examine their own perceptions of the local community and begin to raise their expectations and communicate these clearly to both children and parents. This will include teachers making use of more imaginative and challenging activities for young children and creating an atmosphere within the classroom where academic achievement is expected. It also means communicating that level of expectation clearly to parents so that they not only understand what is expected of their children week-by-week but also so that they are appropriately informed and guided in relation to how they can support their children in this.

This last point leads to the second key issue to be emphasised here in relation to the need to develop effective relationships with parents. As we have seen, working class parents can often feel intimidated by schools and lack the confidence to approach teachers with any concerns they may have. In addition, they may well lack the knowledge and expertise to appreciate what the school is doing with their children. Moreover, they may also not have the level of education themselves to be able to effectively support their children's learning. As the case study has shown, it is all too easy for relationships between schools and parents in areas like North Parade to soon become fixed and entrenched.

There is an onus on the school, therefore, to take a proactive approach to reaching out to parents, making them feel genuinely valued and attempting to build meaningful relationships with them.

Of course, this is not a new point and there are many examples of effective school-based initiatives that are already doing this in a variety of ways (see Shaw *et al.*, 2003; Wilkin *et al.*, 2003). However, the point is that working effectively and meaningfully with parents needs to become a routine practice for all schools – especially those in areas like North Parade where it is much less likely to be taking place, as we have seen.

In practice this means, for example, a school looking at ways of keeping parents fully informed of what it is doing and also what is happening in their own children's classes day-by-day. It will also involve exploring ways in which parents can be invited to play a more significant role within the life of the school, whether this means formally through participation in the Board of Governors and/or in an active Parent Teacher Association or more informally through encouraging parents to help out in class or in relation to specific activities such as school trips or organising the school library. It could also include looking at ways of encouraging parents to use the school building and begin to develop a sense of ownership of it. This could involve, for example, allowing health clinics or advice sessions to be held for parents within the school if there is room available. Moreover, there is a real need for more schools to provide parents with appropriate support – including basic numeracy and literacy support where necessary as North Parade has begun to do – so that they can acquire the key knowledge and skills they need in order to support their children's learning.

This emphasis on schools reaching out and developing meaningful links with parents and the local community is also not new but can be seen in terms of a wide range of relatively successful school-led schemes and programmes that have emerged and which have been collectively labelled as 'Extended Schools' initiatives (Wilkin *et al.*, 2003). A move towards linking such initiatives in a more coordinated way with other social and health care services is also evident in the recent proposals for Sure Start Children's Centres. Further details on these many different initiatives can be found on the companion website to this book. Ultimately, the precise nature of the strategies devised by schools to reach out to parents will depend upon the particular nature of the local communities and the specific circumstances it faces. It will also depend, clearly, upon the resources available to the school. The key point, however, is that schools should prioritise the need to build meaningful relationships with parents. It is only through these that efforts can be made to coordinate the learning strategies adopted at home and school – so important, for example, in relation to encouraging the development of literacy skills in the early years for boys and girls.

The role of the school in challenging dominant forms of masculinity

Alongside recognising the overriding importance of social class, there remains a need for schools to challenge the dominant forms of masculinity that are apparent among their boys and to begin to encourage the development of alternative and more positive and constructive forms of masculinity. As mentioned earlier, this can take place both at the level of the school in terms of its overall ethos and existing policies and practices as well as through more direct work with boys themselves. In terms of the school, it is important to realise that they do not simply represent a neutral venue within which boys and girls tend to construct and express their gender identities. Rather, they tend to actively contribute towards these processes (Kessler *et al.*, 1985; Salisbury and Jackson, 1996; Connolly, 1998a; Skelton, 2001).

In attempting to address this, there is no simple blueprint applicable to all schools. One of the key lessons to learn from the two case studies above is that the nature of the dominant form of masculinity subscribed to by boys will vary from one school to the next (Skelton, 2001). Only two forms of masculinity have actually been described in the preceding chapters. There will be countless others reflecting the particular social class and ethnic backgrounds and also the specific sets of problems faced by each local community. As Skelton (2001) stresses, the first task for any school is therefore to do some research; to study the boys in their school and to identify the dominant form(s) of masculinity prevalent among them. The two case studies used in this book provide one example of how this can be done (for others see Connolly, 1998a; Skelton, 2001).

The next task is then to look at how the school may be contributing to and/or even encouraging such forms of masculinity (Mahony, 1998). In this respect there are a number of things to look out for. First, there is a need to examine the general ethos of the school as it is manifest, for example, through the style and content of school assemblies, the types of school clubs that may be organised and its policies and practices with regard to such matters as bullying. What are the messages being given out to children through all of these?

They certainly provide an excellent opportunity to stress and emphasise values such as mutual respect and understanding, the negative effects of violent behaviour and how it will not be tolerated in school and also the importance of friendship and being inclusive. This can be practically emphasised through child-led approaches to school bullying such as the introduction of peer-counselling and peer-mediation (Cowie and Sharp, 1996; Cowie and Wallace, 2000). Perhaps more significantly, if such messages are not routinely embedded within the ethos of the school then it is quite easy for the school to unwittingly reinforce the existing dominant forms of masculinity that exist among the boys. A preoccupation with the achievements of the school football team (which is invariably male) in school assemblies, for example, can often provide a significant means by which the position and status of the most powerful boys within the school is confirmed (Connolly, 1998a; Skelton, 2001). Banter between male staff and some of the boys in the classroom or playground can achieve the same result as can the tendency to ignore boys' dominance of physical space in the playground or to ignore fighting and aggressive behaviour (Measor and Sikes, 1992; Thorne, 1993). All of these things can lead to the creation of an alternative school ethos that tends, by default, to condone and thus ultimately encourage the existing dominant forms of masculinity already being internalised by the young boys in the school.

Second, and partly related to the first point, there is a need for schools to look carefully at the way that teachers relate to children and, more specifically, the way in which they control and discipline them. As Skelton (2001) has argued, the perceptions that teachers have about the local community can at times influence the way they then tend to control their children. In working class areas that have a reputation for being tough this can lead to teachers adopting rather authoritarian and aggressive ways of reprimanding children. In this way teachers can directly reproduce the dominant forms of masculinity evident in the local community and, as Skelton (2001) points out, this is not only the case for male teachers but female teachers, too, can be 'bearers of masculinity' in the way they interact with children.

The key point from this is that it is difficult to challenge violent and aggressive forms of masculinity among young boys in the school if teachers then routinely deal with them in intimidating and aggressive ways. If we truly accept the Vygotskian notion that children internalise the social relationships that they are engaged in then this should underline the importance of teachers and schools developing approaches to relating to children that are based upon mutual respect and constructive ways of dealing with conflict. It has been shown elsewhere that adopting inconsistent approaches to discipline and/ or reprimanding boys publicly can often simply exacerbate their tendency to reject schooling (Pickering, 1997; Hannan, 1999; Lynch and Lodge, 2002; Ofsted, 2003a).

Third, both case studies have highlighted the need to carefully supervise children's play whether this is in the playground or in the classroom. As has been shown, wherever it takes place there is always the tendency, if left largely unsupervised, for it to provide the space for boys to simply play out and reinforce their existing masculine identities. Teachers and playground supervisors need to think of ways of more positively structuring the children's playtimes and thus encouraging them to diversify their play experiences. Again, this is not a new point and there are plenty of examples of excellent practice in this regard (Blatchford, 1989; Blatchford and Sharp, 1994). However, it is worth touching upon some of the key issues here to stress them as part of the overall approach being advocated. In the playground, for example, this could be done through the introduction and use of a variety of different toys and activities. In the classroom it could also be achieved by paying more attention to the types of activities that the children are encouraged to engage in. Alongside this there is a need for closer supervision of the children's play and for teachers and supervisors to be prepared to intervene more routinely to prevent intimidatory behaviour and negative displays of violence and aggression. As part of a whole school ethos, this could effectively reinforce the message that such forms of behaviour are not to be tolerated.

Fourth, and finally, there is the general issue of the school's and individual teachers' expectations and how these, too, can either challenge or unwittingly reproduce existing gender identities (Skelton and Hall, 2001). It is therefore important to examine expectations at two levels: in terms of expectations regarding the general interests and behaviour of boys and girls and also those surrounding their academic interests and anticipated levels of achievement. As regards the former it is a useful exercise for teachers to conduct a 'gender audit' of their classroom to assess the types of messages that are being conveyed not just through displays, books and other resources but also through how the resources and materials in the classroom are actually being used. Have certain games, toys or activities become defined by the children as appropriate for just girls or boys? Do boys and girls in the class have proper access to a wide range of activities or are their choices effectively restricted due to pressures from their peers? An example of this was given in Chapter 6 with the boy at South Park Primary School who wanted to skip. Formally he had full access to the skipping ropes, just as the girls did. But informally he was effectively prevented from using it because of the 'boundary work' engaged in by his male peers.

Not only should teachers ensure that a range of activities and resources are available to boys and girls in the classroom therefore, representing activities that are traditionally defined as masculine and feminine, but they also need to ensure that methods are used to enable and encourage children to have the opportunity to make use of these differing resources. This could involve, for example, rotating different groups of children around different types of activity. Children may still then use the particular resources in stereotypically-gendered ways (e.g. boys turning the home corner into an army base!) but it is at least one small but important process in attempting to challenge dominant forms of masculinity among the young boys.

The other level of expectation that needs to be considered is that surrounding boys' and girls' academic interests and anticipated levels of attainment. As the example of the middle class parents in South Park showed, a tendency can exist for parents (and teachers) to collude in the gendered behaviour of young boys. Thus rather than simply accepting that boys do not like reading there is a need to have higher levels of expectation – ones that are also effectively communicated to the boys themselves – that they are expected to engage in reading a wide variety of literary forms (Ofsted, 2003b). The key issue then, and following on from the previous point, is that teachers and parents need to ensure that they are actually introduced to a wide variety of stories and literary styles and that the boys' experiences of these are positive and constructive.

Working directly with boys in the 'Critical Gender Zone'

While it is important to challenge the dominant forms of masculinity to be found at the level of the school itself, it is unlikely that this will be effective in its own right (MacNaughton, 1998). As alluded to above, it is not sufficient simply to provide formal equality of opportunity by ensuring children have access to a range of different activities and resources. The fact that gender identities are so engrained will mean that this is unlikely to encourage young boys and girls to actively explore and experiment with those forms of behaviour that transgress their traditional sense of what it means to be masculine or feminine. Indeed, as we have seen, transgressing such boundaries can actually be extremely dangerous. What is required therefore is to also begin to challenge, more fundamentally and directly, the young boys' sense of masculinity that they are actively internalising and coming to increasingly take for granted.

While these may be young children, the evidence from the case studies suggests that they certainly have the skills and social competence to respond positively to some type of work along these lines. As we have seen, for example, these young boys are actively involved in the construction and maintenance of their gender identities. They are not only recognising and picking up the dominant forms of masculinity that surround them but they are also actively appropriating them, forever rehearsing and exploring them and, in the process, continually developing and adapting them to fit into their own social worlds. These are, therefore, not the passive young children simply being trained into stereotypically masculine and feminine roles as much of the traditional sex-role socialisation theories would suggest (see, for example, Davies, 1979; Connell *et al.*, 1982; Skelton and Hall, 2001). Rather, and as shown through the case studies, the children are centrally involved in what Thorne (1993) describes as 'borderwork' and Davies (1989) has called 'gender category maintenance work', whereby they are carefully and continuously attempting to police and reinforce the boundaries that demarcate masculine and feminine behaviour.

With this in mind it is possible to adopt a more proactive strategy whereby teachers and other early years professionals actively encourage young boys to question their taken-for-granted assumptions on gender and to deconstruct their existing masculine identities (Davies, 1989, 1993; MacNaughton, 1998; Francis, 1998, 2000). For such interventions to be successful, however, they need to be grounded in and built upon the young boys' interests and activities. It is with this in mind that we can draw upon Vygotsky's notion of the Zone of Proximal Development (ZPD) and talk of a *Critical Gender Zone* that marks out the parameters of this type of gender work with young boys. In essence, the Critical Gender Zone represents the distance between what a child has already come to internalise in terms of their current experiences of gender relations and the degree to which they are able to reflect upon and deconstruct these with the help of others.

It may seem that children of this age are simply too young to deal with rather complex cognitive activities such as being required to reflect upon their identities and to begin to recognise some of the negative and contradictory aspects of these. However, rather than regarding it as a complete programme of work in its own right it is better to see it as simply the start of a much more long-term process. In this sense Bruner's (1963) concept of the 'spiral curriculum' is a useful one here. The notion of the spiral curriculum suggests that children can understand the principles of a particular subject at increasingly sophisticated levels. Rather than having to wait until children are 'ready' in the Piagetian sense, Bruner claims that children can intuitively grasp the key principles underlying a subject at an early age and then develop an increasingly deep and more complex understanding of that subject as they successively return to it. As Bruner (1963: 33) has argued: 'any subject can be taught effectively in some intellectually honest form to any child at any stage of development'.

In this sense the role of the teacher is to provide the appropriate 'scaffolding', as Bruner terms it, for the young boys in relation to carefully directing their discussions and activities so that they come to recognise some of the negative and contradictory aspects of their masculine identities and behaviour. This can help, with time, to develop their skills of critical reflection and encourage them to slowly develop their thinking beyond the crude and rigid gender categories that tend to dominate children's thought in the early years (Damon, 1977; Lloyd and Duveen, 1992; Francis, 1998).

In doing all of this, the key point, as stressed with the notion of the Critical Gender Zone, is to begin with the day-to-day activities and behaviour and also the interests and concerns that the young boys have themselves. Relations within the playground will clearly provide an ideal opportunity for this as the children continually struggle to create and maintain gender categories and boundaries. Existing preconceptions and behaviour can be challenged in practice by encouraging boys and girls to play games that have become associated with the other sex. Moreover, playground activities and behaviour can also provide a rich source of material for discussion and reflection in the classroom. In this sense the teacher can actively challenge the children's existing gender constructions by promoting, as Francis (1998) advocates, a 'discourse of innate equality' between boys and girls. As some of the discussions with the young boys in the case studies have shown, it is possible to question their taken-for-granted attitudes about gender roles by suggesting that girls can do anything that boys can and encouraging them to try to justify and therefore think through why they do not believe this. From this basis, the young boys can also be encouraged to reflect upon the work they do in school and what they like and do not like. Particular strategies could be developed for encouraging them to try reading carefully-selected stories of a form that they would traditionally reject. They could also be encouraged to view certain aspects of schoolwork in a more positive light, as an achievement and something to be proud of. All of these activities can be seen as encouraging young boys to question their taken-for-granted gender attitudes and identities and thus begin to deconstruct the dominant forms of masculinity that they have tended to subscribe to and internalise.

Ultimately, however, there are no simple lesson plans that can be drawn up for use by early years teachers wishing to engage in such work with young boys. As the notion of the Critical Gender Zone is intended to suggest, the nature of the work will depend very much on where the young boys are currently at and what they are capable of being effectively challenged about. Prior to engaging in any such work it is important therefore to map out the parameters of the Critical Gender Zone for the particular young boys in question. This, in turn, means understanding what the dominant form of masculinity is that is evident among their peer group and how strongly (and in what sense) they tend to police the boundaries between boys and girls.

It also means looking, more fundamentally, at the particular dispositions that the young boys tend to have internalised. For some young boys it may be appropriate to build a significant amount of this type of work around circle time and small group discussions. Indeed it may also be appropriate to encourage some boys to deconstruct their existing attitudes and understandings through story-writing, a technique suggested by MacNaughton (2000) among others. However, it needs to be accepted that these particular ap-proaches will not be appropriate for all groups of boys. It is probably the case, for example, that such methods with their emphasis on academic literacy skills may not sit easily with some of the young working class boys from North Parade whose dispositions, as we have seen, are more likely to be practically- and materially-based.

For these boys it may be more effective to encourage them at this point in time to deconstruct their existing beliefs through practical activities, some of which have been described above.

Conclusions

In conclusion, it has been argued throughout this book that the so-called issue of 'boys' underachievement' is one that should be of central concern to early years teachers and practitioners. All of the key trends and patterns regarding how boys lag behind girls at GCSE can be traced right back to the early years where they are already evident in the patterns of performance in tests at Key Stage 1. As has been argued, however, while there are gender differences these tend to be overshadowed by the effects of social class and ethnicity. At one level, therefore, it is not all young boys who are 'under-achieving' but rather certain groups of boys – particularly working class boys and/or boys from particular minority ethnic groups. These are the real 'underachievers' and the problems they face are actually much more about social class and ethnicity than about gender *per se*. It is therefore always necessary to keep the issue of gender differences in educational achievement in proportion and to refuse to be drawn into the tendency to treat boys and girls as if they constitute two homogeneous groupings.

At another level, however, there does remain a small but significant gender difference in relation to achievement such that boys do tend to lag behind girls whatever social class or ethnic group one looks at. Moreover, for those groups that already suffer from the lowest levels of achievement, masculinity can tend to significantly exacerbate the problems faced by these boys. Strategies are needed, therefore, to address this problem that is rooted, as has been argued, in the dominant expressions of masculinity found among the boys them-selves. Any strategy aimed at addressing the problem posed by boys and achievement therefore needs to focus on the issue of masculinity itself and such a strategy needs to begin in the early years. What this final chapter has attempted to do is to set out some of the guiding principles that should underpin attempts by schools and other early years settings to actively challenge dominant forms of masculinity found among their boys and to begin to encourage them, instead, to adopt alternative forms of masculinity that are more positive and constructive. These have consisted of a series of issues – in relation to addressing the effects of poverty and social disadvantage, school-level policies and practices and direct work with young boys – that need to take place together for them to be effective.

The key point to stress in conclusion is that such attempts need to be seen as part of a long-term process that is simply begun in the early years. In terms of masculinity, they are about challenging and attempting to change deeply engrained habits and unconscious dispositions that young boys have internalised over time. This cannot, by definition, be done overnight. Rather, for it to be successful it needs to be followed up and built upon throughout the boys' educational careers. Just as the problem of boys' levels of achievement cannot be effectively challenged unless we begin the process in the early years, it is equally unlikely that the process will be effective if we just confine it to the early years.

Appendix

Table A.1 Binary logistic regression on whether a school leaver in England and Wales achieved five or more GCSEs grades A*–C or not in 2000/1

	B	SE	Wald	df	Sig	Exp(B)
Gender						
Girls	0.50	0.04	182.60	1	0.00	1.645
Boys						1.000
Social class						
Higher prof.	2.05	0.07	900.49	1	0.00	7.745
Lower prof.	1.42	0.06	601.59	1	0.00	4.131
Intermediate	0.84	0.06	205.29	1	0.00	2.318
Lower supervisory	0.19	0.07	7.41	1	0.01	1.207
Routine						1.000
Ethnicity						
Chinese	1.92	0.35	29.67	1	0.00	6.832
Indian	1.16	0.18	40.34	1	0.00	3.203
White	0.50	0.14	12.35	1	0.00	1.648
Bangladeshi	0.88	0.32	7.53	1	0.01	2.411
Pakistani	0.54	0.21	6.87	1	0.01	1.719
Black						1.000
Constant	−1.56	0.15	110.55	1	0.00	

Model fit: -2LL (intercept only) = 18739.016; -2LL (final model) = 17049.444; $\chi^2(10)$ = 1689.572, $p < 0.0005$ (Percent correctly predicted: 65.4%).

Source: Secondary analysis of Youth Cohort Study of England and Wales 2002.

Notes

1 'Boys' underachievement': the evidence

1 Vocational qualifications, particularly GNVQs, are the most common alternative examinations that are considered as 'equivalents' in the calculation of the GCSE benchmark. For example, an intermediate GNVQ qualification is counted as equivalent to two GCSE passes at grade A^*–C. The government includes GNVQ equivalents in its calculation of the GCSE benchmark (and consequent construction of school league tables). Unless otherwise stated, this is therefore the measure that is used in the analysis to follow. It should be noted that while the incorporation of GNVQs marginally increases the overall levels of performance across the board, it does not significantly affect the overall patterns of performance found in relation to gender, social class or ethnicity.

2 It has been argued, for example, that the use of the GCSE benchmark is a crude device that tends to obscure the more complex patterns of gender differences in achievement that are found when comparing the actual grades achieved by boys and girls (Gorard *et al.*, 1999, 2001). Indeed a more detailed analysis of the actual grades attained by Gorard *et al.* (1999, 2001) has shown that gender differences are most evident in relation to the top grades and that there is little evidence for significant gender differences in performance at lower grades. In other words, for example, while there are differences between the proportions of boys and girls gaining a grade B or above in particular subjects at GCSE the differences tend to become negligible when comparing the proportions of those gaining a grade F or above.

While this argument may be true, I am not convinced that this additional level of complexity adds much to the debate. Indeed, it is rather stating the obvious. To take an analogy of a 100-metre race involving five boys and five girls, it is the same type of reasoning to suggest that gender differences are only evident in relation to the fastest runners. In other words, if we look simply at the fastest three runners then it could be found (for the sake of argument) that two are boys and only one is a girl (boys thus outnumbering girls by a ratio of 2:1). However, if we look at the fastest nine runners then hardly any gender differences may be evident (as these could include five boys and four girls, for example, thus reducing the ratio to 5:4). Of course, if we look at the fastest ten runners then there will be no gender differences at all as there are five boys and five girls! The point is that only those who came in the top three actually receive a medal. Similarly, while all GCSE grades may be considered a 'pass', it is widely accepted that only those graded C or above are recognised as successful.

3   One of the most popular alternative measures is the 'GCSE score' that is calculated for each pupil. This involves allocating a score to each GCSE grade obtained (i.e. A*/A = 7, B = 6, ... F = 2, G = 1) and then adding these individual scores together to provide an overall score for that pupil. Thus a respondent who achieved five B grades would be given an overall score of 30 (i.e. 5 × 6). Similarly, someone who gained just two E grades and one G grade would achieve an overall score of 7 (i.e. 2 × 3 + 1 × 1). It could be argued that the use of this GCSE score is preferable given that it provides a more sensitive picture of the overall achievements of each pupil. However, as Demack *et al.* (2000) found in their analysis of gender, ethnic and social class differences in GCSE performance, remarkably similar overall patterns emerge whether one uses the GCSE benchmark or this alternative GCSE score. This was also found to be the case in this current analysis.

4   A grade of A–C in the former GCE O Level or a grade 1 in the former CSE are counted as equivalent to a current GCSE grade A*–C pass.

5   This is actually the method previously used by Arnot *et al.* (1998: 11) to present such trends in their review of research on gender and achievement and thus this current figure, in effect, provides an 'up-dated' version of their original chart.

6   This figure is gained simply by squaring the correlation coefficient (r) and multiplying by 100. Thus, in this case, 0.964 × 0.964 × 100 = 92.9 or 93 per cent when rounded up.

2 'Boys' underachievement': the explanations

1   For a more detailed and very accessible discussion of these two arguments plus a number of others see Head (1999: Ch. 2). See also Gilbert and Gilbert (1998: 36–46) and Stainton Rogers and Stainton Rogers (2001: Ch. 1).

2   This is evident, for example, in Noble and Bradford's (2000) book. While it is entitled 'Getting it Right for Boys ... *and* Girls' (original emphasis), the book gives very little explicit consideration to girls and, in fact, spends most of its time focusing on boys.

3 Vygotsky, Bourdieu and the social contexts of young children's development

1   It should be pointed out that Vygotsky was a little more ambiguous about the existence of stages than my interpretation of his work implies here. Clearly the logic of his arguments, with their focus on learning taking place through social relationships, refutes the existence of clear and fixed developmental stages. However, some of his writing – especially his emphasis on 'crisis periods' – can be read as implying some recognition of general stages of development (Morss, 1996; Valsiner, 2000). My attempt here is not to offer the 'true' and 'definitive'

reading of Vygotsky's work (if one can ever exist). Indeed I am not particularly concerned with how Vygotsky originally intended to use the particular concepts he developed and that are outlined here. Rather my concern is simply to construct a theoretical framework that is logically coherent and can help to explain what is going on in the two case studies to follow. It is against these latter criteria that my use of these concepts should be assessed.

2 This use of the term 'genetic' here can be misleading given its biological connotations. However, it is derived in this instance from the word 'genesis' indicating development or generation. In this sense Elias (1978) uses the terms sociogenesis and psychogenesis to refer to social and psychological development respectively. Indeed one of Elias's concerns is to show how the two are fundamentally inter-related so that changes to people's ways of thinking (i.e. changes to their habitus) reflect broader social changes.

3 Of course it is here that Bourdieu would use the concept of 'field' rather than figuration. The choice of which concept to use will partly depend upon the precise object of study. In my earlier study of the impact of racism on children's gender identities, the concept of field was a useful one (see Connolly, 1998a, 2000). Bourdieu defines fields primarily in terms of the sets of relationships that exist around particular forms of capital. In this instance I was able to identify dominant forms of masculine cultural capital evident among the boys and feminine cultural capital among the girls and then show how particular discourses on 'race' tended to position Black and South Asian boys and girls differently within their respective fields (i.e. the fields of masculine and feminine peer group relations). However, and as will be seen, such an approach does not lay sufficient stress on the inherently interdependent nature of social relationships and the differing power ratios that exist as found in Elias's notion of figurations. For example, there is an implication that power is simply something that can be owned through the acquisition of masculine/feminine cultural capital. Such an approach suggests that children within their respective field either have power or they do not. Moreover, it is difficult within this framework to understand how boys and girls relate together within the broader field of the children's peer group relations more generally. In terms of gender, it would not be sufficient simply to identify masculinity as the dominant form of capital and thus to conclude that girls lack power simply because they are generally not able to acquire this form of capital. Again, power is not absolute but rather there is a complex interdependent relationship between boys and girls that is more appropriately characterised by the existence of power ratios.

4 The most simple games model Elias uses involves just two people playing a game of chess (for argument's sake). To take the case where one of the players (Player A) is far superior in skill and experience to the other (Player B) then it is clear that Player A will be able to exert a very high measure of control over Player B and the moves they make. However, this control is not absolute. Player A does not have complete control but must also take their bearings from Player B's preceding moves. In this sense Player B therefore exerts some control, however limited. If they exert no control then there would be no game. It is in this way that even where there are clear asymmetries of power and hence Player A exerts a great deal of control over Player B, Player A's consequent actions are still dependent upon what Player B does. In this sense both players are inherently interdependent.

Of course, if Player A and Player B are more evenly matched then the game will eventually take on a life of its own as neither player can exert complete dominance over the direction it takes. Each successive move is predicated on previous ones. While both players therefore have agency and are free to make choices, they do so within the constraints provided by the unfolding logic of the game. Elias (1978) extends this overall analysis with a range of other models involving teams of players operating at differing levels. His key point is that however complex the game becomes and however many players are involved, they are all tied together through webs of interdependent relationships. Moreover, the more complex the game, the less direct control any one individual has over it and the more likely it is that the game will proceed 'as though it had a life of its own' (Elias, 1978: 85).

The main point from all of this is that the starting point for analysing figurations is to identify and understand the particular nature and form that the interdependent relationships take between those involved. Even in cases where there is no 'game' as such, there will always remain relationships of interdependence. If we take the figuration of male peer group relations as an example, then there may be some young boys who choose to 'opt out' of the 'game'. They do not value the dominant forms of masculinity that are at the heart of the competition between the other young boys and thus seek to distance themselves from the whole enterprise. However, even in this case, these boys will still have to make decisions about what they do with the other boys in mind. For example, they may well have to adapt their behaviour in order to avoid drawing attention to themselves and thus possibly being verbally or physically attacked by the other boys. The other boys, in attempting to successfully construct and display their own masculine identities, may do so by picking on and harassing these other boys to distance themselves from them and thus to reinforce their own masculine credentials. Either way, while these two groups of boys are not directly relating to one another, they are still interdependent as they continually behave with reference to and/or in anticipation of the others' actions. Again, and with time, the relationships and forms of behaviour that emerge are never completely planned and under the control of the individual boys involved but partly take on a life of their own.

4 Worlds apart: introducing South Park and North Parade

1 The names of the schools together with the local areas and the names of teachers, children and parents have been altered to maintain anonymity.
2 See http://www.nationalstatistics.gov.uk/methods_quality/ns_sec/default.asp.
3 It is not always possible to simply leave out descriptive details of the schools and their local communities to ensure anonymity. For one thing, the type of qualitative ethnographic methods used here demand a sufficient outline and understanding of the social contexts within which social relationships take place. However, the need to maintain the anonymity of the schools is paramount. With this in mind, some non-essential details regarding the schools and their local communities have been altered in the descriptions that follow. For example, while not applicable in this instance, this could have involved

claiming that there are three high-rise blocks of flats rather than two in the local area. Any minor changes that have been made to the descriptions of the two case studies have been done carefully, however, so as to maintain the overall accuracy and integrity of the 'pictures' being painted. The rule of thumb followed in this regard is that minor alterations have only been made to the descriptions of the schools and local areas if they do not affect the interpretation of the data presented and the points derived from these.

4   The interviews with parents were conducted by two research assistants on my behalf – Julie Healy and Karen Winter – following a similar interview schedule I constructed for both of them. The interviews were tape-recorded and I subsequently transcribed and analysed the interviews myself.

5   This approach is similar to Weber's (1949) notion of the 'ideal type' in that no attempt is made to provide an accurate depiction of reality but, rather, it is simply a heuristic device to help understand real-life situations. As Weber (1949: 93) explains in relation to each ideal typical construct, it is 'neither historical reality nor even the "true" reality … It has the significance of a purely ideal *limiting* concept with which the real situation or action is *compared* and surveyed for the explication of certain of its significant components' (original emphasis). My approach differs, however, to the extent that I am not attempting to accentuate and draw together a set of processes into a unified analytical construct that captures the core features and essence of working class and middle class boys' experiences of and dispositions towards schooling respectively, as an ideal type attempts to do.

6   This paper has been made freely available on the website accompanying this book. See: http://www.routledgefalmer.com/companion/0415298415/.

7   These rankings have been taken from the measures of multiple deprivation calculated for each ward in Northern Ireland (see NISRA, 2001).

8   Figures taken from the 2001 Census of Northern Ireland.

9   See list of abbreviations at the front of the book for the actual titles of each of these groups.

10 The teacher is required to give just one grade for personal, social and emotional development. However, for language development and mathematical development they are required to give three separate grades for each relating to their various aspects. Thus language development is graded separately for talking and listening skills, early reading skills and early writing skills. Similarly, mathematical development is graded separately for ability to talk about maths, understanding of patterns and relationships and grasp of early number concepts. For language and mathematical development respectively, therefore, the grade shown in Table 4.2 is the average (in this case the mode) of the three grades given.

11 The test was taken from Collins Primary Maths and consisted of the 'Assess and Review' test for the second half of the autumn term for Year 1 (or P2 in Northern Ireland). The test was originally marked out of 35 and this was converted into a percentage score for Figure 4.4.

Bibliography

Acker, S. (1999) *The Realities of Teachers' Work*, London: Cassell.

Adler, P., Kless, S. and Adler, P. (1992) 'Socialisation to gender roles: popularity among elementary school boys and girls', *Sociology of Education*, 63: 65–87.

Aggleton, P. (1987) *Rebels Without a Cause: Middle Class Youth and the Transition from School to Work*, Lewes: Falmer Press.

Ahmad, Y. and Smith, P.K. (1994) 'Bullying in schools and the issue of sex differences', in J. Archer (ed.) *Male Violence*, London: Routledge.

Allatt, P. (1993) 'Becoming privileged', in I. Bates and G. Riseborough (eds) *Youth and Inequality*, Buckingham: Open University Press.

Arnot, M. (1991) 'Equality and democracy: a decade of struggle over education', *British Journal of Sociology of Education*, 12: 447–66.

Arnot, M. and Weiner, G. (1987) *Gender and the Politics of Schooling*, London: Unwin Hyman.

Arnot, M., David, M. and Weiner, G. (1999) *Closing the Gender Gap*, Cambridge: Polity Press.

Arnot, M., Gray, J., James, M., Ruddock, J. with Duveen, G. (1998) *Recent Research on Gender and Educational Performance*, London: The Stationery Office.

Ball, S.J. (2003) *Class Strategies and the Education Market: The Middle Classes and Social Advantage*, London: RoutledgeFalmer.

Belotti, E. (1975) *Little Girls*, London: Writers and Readers Publishing Co-operative.

Bernstein, B. (1971) *Class, Codes and Control, Volume 1: Theoretical Studies Towards a Sociology of Language*, London: Routledge and Kegan Paul.

Bernstein, B. (1975) *Class, Codes and Control, Volume 3: Towards a Theory of Educational Transmissions*, London: Routledge and Kegan Paul.

Biddulph, S. (1997) *Raising Boys*, London: Thorsons.

Blatchford, P. (1989) *Playtime in the Primary School: Problems and Improvements*, Windsor: NFER-Nelson.

Blatchford, P. and Sharp, S. (eds) (1994) *Breaktime and the School: Understanding and Changing Playground Behaviour*, London: Routledge.

Bleach, K. (ed.) (1998a) *Raising Boys' Achievement in Schools*, Stoke-on-Trent: Trentham Books.

Bleach, K. (1998b) 'Helping boys do better in their primary schools', in K. Bleach (ed.) *Raising Boys' Achievement in Schools*, Stoke-on-Trent: Trentham Books.

Bleach, K. (1998c) 'Why the likely lads lag behind', in K. Bleach (ed.) *Raising Boys' Achievement in Schools*, Stoke-on-Trent: Trentham Books.

Bleach, K. (1998d) 'What difference does it make?', in K. Bleach (ed.) *Raising Boys' Achievement in Schools*, Stoke-on-Trent: Trentham Books.

Boal, F. (1999) 'From undivided cities to undivided cities: assimilation to ethnic cleansing', *Housing Studies*, 14: 585–600.

Boaler, J. (1997) *Experiencing School Mathematics: Teaching Styles, Sex and Setting*, Buckingham: Open University Press.

Boaler, J. (1998) 'Mathematical equity – underachieving boys or sacrificial girls?', *International Journal of Inclusive Education*, 2: 119–34.

Borooah, V. K. (1993) 'Northern Ireland – typology of a regional economy', in P. Teague (ed.) *The Economy of Northern Ireland: Perspectives for Structural Change*, London: Lawrence & Wishart Limited.

Bourdieu, P. (1977) *Outline of a Theory of Practice*, Cambridge: Cambridge University Press.

Bourdieu, P. (1990) *The Logic of Practice*, Cambridge: Polity Press.

Bourdieu, P. (1993) *Sociology in Question*, London: Sage.

Bourdieu, P. and Passeron, J. (1977) *Reproduction in Education, Society and Culture*, London: Sage.

Bourdieu, P. and Wacquant, L. (1992) *An Invitation to Reflexive Sociology*, Cambridge: Polity Press.

Bradley, B. (1989) *Visions of Infancy: A Critical Introduction to Child Psychology*, Cambridge: Polity Press.

Bradley, J. (1995) 'Economic aspects of the island of Ireland: an overview of the two economies', in J. Bradley (ed.) *The Two Economies of Ireland: Public Policy, Growth and Employment*, Dublin: Oak Tress Press.

Brittan, A. (1989) *Masculinity and Power*, Oxford: Blackwell.

Brooker, L. (2002) *Starting School: Young Children Learning Cultures*, Buckingham: Open University Press.

Broughton, J. (ed.) (1987) *Critical Theories of Psychological Development*, New York: Plenum.

Brown, P. (1987) *Schooling Ordinary Kids: Inequality, Unemployment and the New Vocationalism*, London: Tavistock.

Bruner, J. (1963) *The Process of Education*, New York: Vintage Books.

Bruner, J. (1966) *Toward a Theory of Instruction*, Cambridge, MA: Harvard University Press.

Bruner, J. (1971) *The Relevance of Education*, New York: Norton.

Bulman, J. (2002) 'Patterns of pay: results of the 2002 New Earning Survey', *Labour Market Trends*, 110: 643–55.

Burman, E. (1994) *Deconstructing Developmental Psychology*, London: Routledge.

Burton, F. (1978) *The Politics of Legitimacy: Struggles in a Belfast Community*, London: Routledge and Kegan Paul.

Canaan, J. (1996) '"One thing leads to another": drinking, fighting and working class masculinities', in M. Mac an Ghaill (ed.) *Understanding Masculinities*, Buckingham: Open University Press.

Canning, D., Moore, B. and Rhodes, J. (1987) 'Economic growth in Northern Ireland: problems and prospects', in P. Teague (ed.) *Beyond the Rhetoric: Politics, the Economy and Social Policy in Northern Ireland*, London: Lawrence & Wishart Limited.

Carrigan, T., Connell, R.W. and Lee, J. (1985) 'Towards a new sociology of masculinity', *Theory and Society*, 14: 551–604.

Chetwynd, J. and Hartnett, O. (eds) (1978) *The Sex Role System*, London: Routledge and Kegan Paul.

Christensen, P. and James, A. (eds) (2000) *Research with Children: Perspectives and Practices*, London: RoutledgeFalmer.

Clarricoates, K. (1978) 'Dinosaurs in the classroom: a re-examination of some aspects of the "hidden curriculum" in primary schools', *Women's Studies International Quarterly*, 1: 353–64.

Cohen, M. (1998) ' "A habit of healthy idleness": boys' underachievement in historical perspective', in D. Epstein, J. Elwood, V. Hey and J. Maw (eds) *Failing Boys?: Issues in Gender and Achievement*, Buckingham: Open University Press.

Cohen, S. (1972) *Folk Devils and Moral Panics*, London: Paladin.

Connell, R.W. (1987) *Gender and Power*, Cambridge: Polity Press.

Connell, R.W. (1993) 'The big picture: masculinities in recent world history', *Theory and Society*, 22: 597–624.

Connell, R.W. (1995) *Masculinities*, Cambridge: Polity Press.

Connell, R.W., Ashenden, D., Kessler, S. and Dowsett, G. (1982) *Making the Difference: School, Families and Social Divisions*, London: George Allen and Unwin.

Connolly, P. (1996) 'Seen but never heard: rethinking approaches to researching racism and young children', *Discourse*, 17: 171–85.

Connolly, P. (1997) 'In search of authenticity: researching young children's perspectives', in A. Pollard, D. Thiessen and A. Filer (eds) *Children and Their Curriculum: The Perspectives of Primary and Elementary School Children*, London: Falmer Press.

Connolly, P. (1998a) *Racism, Gender Identities and Young Children*, London: Routledge.

Connolly, P. (1998b) ' "Dancing to the wrong tune": ethnography, generalisation and research on racism in schools', in P. Connolly and B. Troyna (eds) *Researching Racism in Education: Politics, Theory and Practice*, Buckingham: Open University Press.

Connolly, P. (2000) 'Racism and young girls' peer-group relations: the experiences of South Asian girls', *Sociology*, 34: 499–519.

Connolly, P. (2003a) 'The development of young children's ethnic identities: implications for early years practice', in C. Vincent (ed.) *Social Justice, Education and Identity*, London: RoutledgeFalmer.

Connolly, P. (2003b) 'The effects of social class and ethnicity on gender differences in GCSE attainment: a secondary analysis of the Youth Cohort Study of England And Wales 2002', unpublished Paper.

Connolly, P. (2004) *The Historical Context to the Development of Areas Like 'North Parade' and 'South Park' in Northern Ireland*. Online. Available http://www.routledgefalmer.com/companion/0415298415/resources/pdf/HistoricalContext.pdf.

Connolly, P. and Healy, J. (2003) 'The development of children's attitudes towards "the troubles" in Northern Ireland', in O. Hargie and D. Dickson (eds) *Researching the Troubles: Social Science Perspectives on the Northern Ireland Conflict*, Edinburgh: Mainstream Publishing.

Connolly, P., Smith, A. and Kelly, B. (2002) *Too Young to Notice? The Cultural and Political Awareness of 3–6 Year Olds in Northern Ireland*, Belfast: Community Relations Council.

Cormack, R. and Gallagher, A. (1993) 'Education in Northern Ireland', in R. Osborne, R. Cormack, and A. Gallagher (eds) *After the Reforms: Education and Policy in Northern Ireland*, Aldershot: Avebury.

Corrigan, P. (1979) *Schooling the Smash Street Kids*, London: Macmillan.

Corsaro, W. (1997) *The Sociology of Childhood*, Thousand Oaks, CA: Pine Forge Press.

Coulter, C. (1999) *Contemporary Northern Irish Society: An Introduction*, London: Pluto Press.

Cowie, H. and Sharp, S. (eds) (1996) *Peer Counselling in Schools: A Time to Listen*, London: David Fulton.

Cowie, H. and Wallace, P. (2000) *Peer Support in Action: From Bystanding to Standing By*, London: Sage.

Curtis, L. (1984) *Ireland: The Propaganda War: The British Media and the Battle for Hearts and Minds*, London: Pluto Press.

Damon, W. (1977) *The Social World of the Child*, San Francisco: Jossey-Bass.

Darby, J. (1995) 'Conflict in Northern Ireland: a background essay', in S. Dunn (ed.) *Facets of the Conflict in Northern Ireland*, London: Macmillan.

Darby, J., Batts, D., Dunn, S., Harris, J. and Farren, S. (1977) *Schools Apart? Education and Community in Northern Ireland*, Coleraine: University of Ulster.

Davies, B. (1979) 'Education for sexism: moving beyond sex role socialisation and reproduction theories', *Educational Philosophy and Theory*, 21: 1–19.

Davies, B. (1989) *Frogs and Snails and Feminist Tails: Preschool Children and Gender*, Sydney: Allen & Unwin.

Davies, B. (1993) *Shards of Glass: Children Reading and Writing Beyond Gendered Identities*, St Leonards, NSW: Allen & Unwin.

Deem, R. (1980) *Schooling for Women's Work*, London: Routledge and Kegan Paul.

Delamont, R. (1980) *Sex Roles and the School*, London: Methuen.

Demack, S., Drew, D. and Grimsley, M. (2000) 'Minding the gap: ethnic, gender and social class differences in attainment at 16, 1988–95', *Race, Ethnicity and Education*, 3: 117–43.

DE (Department of Education) (2002) *Qualifications and Destinations of Northern Ireland School Leavers, 2000/01, Statistical Press Release*, Bangor: Department of Education.

DfES (Department for Education and Skills) (2002a) *National Curriculum Assessments of 7, 11 and 14 Year Olds by Local Education Authority, 2002 (Provisional)*, Statistical First Release (SFR 25/2002), London: DfES.

DfES (Department for Education and Skills) (2002b) *GCSE/GNVQ Examination Results for Young People in England, 2001/02 (Early Statistics)*, Statistical First Release (SFR 26/2002), London: DfES.

DfES (Department for Education and Skills) (2003) *GCE/VCE A/AS Examination Results for Young People in England 2001/2002 (Provisional)*, Statistical First Release (SFR 07/2003), London: DfES.

Donaldson, M. (1978) *Children's Minds*, London: Fontana Press.

Douglas, J.W.B. (1967) *The Home and the School: A Study of Ability and Attainment in the Primary School*, London: Panther Books.

Duffield, M. (2002) 'Trends in female employment 2002', *Labour Market Trends*, 110: 605–16.

Duncan, N. (1999) *Sexual Bullying*, London: Routledge.

Dunn, S. (1986) 'The role of education in the Northern Ireland conflict', *Oxford Review of Education*, 12: 233–42.

Dunn, S. (1993) 'A historical context to education and church-state relations in Northern Ireland', in R. Osborne, R. Cormack, and A. Gallagher (eds) *After the Reforms: Education and Policy in Northern Ireland*, Aldershot: Avebury.

Dunn, S., Darby, J. and Mullan, K. (1984) *Schools Together?*, Coleraine: University of Ulster.

Duveen, G. (1997) 'Psychological development as a social process', in L. Smith, J. Dockrell and P. Tomlinson (eds) *Piaget, Vygotsky and Beyond: Future Issues for Developmental Psychology and Education*, London: Routledge.

Edley, N. and Wetherell, M. (1995) *Men in Perspective: Practice, Power and Identity*, London: Harvester Wheatsheaf.

Elias, N. (1978) *What is Sociology?*, London: Hutchinson.

Elias, N. (1987) *Involvement and Detachment*, Oxford: Basil Blackwell.

Elias, N. (1994) *The Civilising Process*, Oxford: Blackwell.

Elton Report (1989) *Discipline in School*, London: HMSO.

Elwood, J. (1995) 'Undermining gender stereotypes: examination and coursework performance in the UK at 16', *Assessment in Education*, 2: 283–303.

Elwood, J. (1999) 'Equity issues in performance assessment: the contribution of teacher-assessed coursework to gender-related differences in examination performance', *Educational Research and Evaluation*, 5: 321–44.

Epstein, D. (1997) 'Cultures of schooling/cultures of sexuality', *International Journal of Inclusive Education*, 1 (1): 37–53.

Epstein, D., Elwood, J., Hey, V. and Maw, J. (eds) (1998a) *Failing Boys? Issues in Gender and Achievement*, Buckingham: Open University Press.

Epstein, D., Elwood, J., Hey, V. and Maw, J. (1998b) 'Schoolboy frictions: feminism and "failing" boys', in D. Epstein, J. Elwood, V. Hey and J. Maw (eds) *Failing Boys? Issues in Gender and Achievement*, Buckingham: Open University Press.

Farrell, M. (1980) *Northern Ireland: The Orange State*, second edn, London: Pluto Press.

Fay, M., Morrissey, M. and Smyth, M. (1999) *Northern Ireland's Troubles: The Human Costs*, London: Pluto Press.

Francis, B. (1998) *Power Plays: Primary School Children's Constructions of Gender, Power and Adult Work*, Stoke-on-Trent: Trentham Books.

Francis, B. (2000) *Boys, Girls and Achievement*, London: RoutledgeFalmer.

Frosh, S., Phoenix, A. and Pattman, R. (2002) *Young Masculinities: Understanding Boys in Contemporary Society*, Basingstoke: Palgrave.

Gallagher, A. (2003) 'Education and equality in Northern Ireland', in O. Hargie and D. Dickson (eds) *Researching the Troubles: Social Science Perspectives on the Northern Ireland Conflict*, Edinburgh: Mainstream Publishing.

Gallagher, A. and Smith, A. (2000) *The Effects of the Selective System of Secondary Education in Northern Ireland*, Bangor: Department of Education.

Gallagher, A., Shuttleworth, I. and Gray, C. (1997) *Educational Achievement in Northern Ireland: Patterns and Prospects*, Belfast: Northern Ireland Economic Council.

Gallagher, A., Shuttleworth, I. and Gray, C. (1998) *Improving Schools in Northern Ireland*, Belfast: Northern Ireland Economic Council.

Galton, M., Simon, B. and Croll, P. (1980) *Inside the Primary School*, London: Routledge and Kegan Paul.

Gilbert, R. and Gilbert, P. (1998) *Masculinity Goes to School*, London: Routledge.

Gillborn, D. and Mirza, H.S. (2000) *Educational Inequality: Mapping Race, Class and Gender*, London: Ofsted.

Gorard, S. (1999) 'Keeping a sense of proportion: the "politician's error" in analysing school outcomes', *British Journal of Educational Studies*, 47: 235–46.

Gorard, S. (2001) *Quantitative Methods in Educational Research: The Role of Numbers Made Easy*, London: Continuum.

Gorard, S., Rees, G. and Salisbury, J. (1999) 'Reappraising the apparent underachievement of boys at school', *Gender and Education*, 11: 441–54.

Gorard, S., Rees, G. and Salisbury, J. (2001) 'Investigating the patterns of differential attainment of boys and girls at school', *British Educational Research Journal*, 27: 125–39.

Grenfell, D., James, D., Hodkinson, P., Reay, D. and Robbins, D. (1998) *Bourdieu and Education: Acts of Practical Theory*, London: Falmer Press.

Halsey, A.H. (1972) *Educational Priority. EPA Problems and Policies*, Volume One, London: HMSO.

Hannan, G. (1999) *Improving Boys' Performance*, Oxford: Heinemann Educational Publishing.

Hargreaves, D.H. (1967) *Social Relations in a Secondary School*, London: Routledge and Kegan Paul.

Hatcher, R. (1999) 'Profit and power: business and Education Action Zones', *Education Review*, 13: 71–7.

Head, J. (1999) *Understanding the Boys*, London: Falmer Press.

Hearn, J. (1996) 'Is masculinity dead? A critique of the concept of masculinity/masculinities', in M. Mac an Ghaill (ed.) *Understanding Masculinities*, Buckingham: Open University Press.

Hearn, J. and Morgan, D. (eds) (1990) *Men, Masculinities and Social Theory*, London: Hyman and Unwin.

Heath, S.B. (1983) *Ways with Words: Language, Life and Work in Communities and Classrooms*, Cambridge: Cambridge University Press.

Heath, S.B. (1989) 'The learner as cultural member', in M.L. Rice and R.L. Schiefelbusch (eds) *The Teachability of Language*, Baltimore: Paul H. Brookes.

Henriques, J., Holloway, W., Urwin, C., Venn, C. and Walkerdine, V. (eds) (1984) *Changing the Subject: Psychology, Social Regulation and Subjectivity*, London: Methuen.

HESA (2003) *Qualifications Obtained by and Examination Results of Higher Education Students at Higher Education Institutions in the United Kingdom for the Academic Year 2001/02*. Online. Available http://www.hesa.ac.uk/press/sfr61/sfr61.htm (accessed 17 July 2003).

Hoff Sommers, C. (2000) 'The war against boys', *The Atlantic Monthly*, 285: 59–74.

Hough, J. (1985) 'Developing individuals rather than boys and girls', *School Organisation*, 5: 17–25.

Hyde, J.S. (1981) 'How large are cognitive gender differences?', *American Psychologist*, 36: 892–901.

Jackson, B. and Marsden, D. (1962) *Education and the Working Class*, London: Routledge and Kegan Paul.

Jackson, D. (1998) 'Breaking out of the binary trap: boys' underachievement, schooling and gender relations', in D. Epstein, J. Elwood, V. Hey and J. Maw (eds) *Failing Boys? Issues in Gender and Achievement*, Buckingham: Open University Press.

James, A. and Prout, A. (eds) (1997) *Constructing and Reconstructing Childhood: Contemporary Issues in the Sociological Study of Childhood*, second edn, London: Falmer Press.

James, A., Jenks, C. and Prout, A. (1998) *Theorizing Childhood*, Cambridge: Polity Press.

Jenkins, R. (1983) *Working Class Youth Lifestyles in Belfast*, London: Routledge and Kegan Paul.

Jenks, C. (1996) *Childhood*, London: Routledge.

Johnson, S. (1996) 'The contribution of large-scale assessment programmes to research on gender differences', *Educational Research and Evaluation*, 2: 25–49.

Jordan, E. (1995) 'Fighting boys and fantasy play: the construction of masculinity in the early years of school', *Gender and Education*, 7: 69–86.

Keenan, T. (2002) *An Introduction to Child Development*, London: Sage.

Kelly, E. (1994) 'Racism and sexism in the playground', in P. Blatchford and S. Sharp (eds) *Breaktime and the School: Understanding and Changing Playground Behaviour*, London: Routledge.

Kenway, J. and Fitzclarence, L. (1997) 'Masculinity, violence and schooling: challenging "poisonous pedagogies"', *Gender and Education*, 9: 117–33.

Kessler, S., Ashenden, D.J., Connell, R.W. and Dowsett, G.W. (1985) 'Gender relations in secondary schooling', *Sociology of Education*, 58: 34–48.

van Krieken, R. (1998) *Norbert Elias*, London: Routledge.

Lacey, C. (1970) *Hightown Grammar*, Manchester: Manchester University Press.

Lave, J. and Wenger, E. (1991) *Situated Learning: Legitimate Peripheral Participation*, Cambridge: Cambridge University Press.

Lees, S. (1993) *Sugar and Spice: Sexuality and Adolescent Girls*, London: Penguin.

Lindsey, L. (1990) *Gender Roles: A Sociological Perspective*, London: Sage.

Lloyd, B. and Duveen, G. (1992) *Gender Identities and Education*, London: Harvester Wheatsheaf.

Lucey, H. and Walkerdine, V. (2000) 'Boys' underachievement: social class and changing masculinities', in T. Cox (ed.) *Combating Educational Disadvantage*, London: Falmer Press.

Lynch, K. and Lodge, A. (2002) *Equality and Power in Schools*, London: RoutledgeFalmer.

Mac an Ghaill, M. (1994) *The Making of Men*, Buckingham: Open University Press.

Mac an Ghaill, M. (ed.) (1996a) *Understanding Masculinities*, Buckingham: Open University Press.

Mac an Ghaill, M. (1996b) '"What about the boys?": schooling, class and crisis masculinity', *The Sociological Review*, 44: 381–97.

McGarrigle, J. and Donaldson, M. (1974) 'Conservation accidents', *Cognition*, 3: 341–50.

McGarry, J. and O'Leary, B. (1995) *Explaining Northern Ireland*, Oxford: Blackwell.

McGovern, M. and Shirlow, P. (1997) 'Counter-insurgency, deindustrialisation and the political economy of Ulster loyalism', in P. Shirlow and M. McGovern (eds) *Who are 'The People'? Unionism, Protestantism and Loyalism in Northern Ireland*, London: Pluto Press.

MacKinnon, I. (1993) 'Ulster few enjoy a golden age', *Independent on Sunday*, 8 August.

MacNaughton, G. (1996) 'The gender factor', in B. Creasor and E. Dau (eds) *The Anti-Bias Approach in Early Childhood*, Sydney: Harper Educational.

MacNaughton, G. (1997) 'Feminist praxis and the gaze in the early childhood curriculum', *Gender and Education*, 9: 317–26.

MacNaughton, G. (1998) 'Improving our gender equity "tools": a case for discourse analysis', in N. Yelland (ed.) *Gender in Early Childhood*, London: Routledge.

MacNaughton, G. (2000) *Rethinking Gender in Early Childhood Education*, St Leonards, NSW: Allen & Unwin.

Mahony, P. (1985) *Schools for the Boys*, London: Hutchinson.

Mahony, P. (1998) 'Girls will be girls and boys will be first', in D. Epstein, J. Elwood, V. Hey and J. Maw (eds) *Failing Boys? Issues in Gender and Achievement*, Buckingham: Open University Press.

Martino, W. and Berrill, D. (2003) 'Boys, schooling and masculinities: interrogating the "Right" way to educate boys', *Educational Review*, 55: 99–117.

Martino, W. and Pallotta-Chiarolli, M. (2003) *So What's a Boy?*, Maidenhead: Open University Press.

Measor, L. and Sikes, P. (1992) *Gender and Schooling*, London: Cassell.

Midwinter, E. (1977) *Education for Sale*, London: Allen and Unwin.

Miller, D. (1994) *Don't Mention the War: Northern Ireland, Propaganda and the Media*, London: Pluto Press.

Mirza, H. S. (1992) *Young, Female and Black*, London: Routledge.

Moles, O. (1993) 'Collaboration between schools and disadvantaged parents: obstacles and openings', in N. Chavkin (ed.) *Families and Schools in a Pluralistic Society*, Albany, NY: SUNY Press.

Morrissey, M. and Smyth, M. (2002) *Northern Ireland After the Good Friday Agreement*, London: Pluto Press.

Morss, J. (1996) *Growing Critical: Alternatives to Developmental Psychology*, London: Routledge.

Mortimore, J. and Blackstone, T. (1982) *Disadvantage and Education*, Aldershot: Gower.

Munck, R. (1993) *The Irish Economy: Results and Prospects*, London: Pluto Press.

Munck, R. and Hamilton, D. (1998) 'Politics, the economy and peace in Northern Ireland', in D. Miller (ed.) *Rethinking Northern Ireland*, London: Longman.

Murray, D. (1985) *Worlds Apart: Segregated Schools in Northern Ireland*, Belfast: Appletree Press.

Murtagh, B. (2002) *The Politics of Territory: Policy and Segregation in Northern Ireland*, Basingstoke: Palgrave.

Murtagh, B. (2003) 'Territory, research and policy making in Northern Ireland', in O. Hargie and D. Dickson (eds) *Researching the Troubles: Social Science Perspectives on the Northern Ireland Conflict*, Edinburgh: Mainstream Publishing.

Myhill, D. (2002) 'Bad boys and good girls? Patterns of interaction and response in whole class teaching', *British Educational Research Journal*, 28: 339–52.

Nayak, A. (2003) '"Boyz to men": masculinities, schooling and labour transitions in de-industrial times', *Educational Review*, 55: 147–59.

Newman, D., Griffin, P. and Cole, M. (1989) *The Construction Zone*, Cambridge: Cambridge University Press.

Newson, J. and Newson, E. (1965) *Patterns of Infant Care in an Urban Community*, Harmondsworth: Penguin Books.

NISRA (2001) *Measures of Deprivation in Northern Ireland*, Belfast: Northern Ireland Statistics and Research Agency.

Noble, C. (1998) 'Helping boys do better in their primary schools', in K. Bleach (ed.) *Raising Boys' Achievement in Schools*, Stoke-on-Trent: Trentham Books.

Noble, C. and Bradford, W. (2000) *Getting It Right for Boys ... and Girls*, London: Routledge.

Oakley, A. (1972) *Sex, Gender and Society*, London: Temple Smith.

O'Connor, F. (1993) *In Search of a State: Catholics in Northern Ireland*, Belfast: Blackstaff Press.

O'Donnell, M. and Sharpe, S. (2000) *Uncertain Masculinities*, London: Routledge.

Ofsted (1993) *Boys and English*, London: Ofsted.

Ofsted (2003a) *Boys' Achievement in Secondary Schools*, London: Ofsted.

Ofsted (2003b) *Yes He Can: Schools Where Boys Write Well*, London: Ofsted.

Ofsted/EOC (1996) *The Gender Divide: Performance Differences Between Boys and Girls at School*, London: HMSO.

O'Hearn, D. (1998) *Inside the Celtic Tiger: The Irish Economy and the Asian Model*, London: Pluto Press.

Osler, A. and Vincent, K. (2003) *Girls and Exclusion: Rethinking the Agenda*, London: RoutledgeFalmer.

Paechter, C. (1998) *Educating the Other: Gender, Power and Schooling*, London: Falmer Press.

Piaget, J. (1962) *Play, Dreams and Imitation in Childhood*, London: Routledge and Kegan Paul.

Piaget, J. (1965) *The Moral Judgement of the Child*. Harmondsworth: Penguin.

Piaget, J. (1977) *The Language and Thought of the Child*, London: Routledge and Kegan Paul.

Pickering, J. (1997) *Raising Boys' Achievement*, Stafford: Network Educational Press.

Plewis, I. (1998) 'Inequalities, targets and zones', *New Economy*, 5: 104–8.

Plowden Report (1967) *Children and their Primary Schools*, Volume 1, London: HMSO.

Plummer, G. (2000) *Failing Working Class Girls*, Stoke-on-Trent: Trentham Books.

Power, S., Edwards, T., Whitty, G. and Wigfall, V. (2003) *Education and the Middle Class*, Buckingham: Open University Press.

Power, S. and Gewirtz, S. (2001) 'Reading Education Action Zones', *Journal of Education Policy*, 16: 39–51.

Prout, A. and James, A. (1997) 'A new paradigm for the sociology of childhood? Provenance, promise and problems', in A. James and A. Prout (eds) *Constructing and Reconstructing Childhood: Contemporary Issues in the Sociological Study of Childhood*, second edn, London: Falmer Press.

Raphael Reed, L. (1999) 'Troubling boys and disturbing discourses on masculinity and schooling: a feminist exploration of current debates and interventions concerning boys in school', *Gender and Education*, 11: 93–110.

Reay, D. (1998) *Class Work: Mothers' Involvement in their Children's Primary Schools*, London: UCL Press.

Redman, P. and Mac an Ghaill, M. (1997) 'Educating Peter: the making of a history man', in D.L. Steinberg, D. Epstein and R. Johnson (eds) *Border Patrols: Policing the Boundaries of Heterosexuality*, London: Cassell.

Renold, E. (2002) '"Presumed innocence": (hetero)sexual, homophobic and heterosexist harassment amongst children in the primary school', *Childhood*, 9: 415–33.

Renold, E. (2003) '"If you don't kiss me, you're dumped": boys, boyfriends and heterosexualised masculinities in the primary school', *Educational Review*, 55: 179–94.

Resnick, L.B. and Nelson-Le Gall, S. (1997) 'Socializing intelligence', in L. Smith, J. Dockrell and P. Tomlinson (eds) *Piaget, Vygotsky and Beyond: Future Issues for Developmental Psychology and Education*, London: Routledge.

Rogoff, B. (1990) *Apprenticeship in Thinking: Cognitive Development in Social Context*, New York: Oxford University Press.

Rogoff, B., Mistry, J., Göncü, A. and Mosier, C. (1993) Guided Participation in Cultural Activity by Toddlers and Caregivers, *Monograph of the Society for Research in Child Development*, 236, Vol. 58, No. 8.

Rogoff, B., Mosier, C., Mistry, J. and Göncü, A. (1998) 'Toddlers' guided participation with their caregivers in cultural activity', in M. Woodhead, D. Faulkner and K. Littleton (eds) *Cultural Worlds of Early Childhood*, London: Routledge.

Rolston, B. (ed.) (1991) *The Media and Northern Ireland: Covering the Troubles*, Basingstoke: Macmillan.

Rolston, B. (1992) *Drawing Support: Murals in the North of Ireland*, Belfast: Beyond the Pale Publications.

Rolston, B. (1993) 'The contented classes', *Irish Reporter*, 9: 7–9.

Rolston, B. (2003) *Drawing Support 3: Murals in Transition in the North of Ireland*, Belfast: Beyond the Pale Publications.

Rolston, B. and Miller, D. (eds) (1996) *War and Words: The Northern Ireland Media Reader*, Belfast: Beyond the Pale Publications.

Rowthorn, B. and Wayne, N. (1988) *Northern Ireland: The Political Economy of Conflict*, Oxford: Polity Press.

Salisbury, J. and Jackson, D. (1996) *Challenging Macho Values*, London: Falmer Press.

Segal, L. (1990) *Slow Motion: Changing Masculinities, Changing Men*, London: Virago.

Sewell, T. (1998) 'Loose cannons: exploding the myth of the "black macho" lad', in D. Epstein, J. Elwood, V. Hey and J. Maw (eds) *Failing Boys? Issues in Gender and Achievement*, Buckingham: Open University Press.

Shain, F. (2003) *The Schooling and Identity of Asian Girls*, Stoke-on-Trent: Trentham Books.

Sharp, R. and Green, A. (1975) *Education and Social Control*, London: Routledge and Kegan Paul.

Shaw, C., Harnett, R., Harker, R., Franklin, A. and Olle, H. (2003) *"Becoming Seamless": An Evaluation of Schools Plus Teams Pilot Project*, Research Brief No. 447, London: DfES.

Shirlow, P. and McGovern, M. (1997) *Who are 'The People'? Unionism, Protestantism and Loyalism in Northern Ireland*, London: Pluto Press.

Simpson, D. and Cieslik, M. (2002) 'Education Action Zones, empowerment and parents', *Educational Research*, 44: 119–28.

Skelton, C. (ed.) (1989) *Whatever Happens to Little Women?: Gender and Schooling*, Milton Keynes: Open University Press.

Skelton, C. (1998) 'Feminism and research into masculinities and schooling', *Gender and Education*, 10: 217–27.

Skelton, C. (2001) *Schooling the Boys: Masculinities and Primary Education*, Buckingham: Open University Press.

Skelton, C. (2003) 'Male primary teachers and perceptions of masculinity', *Educational Review*, 55: 195–209.

Skelton, C. and Hall, E. (2001) *The Development of Gender Roles in Young Children: A Review of Policy and Literature*, Manchester: Equal Opportunities Commission.

Skinner, B.F. (1938) *The Behaviour of Organisms*, New York: Appleton-Century-Crofts.

Skinner, B.F. (1968) *The Technology of Teaching*, New York: Appleton-Century-Crofts.

Smith, A. (1995) 'Education and the conflict in Northern Ireland', in S. Dunn (ed.) *Facets of the Conflict in Northern Ireland*, London: Macmillan.

Smith, L. (1996) 'The social construction of rational understanding', in A. Tryphon and J. Vonèche (eds) *Piaget–Vygotsky: The Social Genesis of Thought*, Hove: Lawrence Erlbaum Associates.

Smith, P., Cowie, H. and Blades, M. (1998) *Understanding Children's Development*, third edn, Oxford: Blackwell.

Smith, P., Morita, Y., Junger-Tas, J., Olweus, D., Catalano, R. and Slee, P. (1999) *The Nature of School Bullying: A Cross-National Perspective*, London: Routledge.

Smyth, M. (1998) *Half the Battle: Understanding the Impact of the Troubles on Children and Young People*, Derry/Londonderry: INCORE.

Smyth, M. and Hamilton, J. (2003) 'The human costs of the troubles', in O. Hargie and D. Dickson (eds) *Researching the Troubles: Social Science Perspectives on the Northern Ireland Conflict*, Edinburgh: Mainstream Publishing.

Spender, D. (1982) *Invisible Women: The Schooling Scandal*, London: Writers and Readers.

Stainton Rogers, R. and Stainton Rogers, W. (1992) *Stories of Childhood: Shifting Agendas of Child Concern*, London: Harvester Wheatsheaf.

Stainton Rogers, W. and Stainton Rogers, R. (2001) *The Psychology of Gender and Sexuality*, Buckingham: Open University Press.

Stanworth, M. (1981) *Gender and Schooling*, London: Hutchinson.

Strand, S. (1999a) 'Pupil background and Baseline Assessment results at age 4', *Journal of Research in Reading*, 22: 14–26.

Strand, S. (1999b) 'Ethnic group, sex and economic disadvantage: associations with pupils' educational progress from Baseline to the end of Key Stage 1', *British Educational Research Journal*, 25: 179–202.

Sutton, M. (undated) *An Index of Deaths From the Conflict in Northern Ireland*. Online. Available http://cain.ulst.ac.uk/sutton/index.html (accessed 21 September 2003).

Thorne, B. (1993) *Gender Play: Boys and Girls in School*, Buckingham: Open University Press.

Tizard, B. and Hughes, M. (1984) *Young Children Learning*, London: Fontana.

Troyna, B. (1984) 'Fact or artefact? The "educational underachievement" of black pupils', *British Journal of Sociology of Education*, 5: 153–66.

Urwin, C. (1984) 'Power relations and the emergence of language', in J. Henriques, W. Holloway, C. Urwin, C. Venn and V. Walkerdine (eds) *Changing the Subject: Psychology, Social Regulation and Subjectivity*, London: Methuen.

Valsiner, J. (2000) *Culture and Human Development*, London: Sage.

Vincent, C. (1996) *Parents and Teachers: Power and Participation*, London: Falmer Press.

Vygotsky, L. (1978) *Mind in Society: The Development of Higher Psychological Processes* (edited by M. Cole, V. John-Steiner, S. Scribner and E. Souberman), Cambridge, MA: Harvard University Press.

Walkerdine, V. (1983) 'It's only natural: rethinking child-centred pedagogy', in A.M. Wolpe and J. Donald (eds) *Is There Anyone Here from Education?*, London: Pluto Press.

Walkerdine, V. (1984) 'Developmental psychology and the child-centred pedagogy: the insertion of Piaget into early education', in J. Henriques, W. Holloway, C. Urwin, C. Venn and V. Walkerdine (eds) *Changing the Subject: Psychology, Social Regulation and Subjectivity*, London: Methuen.

Walkerdine, V. (1990) *Schoolgirl Fictions*, London: Verso.

Walkerdine, V. and Lucey, H. (1989) *Democracy in the Kitchen: Regulating Mothers and Socialising Daughters*, London: Virago Press.

Warrington, M., Younger, M. and Williams, J. (2000) 'Student attitudes, image and the gender gap', *British Educational Research Journal*, 26: 393–407.

Weber, M. (1949) *The Methodology of the Social Sciences*, New York: The Free Press.

Weiner, G. and Arnot, M. (eds) (1987) *Gender Under Scrutiny: New Inquiries in Education*, London: Hutchinson.

Wells, G. (1986) *The Meaning Makers*, London: Hodder and Stoughton.

Wertsch, J. (1991) *Voices of the Mind*, London: Harvester Wheatsheaf.

Wilkin, A., Kinder, K., White, R., Atkinson, M. and Doherty, P. (2003) *Towards the Development of Extended Schools*, Research Brief No. 408, London: DfES.

Willis, P. (1977) *Learning to Labour: How Working Class Kids Get Working Class Jobs*, Aldershot: Saxon House.

Wilson, G. (2003) *Using the National Healthy School Standard to Raise Boys' Achievement*, London: DfES.

Wood, D. (1998) *How Children Think and Learn*, second edn, Oxford: Blackwell.

Wood, D., Bruner, J.S. and Ross, G. (1976) 'The role of tutoring in problem-solving', *Journal of Child Psychology and Psychiatry*, 17: 89–100.

Woodhead, M., Faulkner, D. and Littleton, K. (eds) (1998) *Cultural Worlds of Early Childhood*, London: Routledge.

Yates, L. (1997) 'Gender equity and the boys debate: what sort of challenge is it?', *British Journal of Sociology of Education*, 18: 337–47.

Yelland, N. (ed.) (1998) *Gender in Early Childhood*, London: Routledge.

Younger, M. and Warrington, M. (1996) 'Differential achievement of girls and boys at GCSE: some observations from the perspective of one school', *British Journal of Sociology of Education*, 17: 299–314.

Index

Acker, S. 170
Adler, P. *et al.* 2
Aggleton, P. 21, 209
Ahmad, Y. and Smith, P.K. 221
Allatt, P. 129
Arnot, M., *et al.* 2, 10, 13, 16, 38, 40, 43, 48, 52; and Weiner, G. 52

Ball, S.J. 128, 129
Belotti, E. 75
Bernstein, B. 120, 176, 178
Biddulph, S. 33, 35
biological differences, brain structure 34–6; hormones 33–4; as natural explanation 32–3
Blatchford, P. 227; and Sharp, S. 227
Bleach, K. 2, 37, 39, 41–2, 44, 49
Boal, F. 111
Boaler, J. 41, 51
Bourdieu, P. 5, 66, 82–8; and Passeron, J. 21, 120, 138, 169, 176, 178, 209; and Wacquant, L. 86
Boys' Achievement in Secondary Schools (2003) 44
boys–school relationship, and academic competition 155–6; acceptance of routines/internalisation of discipline/control 137–42; boundary work 144–50; dependency aspects 136; engagement in formal lessons 138–41; and

gender comparisons 158–9, 160; interest in/recognition of value of education 142–4; maintenance of order/class rules 141–2; middle class habitus 136–44; and perceptions of school/value of education 186–8; and pupil compliance 186; and reading 156–8, 160–1, 199–201; and teacher control 185–6; uniforms 137, 180–1; working class habitus 179–88
Bradley, B. 71
Brittan, A. 57
Brooker, L. 119, 127, 166, 171
Broughton, J. 71
Brown, P. 54
Bruner, J. 230
Burman, E. 66, 67, 74, 75
Burton, F. 112

Canaan, J. 49
Carrigan, T. *et al.* 57
case studies 5, 213–18; data collection 102; focus of research 102–3; methodology 100–5; middle class/working class contrast 99–100, 103–5; observations/interviews 101–2; qualitative/ethnographic limitations/implications 103–4; South Park/North Parade 105–21, *see also* North Parade; South Park; South Park/